AF340677

FINANCIAL DEREGULATION

Also by Maximilian Hall

*MONETARY POLICY SINCE 1971: Conduct and Performance
 THE FRAMEWORK OF UK MONETARY POLICY (*with
 G. E. J. Dennis, D. T. Llewellyn and J. G. Nellis*)
* THE CITY REVOLUTION

*Also published by Macmillan

Financial Deregulation

A Comparative Study of Australia and the United Kingdom

Maximilian Hall
Lecturer in Economics
Loughborough University

MACMILLAN
PRESS

First published 1987

Published by
THE MACMILLAN PRESS LTD
Houndmills, Basingstoke, Hampshire RG21 2XS
and London
Companies and representatives
throughout the world

Typeset by Latimer Trend & Company Ltd, Plymouth

Printed and bound in Hong Kong

British Library Cataloguing in Publication Data
Hall, Maximilian
Financial deregulation: a comparative
study of Australia and the United Kingdom.
1. Financial institutions—Great Britain
2. Financial institutions—Law and
legislation—Great Britain   3. Financial
institutions—Australia   4. Financial
institutions—Law and legislation—
Great Britain
I. Title
332..1′0941   HG186.G7
ISBN 0–333–43965–1

To all those who helped me retain my sanity
during the writing of this book

Contents

List of Tables, Specimens and Exhibits

TABLES

SPECIMENS

EXHIBITS

Preface

This book arose out of my concern for the prudential ramifications of financial deregulation and a curiosity to see how quickly and to what extent governments presiding over other highly developed financial systems would follow the lead given by the UK authorities in their dismantling of direct monetary control devices during the period 1980–2. The rationale (or lack of it) for such control devices, especially for those that applied in the UK economy, had been extensively analysed in my earlier book on monetary policy,[1] so that this study, in large part analysing the case for different forms of prudential controls, represents a natural extension to the earlier work. The choice of Australia for comparative purposes resulted from a reading of the *Campbell Report* on the Australian financial system which, by virtue of its authoritative analysis of the control regimes applied within the Australian financial system, was obviously going to play a major part in stimulating debate on and accelerating the pace of financial deregulation in Australia. This catalytic role cannot be underestimated, although it took a Labor government, following a commissioned review (the *Martin Report*) of the Campbell proposals, to implement most of the recommendations. As is demonstrated in the text the Australian authorities went a long way in emulating the British eschewal of direct monetary controls and face much the same prudential problems that occupy the minds of supervisors in the UK and the world over.

The broad aims of the book are threefold: (i) to illuminate the programmes of financial deregulation adopted in the UK and Australia; (ii) to assess the implications of these deregulatory moves for the conduct of monetary and prudential policy in the two countries; and (iii) to contrast the developments that took place and the policy problems created in the UK and Australia with a view to providing some guide to other governments engaged in or contemplating financial deregulation as to the difficulties they are likely to encounter and the likely costs and benefits they can expect to enjoy. The intended readership thus embraces students of money, banking and regulation, financial practitioners, politicians, central bankers and lay persons interested in the worldwide trend towards a deregulated, global financial services market.

The format adopted is to present a brief description of the current structure of each financial system, followed by detailed discussion of the regulatory environment, covering both monetary and prudential controls, imposed on deposit-taking financial intermediaries. The programmes of financial deregulation since 1970 are then traced and the implications for monetary and prudential policy assessed. While recognising that other factors such as the fiscal system, financial innovation and technological advances in computing and communications systems, may have been, or are likely to be, equally powerful forces in the shaping of financial systems and the regulatory environment within which they operate, these are only touched upon in order to make the project manageable. Lastly, comparisons are made between developments in the two systems and the policy issues created are contrasted with a view to providing an insight into the likely benefits that other governments with a deregulatory fervour might reasonably expect to reap and the 'costs' they are likely to be asked to pay. In recognition of the absence of a relatively non-technical standard text on the subject, an appendix providing an overview of prudential regulation (in theory and practice) is also provided to facilitate understanding of the material presented in the book.

As a final comment I would like to express my sincere thanks to the Houblon–Norman Fund trustees at the Bank of England, to the British Council and to Loughborough University for providing financial assistance during the course of this study and to the Reserve Bank of Australia and other Australian financial institutions for providing such warm hospitality during my two visits to their shores. Last, but by no means least, my gratitude is extended to Su Spencer for her endeavours in deciphering the untyped text and translating it so magnificently into typed form and to those closest to me who were forced to endure the consequences of my lengthy immersion within the subject.

Loughborough University　　　　　　　　　　　　MAXIMILIAN J. B. HALL

Acknowledgements

The financial assistance of the Houblon–Norman Fund trustees and the British Council (both of which provided me with travel grants to visit Australia to facilitate my research) and hospitality accorded me by the Reserve Bank of Australia during my two visits are gratefully acknowledged.

I am also indebted to the Bank of England for granting me permission to reproduce some of their published work (Specimens 2A–2E in the text).

M.J.B.H.

1 The Australian Financial System[1]

1.1 STRUCTURE

Australian financial intermediaries can be classified under the following broad headings: the central bank; the banking sector; non-bank financial intermediaries (NBFIs). Other useful categorisations distinguish banks which are subject to the 1959 Banking Act from those which are not and deposit-taking NBFIs from the rest. Details are presented in Table 1.1.

Central banking Australia's central bank, the Reserve Bank of Australia, was established by Commonwealth legislation in 1911 as a body corporate with the name 'Commonwealth Bank of Australia'. Initially its purpose was to conduct general banking and savings-bank business, but, after the Second World War, the Commonwealth Bank Act and the Banking Act of 1945 gave full effect to its central-banking functions. Legislation in 1959 brought about the new name 'Reserve Bank of Australia' and non-central banking functions were transferred to banks within the Commonwealth Banking Corporation.

The Reserve Bank Act (1959), the Banking Act (1959) and the Financial Corporations Act (1974) lay down the functions, powers and responsibilities of the Reserve Bank (see RBA, 1983 (a), for a more detailed discussion). These embrace the following: the formulation and implementation of monetary policy; depositor protection and prudential supervision; the provision of banking services to governments, banks and certain financial institutions; the provision of short-term loans (through the Rural Credits Department) to rural marketing authorities and co-operative associations of primary producers; management of the note-issue and stock registries for Commonwealth government securities; distribution of coin; administration of exchange control; and custodian of Australia's gold and foreign-exchange reserves.

The banking sector Intermediaries belonging to the banking sector can conveniently be split into those which are subject to the 1959 Banking Act and those which are not. The former group comprise

1

Table 1.1   Classification of Australian financial intermediaries

1. *Central bank* (the Reserve Bank of Australia)

2. *The banking sector*
   (a) *Banks subject to the 1959 Banking Act*
       (i)   Trading banks
                     major trading banks
                     'prescribed' banks
       (ii) Savings banks
                     public sector
                     private sector
       (iii) Other banks
   (b) *State banks*
       (i)   Trading banks
       (ii) Savings banks

3. *Non-bank financial intermediaries*
   (a) Major
       (i)   Deposit-taking (without issuing a prospectus)
                     permanent building societies
                     credit co-operatives
       (ii) Other   finance companies (and general financiers)
                     terminating building societies
                     money-market corporations (i.e. merchant banks)
                     pastoral finance companies
                     authorised money-market dealers
                     life-insurance companies
                     non-life-insurance companies
                     pension and superannuation funds (public and
                     private)
   (b) Minor   unit trusts, land trusts and mutual funds
               intra-group financiers
               investment companies
               health societies
               friendly societies
               Australian Industries Development Corporation
               Australian Banks' Export and Finance Corporation
               other financial corporations
               retailers
               trustee companies

Source: 'Submission to the Committee of Enquiry into the Australian Financial System', *Occasional Paper No. 7*, **R.B.A.**, 1979.

trading banks (major trading banks and 'prescribed' banks), savings banks (public and private sector) and other banks while the latter, state-regulated group encompass both trading and savings banks.

Following the mergers of 1981[1] there are now three major private sector trading banks: the Australia and New Zealand Banking Group Limited, Westpac Banking Corporation and the National Commercial Banking Corporation. The Australian Bank, licensed in 1981, and the government-owned Commercial Trading Bank of Australia (CTB), make up the major trading bank numbers. The remaining three trading banks subject to the Banking Act are the 'prescribed' banks, comprising one small local bank, the Bank of Queensland Limited and two banks owned by overseas governments – the Bank of New Zealand and Banque Nationale de Paris. Savings-bank facilities are provided by the Commonwealth government-owned Commonwealth Savings Bank of Australia, a number of privately owned savings banks (the majority being wholly-owned subsidiaries of either the major trading banks or the 'prescribed' banks) and state banks in Victoria, South Australia and Western Australia. The remaining intermediaries belonging to the banking sector consist of state trading banks and 'other' ('specific purpose') banks[2] subject to the Banking Act.

The activities of *trading banks* in Australia are diverse. With respect to liabilities, deposits, the major item, may be current, for a fixed term or obtained through the issue of CDs. (In June 1984 the respective deposit shares were 35 per cent, 54 per cent and 11 per cent, 70 per cent of all deposits being interest-bearing and 88 per cent accounted for by the major trading banks.) 'Bills payable' represent roughly one-third of total liabilities, and off-balance-sheet contingent liabilities arising from letters of credit, guarantees, foreign-exchange contracts and bills of exchange are considerable. On the assets side of the balance-sheet nearly half of the portfolio is held in the form of loans and advances (84 per cent of which was accounted for by the major trading banks at end-June 1984). Overdrafts represent the traditional mode of lending, but more recent innovations embrace term loans, personal instalment loans, fully drawn advances, bridging finance, bill-discounting, leasing and charge-card facilities. 'Cash' and liquid (public sector) assets are mainly held to satisfy the Reserve Bank's monetary policy requirements (see Section 1.2) and other security holdings largely reflect the growth in the banks' involvement in bill finance.

Until very recently the activities of *savings banks* have been severely circumscribed by monetary controls. This is reflected in the composition of assets and liabilities. Virtually all liabilities are in the form of deposits from the personal sector, higher interest investment accounts (and deposit stock) representing over 52 per cent of the total at end-June 1984. On the assets side savings banks are major providers of housing funds, both direct and through terminating building societies, and, because of regulations, hold substantial quantities of Commonwealth, local and semi-government securities. Over three-quarters of total savings-bank assets are held by those subject to the Banking Act, the Commonwealth Savings Bank of Australia taking the largest share.[3]

Non-bank financial intermediaries (NBFIs) NBFIs account for over half of all the assets of financial institutions in Australia. Insurance companies and pension funds manage over 40 per cent of NBFI assets, with institutions registered under the Financial Corporations Act – building societies, finance companies and general financiers, money-market corporations, credit co-operatives, authorised money-market dealers, pastoral finance companies, retailers and intra-group financiers – taking a 50 per cent share.

Permanent building societies provide a repository for household savings and mortgage finance for owner-occupied housing. The largest also offer some payments services, such as the acceptance of cheques for collection and the writing of third-party cheques. They are predominantly state-based, co-operative and non-profit-making. Shares and deposits account for about 95 per cent of total liabilities, the bulk being at call, although the 'term' component is gaining in importance – it now represents over a third of the total. Special deposits and investment accounts carrying yields competitive with wholesale money-market rates are also increasing in popularity, and standby facilities, lines of credit and letters of credit may be used to supplement liquidity. On the assets side the major element is secured lending for owner-occupied housing. Investments account for roughly 20 per cent of total assets and are mainly short-term, comprising bills of exchange, promissory notes and public authority securities.

Finance companies (and general financiers) came to the fore in the 1950s when policy and other factors restrained the banking system from fully meeting the demand for finance, especially from the household sector. In the 1960s the finance facilities offered became more broadly based as the trading banks competed to stimulate business investment. Some companies branched out into property investment and recently leasing and factoring activities have become more significant. At end-May 1984 instalment credit and other loans to individuals accounted for 23 per cent of total assets, and leasing, factoring, wholesale financing and bill finance for 49 per cent.

Funding is largely from the general public through subscription to prospectuses covering fixed-interest borrowings by way of debentures and unsecured notes. The larger companies may broaden the funding base by issuing promissory notes or bills of exchange, by taking unsecured deposits or by borrowing overseas or by way of syndicated loans.

Money-market corporations, the equivalent of our merchant banks, emerged as an important group of financial intermediaries in the 1960s. In the early days their growth was associated with the surge in foreign investment, especially in minerals, and the general desire of foreign concerns to seek a presence in Australia in the face of a prohibition on foreign bank entry. Later they branched out into property and short-term money-market activities, in the latter case to exploit their regulatory privileges, especially with respect to their monopoly of the payment of interest on short-term deposits. Today money-market corporations engage in liquidity placements, offer business loans and invest in government and commercial paper. More specialist operations embrace commodities and futures dealing, the acceptance of commercial bills, the underwriting of new corporate and public sector security issues, the provision of financial advisory services and the management of Cash Management Trusts. At end-May 1984 bill (and promissory note) discounts accounted for 28 per cent of total assets, short-term loans and advances for 18 per cent, and leasing, factoring and wholesale finance for 33 per cent. The bulk of their funding needs is met from large-scale, short-term borrowing from the corporate sector by way of prospectuses.

Credit co-operatives, or 'credit unions' as they are sometimes called, are mutual bodies that provide a range of financial services to their members embracing savings facilities, personal loans (especially for the purchase of consumer durables), bill-payment facilities and financial counselling. Members typically represent groups of individuals with a common bond of association established through employment, locality or social affiliation. Their attractiveness to both borrowers and lenders stems from their ability to operate on relatively fine margins. This in turn derives from operating and marketing economies achieved through industry associations in the areas of centralised computer facilities, centralised funds management and the provision of cash and payments facilities.[4] Additionally the common bond between members may offer economies in the collection of funds and the assessment of creditworthiness of borrowers.

Members' deposits represent the major source of funds for credit unions and the bulk – about 60 per cent – are callable. Banks, state Credit Union leagues and state governments may be used to supplement members' deposits. 'Liquid' assets, as required by state legislation, are generally in excess of 10 per cent of borrowed funds, instalment credit and other loans (including secured housing loans) to individuals representing over three-quarters of total assets.

The nine *authorised money-market dealers* (AMMDs) raise funds in the short-term money market from banks, governments and other public sector authorities and business corporations to finance the purchase of short- and medium-term securities. Regulations require that the bulk of security holdings are in the form of Commonwealth government securities with maturities up to five years. Their origins lie in agreements made between a small group of specialised short-term borrowers and the Reserve Bank back in the 1950s under which, in return for certain privileges (not least of which is access to lender-of-last-resort facilities), the group would deepen the market for short-term government securities, develop a more efficient and secure money market and provide the basis for more effective but less direct monetary intervention by the central bank. Having satisfied these original aims the AMMDs continue to attract the support of the Reserve Bank in the face of criticisms of the privileges granted to them.[5] At end-May 1984 53 per cent of total assets were held in Commonwealth government securities, 29 per cent in bills of exchange and promissory notes and 15 per cent in cash and bank deposits.

The final group of non-bank financial intermediaries which solicit short-term funds from the general public are the *Cash Management Trusts* (CMTs). The concept of CMTs was first introduced in Australia by the merchant bank Hill Samuel in December 1980. By the end of 1982 the numbers had mushroomed to sixteen. CMTs operate by raising funds through the sale of units and investing the proceeds in short-term money-market securities (mainly bank-guaranteed). The return to the holder of the unit is the average return on the CMT portfolio less a management charge. Units may be reclaimed at par on very short notice. The attraction for the investor is thus access to money-market yields on a secure and liquid investment. Additionally unit holders are often provided with credit cards, chequing facilities and sweep facilities.

1.2 THE REGULATION OF DEPOSIT-TAKING FINANCIAL INTERMEDIARIES (DTIs)

(a) Monetary controls

(i) On banks subject to the 1959 Banking Act

For the purpose of regulation banks subject to the Banking Act are divided into three groups: trading banks; savings banks; and other banks. Regulation varies according to which group a bank belongs. The controls listed below relate to the situation obtaining at end-August 1984.

Trading banks are subject to the following controls:

- the Statutory Reserve Deposits (SRD) instrument
- the Liquid Assets and Government Securities (LGS) convention
- lending guidelines
- interest-rate ceilings on loans of under $100 000 made in the form of overdrafts or farm development loans or for the purposes of owner-occupied housing. *De facto* bankcard credit charges are limited in a similar fashion although exempt from the directives.

Under the *SRD* regulation trading banks are required to hold a set proportion of their Australian deposits[6] in an SRD account at the Reserve Bank. The volume of required deposits varies with the size of the SRD ratio and the volume of Australian deposits held by the bank. Currently interest is paid on the SRDs (at 5 per cent per annum) but at a below market rate, and the SRD ratio is levied on a uniform basis[7] on all major trading banks. The Banking Act requires the Reserve Bank to inform each bank (other than prescribed banks) subject to the Act at least once each quarter of its forecasts for the current financial year of changes in the aggregate of subject banks' Australian deposits and in the sum of the banks' liquid assets and deposits in SRD accounts. Banks, including prescribed and state trading banks, are also informed, again, in confidence, of the Reserve Bank's intended SRD policy for the remainder of the current financial year.

The purpose of the SRD instrument is to allow the Reserve Bank, through changes in the ratio, to exert influence on interest rates throughout financial markets.[8] The ratio change immediately impinges on subject banks' cash and very short-term assets, wider effects being dependent on the nature of banks' responses to the change. For example, an increase in the SRD ratio causes banks to reduce their holdings of assets (subject to the limitations imposed by the LGS convention – see below) or to bid more strongly for cash reserves and deposits[9,10] or a combination of both. To the extent that banks react by slowing down deposit growth (or reducing deposits in absolute terms), which, to a large degree, will be done through interest-rate rationing of advances,[11] growth in M_3 (the current, operational focus of monetary control – see p. 70) will be slowed. Whatever the pattern of response chosen by the banks the upward pressure on interest rates resulting from asset sales or liability management is transmitted to financial markets more generally through the reactions of banks' customers and competitors in the process of restoring equilibrium in financial portfolios.[12] In this way pressure is imposed on NBFI balance-sheets and financial markets in general.

Since 1956 major trading banks have been party to an agreement with the Reserve Bank under which they observe a uniform, minimum ratio (currently 18 per cent) of *LGS* assets (notes and coin, cash, other than SRDs, with the Reserve Bank, Treasury bills and notes and other Commonwealth government securities and, since August 1984, secured loans at call with authorised money-market dealers[13]) to Australian deposits. Under the arrangement banks may, if necessary, borrow from the Reserve Bank to satisfy the minimum ratio while adjustments are made to their balance-sheets, but the rates charged on such loans are at the discretion of the Reserve Bank. 'Prescribed banks' are not party to the convention but are, nevertheless, asked to provide undertakings to maintain minimum holdings of selected liquid assets. The Reserve Bank undertakes to administer SRD policy so that, providing bank lending is in line with what the Reserve Bank desires, the trading banks will normally be able to maintain their LGS ratio above the prescribed minimum. Moreover, as noted earlier, the Reserve Bank is required to assist the banks further by providing estimates of expected increases/decreases in deposits and in LGS plus SRD assets and details of their intended policy with respect to SRD ratios. In practice SRD ratio changes were normally timed to avoid aggravating banks' seasonal liquidity management problems and, at any rate, since 1981 changes have been infrequent, in accord with the greater emphasis placed on open-market operations for monetary policy purposes.

The SRD instrument, in conjunction with the LGS convention, was used by the authorities as a means of restricting banks' lending and hence monetary aggregate growth. The role played by the LGS convention was to set a floor to banks' holdings of LGS assets and hence reinforce the intended pressure sought by SRD calls or other measures (e.g. sales of Commonwealth securities to non-banks) on financial markets in general and bank lending in particular.[14] In the days before liability management became practicable, this limited the extent to which banks could sell government securities (i.e. reduce their net take-up from the authorities) as a means of raising cash reserves and left them with little option but to curtail growth in advances in order to alter their cash reserve positions.[15] But with the recent moves adopted towards increasing the flexibility of Commonwealth government security yields (Macquarie Banking Centre, Mar 1983) it is not clear that the LGS convention has anything left to offer on the monetary policy front (although it may continue to serve some prudential function – see p. 15). This is because banks no longer have a financial incentive to run down government security holdings first in response to a reserve squeeze nor can they expect to secure more reserves through a reduction in their net take-up of such securities. (In May 1985 the Reserve Bank announced that the LGS convention was to be phased out – see the Addendum, p. 71.)

Under the Banking Act the Reserve Bank is empowered to determine trading and savings banks' advances policy in terms of both volume and direction (other than to a particular person). Prescribed banks are subject to the provisions as well, but state banks are not. The form of *quantitative guidance* given varied over the years, embracing the volume of approvals for new lending, growth in advances outstanding, comments on the desirable course for bank lending or combinations of these. With effect from end-June 1982 quantitative controls on trading bank lending were abolished. However, *qualitative guidance*, though little used in recent times, is occasionally given in relation to housing loans, especially where savings banks are concerned. Again, though, it has not proved necessary to invoke statutory powers.

With the approval of the Treasurer the Reserve Bank may promulgate regulations relating to interest rates payable to or by banks, or to or by others in the course of any banking business carried out by them. Such regulations may also embrace rates of discount chargeable by banks and the periods for which DTIs may pay interest on deposits. In practice formal regulatory powers have not been used, the

Reserve Bank, instead, preferring to inform banks by letter of interest-rate controls established. Following gradual deregulation of interest-rate controls the only restrictions remaining relate to certain types of lending for amounts of under $100 000. Prescribed banks are subject to official interest-rate policy and must consult with the Reserve Bank before determining their interest rates. Savings banks are subject to the same maxima on loans under $100 000.

Savings banks. In addition to the interest-rate controls and lending guidelines discussed above, savings banks are subject, under the Banking Act, to a minimum 15 per cent liquidity ratio (the ratio of cash, deposits with the Reserve Bank and short-term Commonwealth government securities to deposits) and to a limit (of $4 m. plus 2.5 per cent of deposits in Australia) on the amount of funds that can be held with trading banks. Further, under the Banking (Savings Banks) Regulations Act, as amended in August 1982, savings banks are required to keep at least 94 per cent of their Australian deposits in the form of cash on hand in Australia, deposits with the Reserve Bank, deposits with and loans to other banks, Commonwealth and state government securities, securities issued or guaranteed by Commonwealth or state or local government authorities, loans guaranteed by or on behalf of the Commonwealth, a state or a territory, loans for housing or other purposes on the security of land in Australia and secured loans to authorised dealers in the short-term money market. Even this panoply of controls is significantly less than that which obtained until the 1980s – see Table 1.3 (pp. 27–31).

(ii) On state banks

State banks comprise trading and savings banks established by state government. They are not generally subject to Reserve Bank powers, which derive from Commonwealth legislation, but instead operate under state government legislation. Nevertheless their co-operation is sought by the Reserve Bank in ensuring the effectiveness of official monetary policy. As mentioned earlier, state trading banks are informed of SRD policy, as is also the case for lending guidance given to the banks subject to the Banking Act. Generally speaking, state savings banks broadly follow the investment pattern of other savings banks and interest rate controls reflect those impinging on banks subject to the Banking Act.

(iii) On (deposit-taking) NBFIs

Under the Financial Corporations Act of 1974 the Commonwealth government has the power to influence the business activities of certain financial and trading corporations.[16] These comprise: building societies, credit unions, authorised short-term money-market dealers, money-market corporations (i.e. merchant banks), pastoral finance companies, finance companies, general financiers, retailers, intra-group financiers and 'other financial corporations'. These corporations may additionally be subject to state or territory legislation.

The provisions of the Act impose reporting requirements on subject corporations covering monthly returns of assets, liabilities and financial operations of the larger corporations (other than retailers) and quarterly returns of assets and selected liabilities for smaller corporations. Consultations between the Reserve Bank and subject corporations are also formally provided for. Perhaps the most contentious part of the Act is Part IV, which provides for the establishment of regulations giving the Reserve Bank, with the Treasurer's approval, powers relating to the determination of asset ratios, interest rates and lending policies. Provisions for applying different controls to different categories of corporations are included, although any control must apply equally to all corporations within a given category.[17] To date it has not been deemed desirable or necessary to proclaim this part of the Act.

Because of the special market-making roles performed by the *authorised money-market dealers* and the privileged access to Reserve Bank credit given to them, the Reserve Bank specifies both their 'gearing limits' (33 times shareholders' funds) and the types of assets they may hold. Their holdings of non-Commonwealth money-market securities (largely within five years to maturity) are limited to 30 per cent of gearing limits.

(iv) Other

With the adoption of a clean float of the Australian dollar in December 1983 and the simultaneous dismantling of a large part of official exchange control (see Table 1.3, pp. 31–4), *foreign-exchange arrangements* (RBA, 1983 (a), sec. 8) ceased to perform any major monetary policy function. The float, making due allowance for short-term 'smoothing' and limited official intervention to 'test' the market, effectively insulates the domestic money stock from capital flows, removing a major impediment to the successful conduct of monetary policy.[18] And removal of exchange controls (carried a stage further since 1983 – see Table 1.3 on p. 34) ended the debate on their effectiveness in promoting the achievement of policy goals.[19]

(b) Prudential controls imposed on DTIs

Prudential regulation of DTIs is described in detail in Table 1.2 according to the classification system outlined by Dale (1980). The Reserve Bank has no statutory powers to determine such requirements as capital positions or investment policy by banks (other than savings banks), but some direct controls, such as the SRD/LGS mechanism and savings banks' asset ratios, may perform prudential functions. The Banking Act, however, does impose upon the Reserve Bank a duty to protect *banks'* depositors and empowers it to investigate the affairs of a bank which has declared that suspension of payment is imminent or that it is unable to meet obligations[20] and to take over control of its business until repayment of depositors is assured. The Reserve Bank's supervisory role to date (the entry of foreign banks may yet necessitate the embodiment of formal prudential powers within the Banking Act) has centred on detailed discussions with banks' management, analysis of financial data and scrutiny of internal control procedures as the means of ensuring that appropriate prudential standards are adopted.

Although the Financial Corporations Act does not require the Reserve Bank to perform a depositor-protection function with respect to subject corporations, the Bank nevertheless is obliged to preserve the stability of the financial system as a whole. To that end the Reserve Bank is willing to provide liquidity support facilities, where necessary, to 'individual banks which stand behind the liquidity needs of those individual financial institutions which are responsibly managed and have adequate asset backing' (RBA, 1983 (a) p. 30). Moreover the Reserve Bank keeps a careful eye on the activities of the major NBFI groups through the collection and analysis of data, as required by the Financial Corporations Act, and through direct consultations. Because of the importance of their market-making functions the authorised dealers in the short-term money market receive special attention, and agreements have been made with respect to gearing ratios and portfolio composition. Finally, the relevant state or territory legislation determines the prudential arrangements appli-

Table 1.2   Prudential controls operating in Australia on deposit-taking financial intermediaries

Type of control	Details
1. *Market entry*	
(a) Banks	(i) Aside from state banks all organisations wishing to include the title 'bank' in a registered business name must be authorised by the Governor-General under Section 9 of the Banking Act. Approval for bodies corporate is subject to 'such conditions as are specified in the authority' granted, which are likely to embrace the suitability of directors, shareholders and management, an initial minimum capital requirement of $25 m., the adequacy of prudential safeguards, and the proposed range of services to be offered.
	(ii) The Banks (Shareholdings) Act limits individual or associated holdings in an Australian bank to less than 15 per cent of the bank's voting shares unless the Governor-General fixes a higher percentage.
	(iii) Under the Tasmanian Savings Banks Act trustee savings banks may only be formed with the sanction and approval of a judge as prescribed by Court rules.
	(iv) Banks cannot dispose of or effect a restructuring of their business without the consent of the Treasurer.
(b) Authorised money-market dealers	Authorised money-market dealers must be authorised by the Reserve Bank. It is a strong wish of the Reserve Bank that a person or institution should not be a substantial shareholder in more than one authorised dealer company and even then the practice is to allow only indirect equity interests to a maximum of 12.5 per cent (for non-residents the maximum aggregate equity interest is 45 per cent).
(c) Permanent building societies	(i) Must be registered under the relevant state or territory legislation.
	(ii) In all states and territories (except Tasmania) a specified minimum number of persons is required to form a building society.
	(iii) Minimum fund/capital requirements must be satisfied in all mainland states and the Northern Territory (minimum share capital required ranges from $500 000 to $1 m., a varying proportion of which must be non-withdrawable for 10 years).

Table 1.2—continued

Type of control	Details
	(iv) In all mainland states (except Queensland) and in the ACT no person or company is permitted to hold more than 20 per cent of the subscribed capital. (In Victoria a company may hold more with the Registrar's approval; in Western Australia companies may not in aggregate hold more than 50 per cent.)
(d) Credit unions	(i) All credit unions must be registered under the relevant state or territory legislation. The registration requirements are applied by the Registrars in a discretionary manner. As far as formal requirements are concerned, in NSW, Queensland, South Australia and Western Australia a proposed credit union may only be formed by 25 or more persons who have subscribed to its objects and rules which must, however, comply with the Act. In the ACT the minimum number of persons is seven: in Tasmania it is fifteen. No minimum capital requirements are imposed in the states or the ACT.
	(ii) In NSW, Western Australia and the ACT no shareholders may hold more than 20 per cent of paid-up share capital. In South Australia all members must hold the same number of shares and in Queensland natural persons are limited to a shareholding of $2000 unless the Governor-in-Council approves a greater amount.
2. Capital adequacy	
(a) Banks	The Reserve Bank monitors the capital gearing of all banks subject to the Banking Act on a consolidated basis (i.e. domestic operations and those of overseas branches and subsidiaries and domestic financial associations are considered) and uses moral suasion to ensure 'appropriate' levels are maintained. (Subordinated debt is excluded for this purpose.)
(b) Authorised money-market dealers	Authorised money-market dealers are subject to gearing limits whereby borrowings are limited to 33 times shareholders' funds.
(c) Permanent building societies	Subject to some form of gearing ratio in all mainland states and territories. Deposits with and loans to societies (i.e. as distinct from share capital) are not permitted to exceed:

- 4/5 of loans outstanding to members in NSW;
- 2/3 of loans outstanding in South Australia and the Northern Territory;
- 5 times share capital in Victoria;
- 4 times paid-up share capital and reserves in Queensland;
- 4 times share capital in Western Australia;
- $\frac{1}{2}$ of unpaid capital, plus 4/5 of loans outstanding, plus $\frac{1}{2}$ of other assets (excluding goodwill), less $\frac{1}{2}$ of debts owing by the society in the ACT, where they have been received from persons other than members holding fully paid-up shares to the value of $10.

(d) Credit unions

Credit unions in NSW, South Australia and Western Australia may not accept loans from non-members in excess of 25 per cent of members' funds (defined to include share capital and deposits in NSW and Western Australia and share capital, deposits and reserves in South Australia). Credit unions in the ACT are subject to the same constraints on borrowing as permanent building societies. In Queensland credit unions may not borrow more than the aggregate amount specified in its rules (or as prescribed in the Act).

3. *Liquidity adequacy*

(a) Banks

(i) The SRD/LGS mechanism applied to trading banks, in so far as it contributes to the stability of, and public confidence in, banks, can be regarded as a prudential device. (The current minimum LGS ratio is 18 per cent.)

(ii) The Reserve Bank is currently seeking to establish a framework for the prudential supervision of trading banks' liquidity.

(iii) Under the Banking (Saving Banks) Regulations, as amended on 26 August 1982, each savings bank is required to invest a minimum of 15 per cent of depositors' balances in cash, deposits with the Reserve Bank and Commonwealth government securities.

(b) Permanent building societies

Permanent building societies in the mainland states are not permitted to approve loans unless they hold 'liquid assets' equivalent to 10 per cent (in Queensland 7.5

Table 1.2—*continued*

Type of control	*Details*
	per cent) of the sum of paid-up share capital and deposits (Victoria, South Australia and Western Australia also include societies' unsecured borrowings). In the ACT building societies meet this requirement voluntarily, although a formal requirement is planned. In Tasmania building societies wishing to have their deposits accorded trustee status are required to meet the liquid asset ratio specified in terms of deposits (i.e. share capital is excluded). The definitions of 'liquid assets' vary between the states – see Interim Campbell Report, table 15.1.
(c) Credit unions	Credit unions are required to hold 'liquid assets' (see Interim Campbell Report, table 15.2, for varying definitions) equivalent to a prescribed proportion (7 per cent in NSW and Western Australia, 9 per cent in South Australia and 10 per cent in the ACT) of the sum of their share capital and deposits (also loans in South Australia, but excluding deposits fixed for a term of more than 2 years in Western Australia). In NSW, Western Australia and the ACT, credit unions may not make/approve loans if their holding of liquid assets falls below the prescribed proportion.

4. *Restrictions on business activities*

(a) Banks	(i) Although in August 1984 the Reserve Bank withdrew the restraint on the maximum allowable equity interest in a merchant bank (at 60 per cent it was thought low enough to discourage the transfer of business to the less regulated merchant banks but high enough to allow effective management control) the Reserve Bank stated that it did not want a bank subsidiary to become large relative to the bank itself. Further, the Reserve Bank prefers that there should not be a proliferation of relationships between financial institutions, particularly in the same broad financial area.

(ii) Following understandings reached in 1963, banks are requested to consult with the Reserve Bank on any proposals to form associations with non-bank institutions. Management or sponsorship of cash management trusts by banks or their wholly-owned subsidiaries is prohibited.

(iii) Banks' associations with official short-term money-market dealers and property subsidiaries are specifically limited by the Reserve Bank. Banks have been asked not to enter into direct and permanent associations with official dealers. Guidelines are provided pertaining to wholly-owned property subsidiaries covering function, maturity structure of public borrowings and relationships with the parent bank.

(iv) Banks have been asked not to give letters of comfort, general guarantees, etc., regarding the repayment of liabilities issued by their subsidiaries other than savings banks.

(v) Banks are subject to interest-rate ceilings on small ($<$\$100 000) overdrafts, housing loans and farm-development loans and to the LGS/SRD convention. They are also subject to lending guidelines, as specified by the Reserve Bank.

(vi) Savings banks are restricted in the range of assets they can acquire. Since August 1982 they have been required to observe a minimum 15 per cent liquidity ratio (involving minimum holdings of cash, deposits with the Reserve Bank and Commonwealth government securities) and to hold a minimum of 94 per cent of depositors' balances in Australia in the form of liquid assets (as defined for the liquidity ratios), state or state-guaranteed securities, government-guaranteed loans, secured short-term loans to authorised money-market dealers, deposits with or loans to prescribed banks (up to a maximum of \$4 m. plus $2\frac{1}{2}$ per cent of its deposits in Australia) and loans for housing or other purposes on the security of land in Australia. Finally, they are subject to Reserve Bank suasion as to the pattern of their lending, especially with respect to housing.

(vii) Trustee savings banks are limited in the investments and loans they can make. They are subject to the Banking Act and the Tasmanian Savings Bank Act and, under the latter, are permitted to make investments in or loans upon any security authorised by the Trustee Act for the investment of trust moneys, to make unsecured loans to

Table 1.2—continued

Type of control	Details
	depositors and to hold a maximum of 30 per cent of their assets in fixed deposits with other banks. Although required by the Banking Act to hold assets in Australia at least equal to their deposits, they escape the 15 per cent liquidity requirement placed on savings banks.
	(viii) Unless authorised by the Reserve Bank, banks are required under the Banking Act to hold assets (other than goodwill) in Australia of a value of not less than the total amount of their deposit liabilities in Australia. The requirement applies to all savings banks (but the figure is reduced to 94 per cent of deposit liabilities), but does not apply to trading banks incorporated in the Queen's dominions.
(b) Authorised money-market dealers	The assets structures of authorised money-market dealers are restricted. From 1 July 1982 up to 30 per cent of a dealer's gearing limit may be held in assets within 5 years to maturity in the form of bank CDs, acceptances and public authority marketable securities or in 'other assets' (including Commonwealth government or other securities with 5 or more years to maturity), provided these do not exceed 2.5 per cent of the gearing limit. The remainder of a dealer's assets must be Commonwealth government securities within 5 years of maturity (in normal circumstances, these will be the only assets accepted as collateral for loans made under Reserve Bank lines of credit to authorised dealers).
(c) Permanent building societies	State Acts, Territory legislation and tax requirements contain a range of provisions relating to the loans and investments which societies may make, source and denomination of borrowings, maturity of assets and liabilities and restrictions on fund-raising procedures.
	(i) *Loans.* All states and territories permit loans to members (and others in Victoria and the Northern Territory) on security of mortgage over land. NSW, Victoria, Queensland, the ACT and the Northern Territory also permit loans to members on security of their shares (or deposits in NSW, and to non-members in Queensland).

In all mainland states loans may not exceed 75 per cent of valuation of the property unless additional security is taken (for a loan in excess of $25 000 in NSW). In all mainland states 'special advances' or 'restricted loans' (e.g. to a body corporate or in excess of a certain amount) are limited to a maximum of 10 per cent of the value of total loans advanced in any one year. Some states restrict lending on the security of vacant land. Different provisions relate to lending to other building societies according to Registrar decisions in each state (in practice, building societies rarely lend to societies in other states).

(ii) *Investments.* Relevant Acts specify the forms of investment where funds not immediately required for making loans may be held. These normally include bank deposits, other trustee-type investments in the state of operation and acceptances. In NSW shares in a co-operative insurance company to a limit of £100000 may be held; in South Australia investment in company shares up to a limit of 1 per cent of paid-up share-capital is authorised. In Queensland and Western Australia the purchase of mortgage debts from other societies is allowed and, in the former, societies may invest in the Building Societies Contingency Fund.

(iii) *Source of borrowings.* To be taxed as a co-operative a building society must have as a primary objective the obtaining of funds from its shareholders for on-lending to its members. In practice the Commissioner of Taxation accepts that this requirement is satisfied so long as at least 20 per cent of the funds used for making housing loans is obtained from the society's own members.

(iv) *Maturity of assets.* Investments in trustee securities and *ARDB* transferable deposits must be within 10 years of maturity in NSW. In South Australia all securities must be within 15 years of maturity.

(v) *Maturity of liabilities.* In NSW and South Australia building societies may possess the power not to repay share capital at any specified date or time (although in practice this right is not exercised). In NSW and the ACT building societies may not receive deposits except on the terms that no less than one month's notice may be required before repayment. In Queensland the term of loans to societies and deposits (as distinct from shares) may not be less than two months (although, in practice, deposits are repaid on demand after expiry of the term of deposit).

Table 1.2—continued

Type of control	Details
	(vi) *Denomination of borrowiwngs.* In Victoria, South Australia and Western Australia they may only borrow and repay moneys denominated in Australian currency.
	(vii) *Fund-raising restrictions.* For a society seeking registration the contents of advertisements seeking members, share capital or deposits must be approved by the Registrar. Once registered, approval to commence advertising must be obtained from the Registrar (or the Advisory Committee in the case of NSW).
(d) Credit unions	(i) *Loans.* Similar restrictions to those imposed on building societies are borne by credit unions. Most states and the ACT restrict loans to members as specified in their rules (in Western Australia loans may also be made to other credit unions). Legislation normally provides also for the Board of a credit union to set a maximum amount that may be advanced on a secured or unsecured basis.
	(ii) *Investments.* Surplus funds may be invested in trustee securities and deposits/shares with specified banks and credit-union associations in all mainland states. In addition investments in other designated assets are allowed, the assets varying according to state location. In the ACT credit unions are permitted to hold the same range of investments as permanent building societies provided they hold liquid assets amounting to at least 10 per cent of withdrawable funds.
	(iii) *Source of borrowing.* To be taxed as a credit union it must have the raising of moneys from its members for lending to its members as its principal object. No minimum proportion of funds to be obtained from members is specified under the Income Tax Assessments Act, however. In NSW, South Australia and Western Australia credit unions may only receive deposits from members. They may also borrow from non-members up to a maximum of 25 per cent of members' funds.
	(iv) *Maturity of assets.* In NSW investments in trustee securities must be within 10 years of maturity and loans may not be made for a period exceeding 15 years. In South Australia the maturity date of any investment must be less than 15 years.

(v) *Maturity of liabilities.* In South Australia one month's notice may be required before withdrawal of share capital from a credit union. In other mainland states and the ACT credit unions may not receive deposits except on terms requiring the giving of at least 1 month's notice before withdrawal.

(vi) *Fund-raising restrictions.* In South Australia the Registrar's consent is required prior to the issue of an advertisement, which must contain any information he stipulates. In NSW, South Australia and Western Australia, with the approval of the Minister, the Registrar may prohibit the publication of any advertisement and/or require its withdrawal.

5. *Loan concentration*

(a) Banks

The major banks have 'in-house' rules for loan concentration which are considered by the Reserve Bank in their periodic discussions with management.

(b) Permanent building societies

In all mainland states 'special advances' or 'restricted loans' are limited to a maximum of 10 per cent of the value of total loans advanced in any one year.

6. *Country risk*

The Reserve Bank can afford to take a relatively relaxed attitude to 'country risk' as Australian banks' exposure arising from international lending by their offshore offices is quite widely spread and does not appear to be unduly large relative to their resources (at end-March 1983 aggregate exposure to Mexico was about 0.4 per cent of total bank assets, Latin America as a whole, 0.6 per cent and Eastern Europe, 0.3 per cent). Nevertheless the Reserve Bank seeks to ensure that banks apply 'appropriate' limits and guidelines to country risk and that management-control systems are adequate in this respect.

7. *Foreign currency exposure*

The Reserve Bank seeks to ensure that banks apply appropriate limits and guidelines to foreign currency exposures (and maturity mismatching) and checks that management-control systems are adequate in this respect. Details are sought on both a global and an individual centre basis.

Type of control	Details
8. *Official liquidity/solvency support arrangements* (covering 'lender-of-last-resort' facilities and compulsory levy-financed fund-pooling arrangements established under legislation and/or entailing explicit government financial support).	
(a) Banks – 'lender-of-last-resort' facilities	(i) In order to preserve confidence in, and hence the stability of, the financial system, under Section 26 of its own Act the Reserve Bank may find it necessary, possibly in conjunction with others, to support individual banks. This liquidity support would be additional to that required under the LGS convention. As a guide to how, in practice, this might be achieved one is able to turn to the example of the Bank of Adelaide which, in 1979, received liquidity assistance direct from the Reserve Bank and, at the behest of the Reserve Bank, from a number of major trading banks also. This injection of capital enabled the Bank of Adelaide to deal with the affairs of its wholly-owned finance company Finance Corporation of Australia Ltd (which had suffered from a dramatic fall in the value of its development land holdings) by making substantial specific and general provisions against possible losses. Subsequently, again at the suggestion of the Reserve Bank, the Bank of Adelaide was merged with the ANZ Banking Group Ltd. (ii) Arrangements also exist whereby, against the background of the Reserve Bank's support for banking liquidity, banks may stand behind financial institutions which are responsibly managed and have adequate asset-backing. An example of such an operation arose in 1977 when, following the placing of a large Queensland building society in the hands of an administrator, a general erosion in confidence in Queensland building societies set in. This necessitated the bankers of one large Queensland society making available, with the support of the Reserve Bank, a substantial line of credit to that society. (iii) State banks' liabilities are guaranteed by the respective state governments and the liabilities of member banks of the Commonwealth Banking Corporation are guaranteed by the Commonwealth government.

(b) Permanent building
     societies

In Victoria the Building Societies' General Reserve Fund was established in 1976 under the Building Societies Act for: (i) the protection of members of societies which are being or have been wound up, as well as persons who give credit or lend to, or deposit money with such societies; and (ii) the provision of 'temporary financial assistance' to societies which normally maintain an acceptable level of liquidity. The Fund is financed primarily by levies on societies, payable each year, equivalent to 0.1 per cent of the sum of withdrawable share capital, deposits and loans to societies. As well, societies may be subject to compulsory levies or required to make loans to the Fund at a prescribed rate of interest. If necessary funds may also be borrowed from other sources, as approved by the Minister. There is no explicit government backing for the Fund.

In Queensland the Permanent Building Societies Contingency Fund was established in 1976 under the Building Societies Act to provide protection to persons acquiring shares in or lending to permanent building societies and creditors of those societies. The Fund is financed by levies on societies, payable montly, at an annual rate of 0.25 per cent of the sum of withdrawable share capital, deposits and funds obtained on loan (but excluding certain prescribed loans). Additional levies may be called for (up to a maximum of an additional 0.75 per cent of the sum of withdrawable share capital, deposits and funds on loan) and societies may also be required to make compulsory loans to the Fund. The Fund has no explicit government backing.

(c) Credit unions

In NSW the Credit Union Savings Reserve Fund was established in 1978 to provide financial assistance to credit unions and to meet the claims of any credit union that is unable or refuses to satisfy any lawful demands with respect to their share capital or deposits. Subscriptions equal to 0.75 per cent of share capital and deposits are required and must be maintained at this level. In addition further levies (not exceeding 0.5 per cent of share capital and deposits in any 12-month period) may be made if the capital of the fund needs replenishing. In South Australia the Credit Union Stabilisation Fund was established under the Credit Union Act to meet the claims of members of any credit union which fails to satisfy any demands with respect to their share capital or deposits, as long as the claim is made within 6

Table 1.2—continued

Type of control	Details
	months of that failure. Credit unions contribute the equivalent of 2 per cent of their share capital and deposits and are required to maintain the Fund at this level. Additional levies (not exceeding 0.2 per cent of share capital and deposits in any calendar year) may also be required. Additional borrowings from or with the concurrence of the State Treasurer (who guarantees such borrowings) are also sanctioned. In Victoria the Credit Societies General Reserve Fund was established in 1976 to protect members and others who lend to or deposit money with credit societies as well as providing temporary financial assistance to societies experiencing financial difficulties. Annual levies of 0.1 per cent of aggregate liabilities are required until the Fund reaches $10 m. (or as prescribed). Additionally annual contributions are required to maintain its total contribution at a level at least equivalent to 1 per cent of aggregate liabilities. Compulsory levies and/or loans may also be required by the Minister.

9. *Industry-based liquidity/solvency support arrangements (including deposit insurance)*

Type of control	Details
(a) Banks	No formal industry-based support arrangements exist although the Bank of Adelaide affair of May 1979 involved loans by banks belonging to the Australian Bankers Association and the Commonwealth Trading Bank (but organised under the auspices of the Reserve Bank).
(b) Permanent building societies	In February 1980 the Commonwealth government announced that it had endorsed the framework for a private industry-based deposit insurance scheme for permanent building societies. The scheme involves the establishment of a private national insuring corporation (**ABSSDIC**, established 1984), with building societies that choose to become members (state governments may insist on membership) subscribing the capital and paying the premiums. The insuring corporation will have the power to borrow or arrange standbys and lines of credit from normal

commercial sources and have discretion to arrange liquidity support for insured societies which may be experiencing temporary loss of liquidity. In New South Wales the Building Society Indemnity Fund Ltd was established in 1967 as a private organisation to guarantee the liquidity (as distinct from the solvency) of its member societies. Its aim is that member societies should have access to meet withdrawals of $10 000 for each investor. Each member society allocates 'liquid assets' equivalent to 2 per cent of its withdrawable funds to the Fund (which is permitted to ask for up to 3 per cent). In the event of liquidity assistance being sought by member societies, securities to the appropriate value would be liquidated. In Victoria the Building Society Resources Ltd was established in 1967 to provide a source of liquidity and mutual assistance for its members. The company has established lines of credit and also borrows in the financial market against the security of investments owned by societies. In addition it has created an internal secondary market for the purchase and sale of mortgages to and from its members. Membership is voluntary and members must invest 0.2 per cent of their assets as at end-1977 in the share capital of the Corporation.

(c) Credit unions

The Australian Federation of Credit Union Leagues Ltd was established in 1966 to represent the interests of a significant proportion of Australia's credit unions, comprising 5 member leagues operating in South Australia, Victoria, Queensland, NSW and the ACT, to which a varying number of credit unions operating in those states belongs. There is also a credit-union association in Western Australia which is not affiliated with AFCUL and a number of smaller credit-union associations operate in some states. Differing legislation in the states sets out the objectives of the associations and determines issues such as the subscription of share capital, the investment of surplus funds, borrowing facilities and the building up of reserves.

cable to permanent building societies and credit unions, the major deposit-taking NBFIs.

1.3 FINANCIAL DEREGULATION IN AUSTRALIA

Fortuitously the whole issue of financial deregulation in Australia has been surveyed in two recent reports, the Campbell Report ('Report of the Committee of Enquiry into The Australian Financial System', 1981) and the Martin Report ('Australian Financial System: Report of the Review Group', 1983). The former report was the result of deliberations of a committee, chaired by Mr J. K. Campbell, charged with the responsibility of analysing and reporting (with recommendations) on the structure and methods of operation of the Australian financial system. The terms of reference emphasised the importance of 'efficiency' considerations in the committee's deliberations. In contrast the Report of the Review Group represented the outcome of deliberations by a group chaired by Mr V. E. Martin (established by the incoming Labor government), which were required to take into account not just efficiency and stability objectives, but also the government's social and economic objectives (especially in relation to housing finance and rural and small business sectors), in reviewing the recommendations of the Campbell Committee.

Before attempting to provide a broad assessment of the recommendations made by these two bodies it is important to appreciate the extent to which the financial system had already been deregulated, a process undoubtedly speeded up since publication of the two reports. Brief details of the major moves are recorded in Table 1.3. In addition to monetary deregulation, financial deregulation also covered the securities industry and other areas such as participation, foreign and domestic, in banking and bank diversification. Though interesting in their own right, these other areas will only be considered to the extent that they hold prudential ramifications.

Critique of the Campbell and Martin Reports

For the purposes of this discussion the arguments will focus on two areas, namely monetary and prudential regulation. While the necessarily brief analysis,[21] given the scope of this book, cannot hope to do justice to the vast amount of material covered by these two reports,

Table 1.3   Australia: the programme of financial deregulation since 1970

A. Monetary Controls

Date of announcement	Subject-matter	Details
December 1970	Trading bank deposit facilities	Approval was given for the extension from 2 to 4 years of the maximum allowable period for which trading banks can take fixed deposits.
January 1972	Short-term money markets	The requirement that authorised dealers should hold amounts of government securities ('margins') with the Reserve Bank additional to security lodged with lenders was withdrawn from 1 February.
February 1972	Trading bank interest rates	Henceforth the maximum overdraft rate would apply only on loans drawn under limits of less than $50 000.
November 1972	Trading bank Farm Development Loan Funds lending	General arrangements for this form of lending were widened and the limitations on the type of rural lending from the Funds were lifted with interest rates charged on new longer-term lending to be at commercial rates.
September 1973	Trading bank interest rates	The ceiling on rates payable by banks on certificates of deposit was removed and their maximum term was extended from 2 to 4 years. Previous requests to banks to offer concessional rates on certain categories of loan (e.g. to exporters and rural producers) were withdrawn.
January 1976	Trading bank and savings bank interest rates	The maximum rate of interest chargeable on 'small' overdrafts was extended from overdrafts drawn under limits of less than $50 000 to overdrafts drawn under limits of less than $100 000. The maximum interest rates chargeable on 'small' savings bank loans are similarly extended to loans under $100 000.
May 1977	Savings bank regulations	The Banking (Savings Banks) Regulations were amended to allow, from 27 May, a reduction from 50 to 45 per cent in the

Table 1.3—*continued*

		proportion of depositors' balances required to be held in certain prescribed assets (mainly liquid assets and public sector securities). On 15 June three further technical amendments were made concerning the nature of securities in which savings banks may invest and their eligibility as prescribed assets.
August 1978	Savings bank regulations	An amendment to the Banking (Savings Banks) Regulations reduced from 45 to 40 per cent the proportion of depositors' balances required to be held in prescribed asset form.
April 1979	Marketing of Commonwealth securities	The Loan Council agreed to a new system of issuing Treasury notes by periodic tender through the Reserve Bank and to a replacement of the present system of selling Commonwealth bonds in periodic cash loans with a 'tap' issue system, making new securities available more or less continuously to investors.
May 1979	Marketing of Commonwealth securities	In addition to its other arrangements for trading in Commonwealth Government securities the Reserve Bank announced it would make securities available through authorised money-market dealers and stock-exchange brokers.
December 1979	ditto	Arrangements were announced whereby Treasury notes would be sold by a tender system rather than the old system when they were continuously on sale at predetermined prices. The first tender was held on the 19 December.
April 1980	ditto	Arrangements were announced for the tap system for the marketing of Treasury bonds. The first two tap stocks were on issue from 30 April.
December 1980	Trading and savings bank deposit interest rates	Effective 3 December, the ceilings on interest rates offered by trading and savings banks on deposits were to be removed.
August 1981	Minimum term of issue for bank CDs	Reduced from 3 months to 30 days.

November 1981	Marketing of Australian savings bonds	From 9 November investors were permitted to reinvest into a later series of Australian Savings Bonds without giving, as was required before, one month's notice of their intention to do so.
March 1982	Trading bank fixed deposit terms control	The minimum period for which trading banks may offer fixed deposits and CDs was reduced from 30 days to 14 days for amounts of $50 000 and over and from 3 months to 30 days for fixed deposits of under $50 000.
March 1982	Savings bank fixed deposit terms control	Savings banks were authorised to offer fixed deposits of less than $50 000 for terms of 30 days to 4 years. In addition they need no longer require a minimum period of 1 month's notice of withdrawal on their savings investment accounts.
May 1982	'Last-resort' loans to authorised money market dealers	Loans are now repayable between 7 and 10 days (previously 7 and 30 days) and the Reserve Bank reserves the right to offer loans of less than 7 days.
May 1982	Interest paid on SRDs	Increased from 2.5 per cent to 5 per cent per annum as a move towards paying a competitive rate on SRDs.
June 1982	Arrangements with authorised money market dealers	Effective 1 July, dealers were allowed more flexibility (i.e. could hold up to 30 per cent rather than 20 per cent of their gearing limits in non-Commonwealth government securities) in the composition of their portfolios. However the range of securities accepted by the Reserve Bank as collateral for last-resort loans was reduced to comprise, in normal circumstances, only Commonwealth government securities within 5 years to maturity (previously some other public-sector securities were accepted).
June 1982	Loan Council decisions	1. The tap system of selling Commonwealth Treasury bonds was replaced with a tender system. Under this system the Treasurer has the power to decide the timing of each tender and the maturity, coupons and quantities of stock to be offered (as well as the power to allot up to the full amount

Table 1.3—*continued*

		offered at each tender) at yields bid in the tender. 2. The power to determine the terms and conditions of Australian Savings Bonds was delegated to the Treasurer. 3. Major electricity authorities were freed, in respect of their domestic borrowing, from Loan Council controls.
June 1982	Lending requests	With effect from the end of June the request, made on 15 September 1981, to trading banks to keep growth in their advances to not more than 12 per cent per annum was withdrawn. This represented the abolition of quantitative controls on trading-bank lending (in force since 1975).
July 1982	Marketing of Commonwealth securities	The first Treasury bond tender was announced.
August 1982	Savings bank regulations	Effective 31 August, the 40 per cent 'prescribed assets ratio' was abolished but, henceforth, each savings bank was required to invest a minimum of 15 per cent of depositors' balances in cash, deposits with the Reserve Bank and Commonwealth government securities. For a transitional period to 30 June 1983 banks had the option of observing this or the previous $7\frac{1}{2}$ per cent requirement. In addition savings banks were allowed to invest 6 per cent of deposits in assets (other than fixed assets) of their choice, and restrictions on sources of deposits were relaxed to allow the acceptance of deposits from trading or profit-making bodies up to a maximum, for each entity, of $100 000.
July 1983	Loan Council controls	The Loan Council discontinued arrangements whereby the terms, conditions and timing of domestic borrowings by larger authorities were subject to Loan Council control.

April 1984	Maturity controls on bank deposits	Effective 1 August, all maturity controls on trading and savings banks are to be removed. This ended the monopoly enjoyed by the merchant banks for deposits of less than 14 days to maturity and allows banks to accept deposits of more than 4 years to maturity.
April 1984	Payment of interest on chequing accounts and call money	Effective 1 August, banks are to be permitted to offer interest on chequing accounts and call money (the first bank to take advantage of this was the Commonwealth Bank of Australia which, from 1 August, 1984, paid 4 per cent interest on balances of between $2000 and $4999 and 7 per cent on balances of $5000 and over).
April 1984	Amendment to the Banking (Savings Bank) Regulations	Amended to allow, from 1 August: – savings banks to offer cheque facilities on all accounts; – removal of the $100 000 limit on deposits by a trading or profit-making body. At the same time the Reserve Bank announced the removal of the control on the maximum size ($50 000) of fixed deposits offered by savings banks.
June 1984	LGS convention	Effective 1 August, major trading banks would be allowed to count their loans to authorised dealers (on the security of Commonwealth government securities) as LGS assets for the purposes of the LGS convention.
September 1984	'30/20' rule	It was abolished because it was no longer thought to have any significant effect on Commonwealth and semi-government security yields yet involved considerable administrative costs.

B. Foreign Exchange Arrangements

Date of announcement	*Details*
September 1971	Banks were given greater discretion to deal with their customers in sterling forward exchange at rates determined by them and, within limits, to vary the exchange rates at which they dealt with

Table 1.3—continued

	the public in spot transactions in sterling. The measures were designed to stimulate competition in the foreign-exchange field.
July 1972	Australian residents could arrange to receive payments from and make payments to overseas countries in any foreign currency. Previous arrangements required foreign currency settlements to be in currencies appropriate to the monetary area in which a particular country was situated.
September 1973	New outer limits were set for banks' spot exchange transactions with the public in US dollars. Banks' rates of exchange for other currencies were to reflect the change in the market rates in the US dollar.
September 1974	The Australian dollar was devalued by 12 per cent. The fixed link to the US dollar (adopted in December 1971) was discontinued, with the exchange rate for the Australian dollar henceforth being determined by changes in an average of foreign currency values weighted in accordance with trading significance to Australia, in order to maintain a constant effective (trade-weighted) rate of exchange.
November 1976	The Australian dollar was devalued by 17.5 per cent and changed arrangements for adjusting the exchange rate were introduced whereby a small group of officials would review developments and make adjustments where necessary, with a view to making adjustments smaller and more frequent.
April 1977	Controls on indirect overseas borrowings were modified to permit reinvestment of maturing interest-bearing deposits and fixed-interest securities, including Commonwealth government securities, without application of variable deposit requirement or embargo where funds were originally received in Australia prior to 17 January 1977.
July 1977	The operation of the variable deposit requirement, imposed on 14 January, was suspended. The embargo on short-term overseas borrowing was reduced from 2 years to 6 months, reverting to the position prior to 14 January.
June 1978	Some procedural requirements for smaller foreign investments were relaxed, existing foreign-investment guidelines were modified and the embargo on overseas borrowings for periods of less than 6 months was suspended.
December 1978	The Banking (Foreign Exchange) Regulations were amended to allow for the abolition of export licensing and the introduction of new arrangements for the control of export proceeds.

January 1979	Some changes were announced in the conditions which apply to exchange-control authorities for direct investment overseas by Australian residents. The main change was that earnings from such investments may be retained for use overseas in the financing of growth in working capital, and for firmly planned future expansion, without specific prior exchange-control authority.
March 1980	Exchange controls relating to portfolio investment overseas by Australian residents were relaxed. Effective 1 April, limits were increased for overseas equity and real-estate investment, and the range of eligible investments was widened to include certain marketable fixed-interest securities.
July 1981	Effective 20 July, the limits on the amounts that Australian residents may invest overseas in equities and real estate were removed. The limits for investment overseas in fixed-interest securities remained unchanged.
December 1982	The need for exchange-control forms was eliminated on most categories of current payments or travel funds abroad for amounts up to $10 000.
October 1983	From 31 October the Reserve Bank will no longer underwrite the forward foreign-exchange market. Banks will no longer be required to clear their forward positions with the Reserve Bank and will be authorised to hold spot assets or liabilities as cover against exchange risk incurred on net forward positions subject to the establishment of 'spot against forward' currency limits. (As from 31 October the requirement that eligible forward risks had to be covered within 7 days of first being acquired ceased to apply.) In addition banks can now engage in spot US dollar transactions with customers at negotiated rates rather than within a fixed spread around a rate announced by the Reserve Bank, as previously (banks are already free to set all other rates of exchange). Banks clear to the Reserve Bank any net currency positions beyond the 'open-position' limits established.
November 1983	In a clarification of its rules the Reserve Bank stated that Australian banks may maintain foreign-currency balances for their own account 'sufficient for reasonable operating flexibility'. Six months prior to this the central bank had banned all dealings in foreign currencies without customer orders.
December 1983	Effective from 12 December the Australian dollar is to be allowed to float freely (the immediate desire was to halt heavy speculative capital inflows which were pushing up recorded monetary growth figures) and exchange controls were largely dismantled. The exchange controls

Table 1.3—continued

	retained related to tax havens, foreign-investment policy and interest-bearing balances held in Australia by foreign official institutions and banks. The requirement introduced in August 1971 that banks cover their net spot positions with the Reserve Bank at the end of each day lapses. Banks can now hold foreign currency positions within limits established for each bank.
April 1984	As a quid pro quo for opening up the short-term deposit market to the trading banks from 1 August 1984 it was decided that merchant banks be allowed to obtain *foreign-exchange licences*, subject to meeting a minimum capital requirement of $10 m. and demonstrating competence in foreign-exchange dealing. It was originally envisaged that about 20 licences would be granted but, in the event, 40 non-bank financiers had applications approved by the Treasurer by 19 June.
June 1984	Effective 25 June:

(i) Banks ceased to be agents of the Reserve Bank for the purposes of the Banking (Foreign Exchange) Regulations.

(ii) The need to submit exchange-control applications for approval was removed for all transactions except
 – investment in Australia by foreign governments or foreign banks
 – the taking or sending out of Australia of Australian notes and coin.

(iii) New tax-screening arrangements were introduced to cover certain payments abroad or to non-residents.

C. Other

Date of announcement	*Subject-matter*	*Details*
May 1980	Banks' shareholdings in money-market corporations	The Reserve Bank confirmed that, on a case-by-case basis, it was willing to extend the maximum allowable equity interest from $33\frac{1}{3}$ per cent to 60 per cent.

February 1981	Bank authorisation	The Governor-General granted the Australian Bank Ltd unconditional authority to carry on banking business in Australia.
June 1981	Authorisation of bank mergers	Under Section 63 of the Banking Act the proposed amalgamations between the Bank of New South Wales and the Commercial Bank of Australia Ltd (to be known as Westpac Banking Corporation) and between the National Bank of Australia Ltd and the Commercial Banking Company of Sydney Ltd (to be known as the National Commercial Banking Corporation) were approved.
1982	Savings bank authorisation	The Bank of Queensland received a savings bank licence (it commenced operations in September 1983).
April 1984	Foreign bank entry	Hill Samuel, the London merchant bank, announced that it is to reduce its voting shareholding in its wholly-owned Australian subsidiary to 9.9 per cent to allow a new bank, the Macquarie Bank, to be formed around Hill Samuel Australia's merchant banking operations. The application for a new banking licence has already been approved in principle.
July 1984	Bank merger	The merger of the Savings Bank of South Australia and the State Bank of South Australia (both state-owned) came into effect in July 1984.
July 1984	Foreign bank entry	Under the policy endorsed by the Australian Labor party at its conference in July, between 6 and 10 new foreign banks will get full banking licences by end-1984. Prospective licensees will be expected to offer significant benefits by way of new facilities and make every effort to achieve 50 per cent Australian ownership of their local units.
August 1984	Banks' equity investment in merchant banks	The restraint (maximum equity interest was set at 60 per cent) was withdrawn.

Table 1.3—continued

| September 1984 | Foreign bank entry | The Bank of China was provided with a limited licence and the criteria for (foreign) bank entry were clarified. These embraced requirements for a $25 m. minimum paid-up capital, local equity participation, local incorporation, demonstration of management suitability and expertise, limitations on involvement in other Australian financial intermediaries and observance of specified prudential controls. |
| February 1985 | Foreign bank entry | The names of the 16 foreign concerns to receive bank licences were announced. |

selectivity allows, to some degree, attention to be centred on issues of general importance to the development of financial systems outside Australia, thereby facilitating comparative study.

Monetary control. The first obvious trend pervading *monetary policy* prescriptions is the acceptance of the virtues of the free market-place. Accordingly, efficiency ('allocative', 'operational' and 'dynamic' – Campbell Report, p. 2) and equity gains are thought likely to result from deregulation, even of a financial system characterised (and likely to remain so – Tobin, 1984) by market imperfections[22] such as instability, imperfect information and risk assessment, barriers to entry and exit and lack of homogeneity in products offered.[23] The burden of proof was thus shifted to demonstrating the need for controls and regulations rather than justifying their removal.[24]

The Campbell Committee (ch. 4) came out strongly against the use of direct controls for monetary policy purposes.[25] They were criticised as being: (i) distortive (disintermediation through the inter-company market and, with respect to mortgage lending, through solicitors, occurred; banks switched business to their unregulated subsidiary finance houses and merchant banks; and 'hard arbitrage' opportunities were created for those able to draw-down overdrafts to redeposit in the short-term money markets); (ii) ineffective (the overdraft system could be used to avoid or delay the impact of restrictive measures and credit could still be obtained from the unregulated sector); (iii) responsible for a misallocation of resources (e.g. interest-rate controls induce growth in 'wasteful' non-price competition in the shape of unnecessarily large branch networks and advertising); and (iv) responsible for a loss of *allocative* (savings are prevented from gravitating towards outlets offering the highest, risk-adjusted, rates of return) and *dynamic* (the operational flexibility of institutions subject to the controls is impaired) efficiency. Moreover, to the extent that such controls (e.g. savings banks' prescribed asset ratios and lending ceilings[26] in connection with the provision of housing finance) are used to provide sectoral assistance or to secure social objectives, it would be preferable if the fiscal system were used to provide explicit subsidies instead. The Martin Group concurred with most of these points except that it did not rule out, because of the importance of the government's social objectives, the use of prescribed assets ratios on savings banks nor, as a second-best solution, interest-rate ceilings on housing loans.[27]

Notwithstanding these criticisms a case can be made for retaining the SRD instrument, or similar variable reserve ratio,[28] based upon the following two arguments. First, that it may be necessary, on occasions, to supplement open-market operations in Commonwealth bonds or Treasury notes with some form of direct control. This argument hinges largely upon a belief in the segmentation of financial markets which might account for differing interest-rate responses (and associated real effects) to open-market operations and reserve ratio changes (Davis, 1981). Alternatively it may be believed that additional benefits may arise from the 'announcement effects' that accompany changes in the SRD ratio. And, second, it might prove necessary at some point in the future to ensure that banks maintain *some* holdings of cash reserves to serve as a fulcrum either for a cash-based system of money-supply control (such as *monetary base control*) or for a system reliant upon interest-rate control of the demand for money and bank credit effected through open-market operations. The need might arise as, in a completely deregulated world, the demand for cash might fall to zero if small transactions are accommodated by transactions in tradeable bank paper and EFT/POS systems account for the electronic execution of the rest (Harper, 1984). Finally it is possible to argue for the retention of some form of direct control on the grounds that it might have a speedier and more predictable impact on the targeted aggregate, considerable virtues when annual targets are specified and policy judged accordingly by the markets and where inflation expectations are encouraged to rest so heavily on the achievement of the target!

Prudential regulation. The *Campbell Committee* argued that a functional approach, making due allowances for differences in risk attaching to different business operations, to regulation would best serve considerations of 'competitive neutrality' and efficiency and duly proposed that financial intermediaries soliciting funds from the public should, for the purposes of prudential regulation, fall into five categories: banks; authorised dealers; non-bank DTIs which solicit small deposits from households without issuing prospectuses; institutions which solicit small investments from households through the issue of prospectuses; and other institutions which only accept large deposits, predominantly from the business sector (19.17). In respect of banks the proposed schema of controls (see Table 1.4) embraced capital and liquidity adequacy, liquidity support and risk-asset limits.

Interest-rate controls and restrictions on business activities, on either side of the balance-sheet, were eschewed.[29] Banks would continue to be regulated under the Banking Act which should

Table 1.4   Proposed prudential regulation of DTIs

Prudential control	Purpose/drawbacks	Campbell Committee (from the final report unless otherwise stated)	Martin Group
1. Entry controls (a) On any institution, domestic or foreign.	(i) To protect depositor from the incompetent and the untrustworthy. (ii) To prevent destabilising competition increasing the risk of failure and more generalised instability. Drawbacks: stifle competition and innovation; protect the inefficient (although any economies of scale present would, eventually, cause the exit of the small and inefficient); encourage disintermediation.	(i) 'New domestic banks should be required to demonstrate that they have: an appropriate capital base; and management of an acceptable quality, including their capacity to meet prudential standards laid down for established banks' (para. 19.190). (ii) 'eligibility for recognition as a bank should not require a broad-ranging banking and financing operation as a precondition; conversely, and subject to appropriate prudential safeguards, authorised banks should not be precluded from diversifying their operations as market opportunities permit' (para. 24.34(b)). (iii) 'It should not be mandatory for new banks to adopt a joint-stock corporate struc-	(i) A presumption would be that new trading banks undertake a wide range of banking business, without requiring that they undertake all the activities regarded as the general business of banking (para. 6.18) (ii) The Group proposes a one-off 'tender' arrangement for a limited number of new banking authorities: – applicants would be required to meet the normal requirements for the grant of a banking authority and to demonstrate the extent to which they would increase competition in banking and contribute to other government economic and social objectives (para. 10.4); – consideration would be given to exemptions to the

Table 1.4—continued

Prudential control	Purpose/drawbacks	Campbell Committee (from the final report unless otherwise stated)	Martin Group
		ture. Subject to appropriate prudential safeguards, registered co-operative institutions (or central institutions owned by a group of co-operatives) should be eligible for authorisation as a bank' (para. 24.34(c)). (iv) 'official policy should not be discouraging to the entry and participation of resident-owned non-bank financial intermediaries' (para. 24.40). (v) New non-bank DTIs should be required to: – have a significant non-withdrawable capital base; – demonstrate satisfactory quality of management; – be able to meet prudential standards laid down for established DTIs. (vi) 'Primarily non-finance corporations engaged in a	limit on individual shareholdings under the Banks (Shareholdings) Act, up to a maximum of 50 per cent, to interests of undoubted financial strength (para. 10.1); – subject to receipt of sufficient applications of the necessary quality, consideration should be given to the granting of 4 to 6 banking authorities (para. 10.2); – applicants could be made by both domestic and foreign interests; – banking licences should not be confined to organisations in the form of joint-stock corporations. (iii) To the extent controls remained in operation, it would be appropriate to expect new participants to give similar support to busi-

		financial intermediation in operation in a substantial way should be required to supply statistics on that operation as if it were separately incorporated' (para. 24.43).	ness in controlled areas as existing banks.
(b) On foreign institutions.	(i) To preserve financial and economic stability. (ii) To prevent a socially unacceptable loss of resident ownership and control. Drawbacks: (i) stifles competition and innovation; (ii) invites retaliatory treatment for domestic banks wishing to expand abroad.	(i) 'the existing embargo on non-resident participation in Australian banking should be removed' (para. 25.24). (ii) 'initially, the rate of entry of foreign banks should be carefully managed' (para. 25.26). (iii) 'Foreign bank participation in domestic banking should only be restricted through the number of licences granted. Banking licences issued to non-residents should carry no encumbrances additional to those attaching to licences held by residents; both resident- and non-resident-owned banks should have the same privileges and responsibilities' (para. 25.50). (iv) 'banking licences issued to non-residents should not	(i) Under the proposed tender for new licences, foreign interests would be subject to foreign investment policy guidelines as follows: – proposals involving foreign ownership of $33\frac{1}{3}$ per cent or less to be fully acceptable; – proposals involving foreign ownership between $33\frac{1}{3}$ per cent and 50 per cent would be considered, but against the background of a Government preference, other things being equal, for lower rather than higher levels of foreign ownership. Some trade-off between the extent of foreign ownership and control and the expected benefits would be accepted (para. 9.15). (ii) The Group recommends that the Government adopt, at least for a period, a more

Table 1.4—continued

Prudential control	Purpose/drawbacks	Campbell Committee (from the final report unless otherwise stated)	Martin Group
		be subject to mandatory resident equity participation requirements' (para. 25.59). (v) 'foreign banks should be permitted to establish agencies in Australia which would be restricted to an 'offshore' lending role, with no authority to borrow on Australian markets or undertake foreign exchange business' (para. 25.76). (vi) 'the Committee has no reason to suggest any change in present policy concerning non-resident equity investment in Australian non-bank financial intermediation; this policy tests proposals against the prospect of substantial net economic benefit to Australia' (para. 25.83).	flexible approach to foreign investment policy in the NBFI sector, having special regard to the need for restructuring in the light of changing circumstances (paras. 3.5–3.8).

2. Ownership restrictions

(a) Under the Banks (Shareholdings) Act (1972) individual or associated holdings in an Australian bank are limited to less than 10 per cent of the voting shares (unless decreed otherwise by the Governor-General).

(i) An original concern was foreign ownership now dealt with under the Foreign Takeovers Act. (ii) To limit concentration of ownership in the financial sector. (iii) To ensure reasonable independence and continuity of management (by widening ownership) and thus contribute to instilling confidence in banks. (iv) To ensure that depositors' funds are not used primarily for the benefit of particular shareholders. (v) To prevent the transfer of ownership to new owners who, themselves, may not be of sufficient stature to obtain a licence. (vi) To ensure that any capital increases required would not fall too heavily on any one shareholder.
Drawbacks: dispersion of shareholdings may give unwarranted security of tenure to management, which might inhibit efficiency and

On prudential grounds the restriction on the ownership of banks is unnecessary. Accordingly 'the Banks (Shareholdings) Act should be repealed' (para. 19.56). However the Committee also recommends that:
– the Banking Act should require that anyone acquiring a substantial shareholding in a bank (>10 per cent of voting shares) or increasing an existing substantial shareholding notify the Reserve Bank within two business days of that shareholding being acquired;
– the Reserve Bank should be empowered to order divestment of shares held in excess of the 10 per cent benchmark where, in its view and in the view of the Treasurer, this would be in the best interests of depositors (para. 19.58).

The Group believes that the policy presumption in favour of dispersion in shareholdings of banks inherent in the Banks (Shareholdings) Act should be retained for the protection of depositors (para. 6.9). It proposes, however, several amendments to the Act, directed at easing certain requirements and increasing administrative flexibility:
– maintenance of the basic threshold limit on individual shareholdings of 10 per cent for existing banks;
– an increase to 15 per cent in the basic threshold limit for new banks;
– a requirement that no single party or associated group(s) of parties be allowed to hold on interest of 10 per cent or greater in more than one bank;
– incorporation in the Act of the criteria for granting

Table 1.4—*continued*

Prudential control	Purpose/drawbacks	Campbell Committee (from the final report unless otherwise stated)	Martin Group
	innovation – with adequate prudential safeguards, discontinuity of management may well be advantageous; the backing of large prestigious shareholders tends to promote confidence; in a competitive, deregulated market, concentration concerns are less valid.		exemptions; – a requirement for approval of any proposal for an equity interest, or an increase in an equity interest, of 3 percentage points or more in a bank.
(b) Prohibition on ownership of cash management trusts by banks or their wholly-owned subsidiaries.	To limit the risks, for depositor protection purposes, associated with diversification into an area initially viewed with some official concern as to its long-term viability.		The Group recommends removal of the restriction on involvement in cash management trusts (para. 6.27). However, with respect to general diversification by banks, the Group considers it appropriate for the Reserve Bank to ensure that the affiliates of banks do not expand to the point where they are so large in relation to the bank itself that, in the event of their failure, the parent bank's viability would be threatened (para. 6.14).

(c) Limits on equity interests in authorised money market dealers. [12.5 per cent (indirect) for residents and 45 per cent for non-residents in total].	(i) To restrict concentration of economic power. (ii) To stop banks from getting more direct access to central bank liquidity support facilities. (iii) To avoid conflicts of interest arising. Drawbacks: each of the above points can, if thought significant, be dealt with in other ways.	'The policy of discouraging banks from holding, directly or indirectly, ownership interests in authorised dealer companies should be kept under close review to ensure it remains appropriate in a changing financial environment. Ultimately there may be no need for a formal restriction but initially the Committee believes that a restriction can be justified.' (para. 9.75).	Because significant ownership of authorised dealers could create conflicts of interest and impair competition in the wholesale market for low-risk deposits, the Group endorses the rationale for the existing restriction of banks' ownership. The Group suggests that the Reserve Bank should keep the limit under review in the light of changes proposed in their Report (paras 6.33–6.34).

3. Asset restrictions

(a) On banks.	To protect depositors from the consequences of imprudent investment decisions. [This is distinct from a more general desire to provide sectoral assistance.] Drawbacks: such restrictions are likely to result in segmentation of financial markets, leading to inefficiency and inflexibility.	'There should be no official prohibitions (on prudential grounds) on the nature of financial intermediation undertaken by banks or on the kinds of assets they may hold arising therefrom' (para. 19.61).	The Group recommends that the 'free tranche' of assets available for investment at saving banks' discretion be increased from 6 per cent to 10 per cent (para. 4.45). Having regard to the government's sectoral assistance objectives for housing, the Group does not propose further relaxation of asset restrictions on savings banks at this stage (para. 4.46).

Table 1.4—*continued*

Prudential control	Purpose/drawbacks	Campbell Committee (from the final report unless otherwise stated)	Martin Group
(b) On non-bank DTIs.		(b) 'Non-bank DTIs should be: – unrestricted in the range of lending they may undertake and investments they may hold; and – free to lend interstate, where they cannot already do so. If an existing DTI chooses to broaden substantially its asset structure, it should first seek the consent of its shareholders and, where appropriate, its depositors' (para. 19.198). Further, 'non-bank DTIs should not be subject to restrictions on the maturity of their investments, other than in respect of those assets held to meet prescribed liquidity requirements' (para. 19.200).	

| (c) On authorised money-market dealers. | In order to justify the special arrangements provided by the Reserve Bank it is necessary to ensure that they continue to provide a specialist market-making function by requiring substantial holdings of Commonwealth securities. | 'Authorised dealers should be required to invest at least 70 per cent of their portfolios in Commonwealth securities with terms to maturity of up to five years.' (para. 9.63). However, they should be permitted to hold up to 30 per cent of their deposits in securities of approved major public authorities, bank CDs and bank bills (all with maturities of up to 5 years) but the relevant proportions held within the 30 per cent tranche should be left to their discretion (para. 9.65). | |

4. Capital requirements

| (a) For banks. | To ensure the availability of resources to repay creditors, especially depositors, in the event of liquidation. | 'Individual banks should be subject to appropriate capital adequacy requirements. Consideration should be given to the introduction of a two-tier capital ratio. The ratios should have regard for the interrelationship between capital and other criteria such as the quality of a bank's | The Group accepts the fundamental importance of capital for a sound banking operation (para. 7.21). As to the definition of capital, the Group believes that general debt provisions, to the extent that they are freely available to absorb future losses, should be included (para. |

Table 1.4—continued

Prudential control	Purpose/drawbacks	Campbell Committee (from the final report unless otherwise stated)	Martin Group
		assets, its management, earnings performance and the maturity structure of its liabilities'. (para. 19.79). The 'broad criteria used in determining the ratios should be publicly available, though the specific ratio for each bank should not be publicly disclosed' (para. 19.80)	7.17). The Group recommends a review by the Reserve Bank of the extent to which subordinated debt, which is medium- to long-term, should be taken into account (para. 7.19).
(b) For non-bank DTIs.		'Non-bank DTIs should be subject to appropriate capital ratios. The precise ratio for individual institutions should be determined having regard to the quality of their assets and management, the maturity structure of their liabilities and their earnings performance.' (para. 19.209).	

5. Liquidity requirements

(a) For banks.

To ensure the availability of funds in an 'on-going' business situation.

'Each bank should be required to meet a liquidity ratio for prudential purposes. The liquidity ratio should be generally maintained at or above the required level. An averaging process would apply over short periods. The eligibility of assets for a bank's liquidity ratio should be determined having regard to their period to maturity and their quality.' (para. 19.119).

(i) The Group proposes the replacement of the LGS ratio for trading banks by a liquidity requirement set for prudential purposes. The Group recommends that the Reserve Bank review banks' liquidity requirements, taking into account differences in the circumstances of banks (para. 7.27).
(ii) Because of the benefits for banks' operational flexibility, the Group sees merit in modest relaxation in the basis for observance of a liquidity ratio for prudential purposes, e.g. to allow the ratio to fall below the 'minimum' level by up to, say, 2 percentage points but subject to a requirement that the minimum level be observed on a weekly-average basis over the month (para. 7.30).
(iii) The appropriate liquidity standard for a bank depends on the totality of its balance-sheet structure, including the

Table 1.4—continued

Prudential control	Purpose/drawbacks	Campbell Committee (from the final report unless otherwise stated)	Martin Group
			maturity structure of its assets and liabilities. Non-deposit liabilities, and bill acceptances in particular, should be taken into account. The Reserve Bank should give consideration to these views in the design of liquidity requirements (para. 7.32).
(b) For non-bank DTIs.		'The liquidity ratio of each non-bank DTI should have regard to the maturity structure of its assets and liabilities. The ratio should be maintained in normal circumstances at (or above) the required level. An averaging process would apply over short periods. The eligibility of assets for a liquidity ratio should be determined on a consistent national basis, and should have regard for their quality, their period to maturity and their marketability.' (para. 19.216).	

6. Risk-asset limits

(a) For banks.

To protect depositors by ensuring that the holding of risky assets beyond a certain level is financed from equity rather than depositors' funds.

'Loans by a Bank to a single customer should not exceed a prescribed proportion of its capital, with a specified number of the largest loans, in aggregate, being limited to a prescribed proportion or multiple of bank capital' (para. 19.88).

'Loans to "controlling" shareholders and directors should be subject to a conservative risk asset limit.' (para. 19.92).

'Consideration should be given to the imposition of risk-asset limits in respect of investments in, or aggregate lending on the security of, certain classes of property (such as low or non-income-producing property of a developmental or speculative nature).' (para. 19.95).

'The Reserve Bank might consider the application of risk-asset limits for banks in respect of:
their spot dealing exposure in each individual foreign currency;

Table 1.4—*continued*

Prudential control	Purpose/drawbacks	Campbell Committee (from the final report unless otherwise stated)	Martin Group
(b) For non-bank DTIs.		the aggregate of those individual spot exposures; their forward dealing exposure in each individual foreign currency; and aggregate forward dealing exposure.' (para. 19.103). 'Risk-asset limits (RALs) should be applied in certain circumstances (e.g. in respect of loans to a single customer) in preference to asset restrictions.' (para. 19.210).	
7. Liability restrictions			
(a) On banks.	Normally seen as limiting the volatility of particular elements of deposits. Drawbacks: the above desire would be better achieved by removing interest-rate controls; discourages innovation and causes inflexibility in operating procedures.	'The restrictions on sources of savings bank deposits should be removed.' (para. 19.123).	(i) The Group recommends removal of the $100 000 limit imposed on savings banks on deposits from a trading or profit-making body at the time of elimination of the short-term maturity control on trading bank deposits (para. 2.24).

(ii) The Group recommends immediate freedom for savings banks to accept fixed deposits without restrictions on their minimum term or their size.
(iii) The Group recommends removal of the control prohibiting trading and savings banks from offering interest-bearing fixed deposits of more than 4 years to maturity (para. 2.22).

(b) On non-bank DTIs.

(i) 'No notice-of-withdrawal requirements or restrictions should be imposed by governments on the right of a depositor to be repaid at any specified date or time.' (para. 19.220).
(ii) 'Building societies and credit unions should be free to borrow on whatever terms and from whatever sources they wish.' (para. 19.219).
(iii) If withdrawable funds deposited with non-bank DTIs are to be classified as "shares", the distinction between "shares" and "deposits"

Table 1.4—continued

Prudential control	Purpose/drawbacks	Campbell Committee (from the final report unless otherwise stated)	Martin Group
(c) On authorised money-market dealers (i.e. gearing ratios).	To ensure expansion is adequately backed by capital.	should be made clear to investors' [shares rank behind deposits] (para. 19.222). 'Assuming that no significant changes are made to the assets authorised dealers are permitted to hold, the Committee believes the quality of these assets justifies a continuing high gearing ratio.' (para. 19.254).	
8. Interest rate controls, e.g. on loans	To discourage the taking of riskier, higher-yielding assets (and/or operating on finer margins) so as to preserve stability for the industry as a whole. Drawbacks: such controls may increase risk by impairing the flexibility of banks to adjust to changing market conditions and by inhibiting	'There is insufficient justification for retaining interest-rate controls as an instrument of prudential policy.' (para. 19.127). This is true for controls on both banks and non-bank DTIs.	The Group does not consider controls over bank interest rates as appropriate for either monetary policy or prudential purposes; indeed, their use could be counter-productive (para. 3.14). The Group recommends the removal of all interest-rate controls applying to trading and savings banks. Even if

	their ability to charge fully for the risk inherent in various loans.		the government were to decide that its social and economic objectives warranted the retention of some interest-rate controls, this should not prevent decontrol of interest rates on all forms of lending to personal customers for purposes other than housing (paras 2.36–2.40).
	If the process of exit from the industry is carefully controlled following the introduction of freer interest-rate competition, the stability of the industry as a whole need not suffer.		
9. Solvency support arrangements			
(a) For banks.	To preserve financial stability.	'In the interests of public education and competitive neutrality, the Reserve Bank Board, in its Annual Report, and the Governor in his public addresses, should seek to explain the extent of the Bank's responsibility to bank depositors.' (para. 19.143).	
(b) For non-bank DTIs.		'State Registrars should, in their Annual Reports and public addresses, seek to explain the extent of their responsibilities for the protection of depositors.' (para. 19.237).	

Table 1.4—*continued*

Prudential control	Purpose/drawbacks	Campbell Committee (from the final report unless otherwise stated)	Martin Group
10. Liquidity support arrangements			
(a) For banks.	To preserve financial stability.	'Any official agreements or arrangements (such as the LGS convention), which might be viewed as providing an individual bank with access, at its discretion, to Reserve Bank liquidity in certain circumstances, should be avoided. Provision of liquidity support by the Reserve Bank to an individual bank (like any other DTI) should be provided only at the Reserve Bank's discretion and subject to: – The Reserve Bank satisfying itself that the bank is viable and well-managed, and that it cannot meet its liquidity needs (e.g. from the sale of assets) without jeopardis-	

ing market confidence in its viability; and
– the imposition of a substantial penalty, except where the circumstances involved are clearly beyond the influence of the bank.
Details of any liquidity support provided, including the size of the loan and associated terms and conditions, should be publicly disclosed, with a discretionary lag which would have appropriate regard for the potential impact of disclosure on confidence in the bank.' (para. 19.146).
'The Government should explore with state governments the feasibility of encouraging the establishment of industry-based liquidity support instrumentalities for non-bank DTIs by permitting certain funds lodged with such instrumentalities to count towards prescribed liquidity requirements. The Reserve Bank should be prepared to make loans, at its

(b) For non-bank DTIs.

Table 1.4—continued

Prudential control	Purpose/drawbacks	Campbell Committee (from the final report unless otherwise stated)	Martin Group
		discretion, to any industry-based liquidity instrumentality, subject to conditions similar to those applying in the case of banks. Any such instrumentality should be subject to supervision by the Reserve Bank and be fully accountable to the Bank for any liquidity support provided.' (para. 19.245).	

'provide for the capacity to impose prudential requirements by regulation, but in the expectation that formal regulation would not generally be used' (19.158). In the case of non-bank DTIs the underlying principles of prudential regulation[30] were held to be the same suggesting that comparable, but perhaps less rigorous, treatment to that given to banks was necessary. Supervision was to remain a state responsibility, but a rationalisation and standardisation of state controls were called for.

The *Martin Group* agreed with many of the sentiments embodied within the Campbell submission and with most of the proposals suggested (see Table 1.4). For instance it argued that banks should be placed in a special category for prudential supervision, that formal prudential powers should be incorporated within the Banking Act (but with the expectation that moral suasion would suffice so that the powers would not generally need to be invoked), that prudential requirements, incorporating capital and liquidity controls and liquidity support facilities, should be tailored to the particular risk characteristics of individual institutions' balance-sheets and that regulation of non-bank DTIs should remain a state responsibility. The Group, however, opposed the consolidation principle espoused by the Campbell Committee, demanded the imposition of tougher restrictions on bank entry, and supported the retention (subject to greater flexibility) of asset controls on savings banks.

Criticisms of the Campbell proposals, and by implication, given their similarity, the Martin Group's proposals also, are numerous. For example, it can be argued that the committee's proposals are inconsistent with a general thrust towards a deregulated and more efficient financial system. As Hogan and Sharpe see it, the

> lack of a basic understanding of the nature of risk in financial intermediation, of the effects and functions of regulations, and of the interdependencies between economic variables has led the Committee to propose a panopoly of overlapping and unnecessary controls of dubious effectiveness for investor–depositor protection. Furthermore, in terms of other policy objectives, the Committee's prudential controls will have a deleterious impact on monetary control, segment financial markets so reducing market efficiency and the effectiveness of open market operations, encourage disintermediation, and reduce the spectrum of risk-return investment opportunities available to investors (1983, p. 160)

A possible justification for the recommendation of a formal system of prudential controls is that the Committee hoped, in the process, to make some of its other proposals more workable and acceptable.[31] For instance, some of the foreign banks admitted under new entry proposals might be smaller and less experienced than the domestic trading banks, requiring strict surveillance. Moreover, most would want to 'play' the game of banking strictly by the rule book, allowing less room for moral suasion.[32] A second general criticism relates to the fact that the role of deposit insurance and other non-regulatory approaches to depositor protection was overlooked (Hogan and Sharpe, 1983; Perkins, 1982; Wood, 1982). And, third, the proposals were taken to task for allowing too much discretion to policy-makers, for example in the granting of banking licences, activating support facilities or in specifying capital ratios, thereby creating uncertainty.

On the question of participation in the domestic cheque payments system, the two Reports were unequivocal; only banks should be able to have their cheques cleared through the clearing system (Campbell Report, para. 23.54; Martin Report, ch. 7, para. 2.31).[33] The reasons given were the same in both cases – confidence in the payments system must be above suspicion so that only those subject to 'banking' prudential standards are eligible for consideration. The recommendations were made in spite of an acknowledgement that the principle of 'competitive neutrality' would be breached:

> the provision of payments system facilities – both domestic and international – makes it easier for an institution to also provide related financial facilities; this is particularly so at the retail end of financial markets where the convenience and time saving involved in 'one stop' banking offer powerful attractions. The right to provide payments system facilities thus has significant implications for competitive balance across a wide spectrum of financial inter-mediation. (Campbell Report, para. 23.45)

A carrot, in the shape of access to electronic funds transfer, was however offered to non-bank DTIs in the belief that developments on this front would erode the advantages pertaining to membership of existing payments systems.[34] As far as new banks are concerned, both Reports advocated that the Reserve Bank oversee negotiations for membership of the cheque-clearing houses or for the provision of agency facilities for non-clearing banks by clearing banks, in the latter case to ensure their availability on reasonable and commercial terms.

The decision to support continued denial of direct access to the cheque clearing system to non-bank DTIs may be challenged on two grounds. First, given the willingness of both bodies to contemplate wide-ranging reform of prudential regulation, it is not clear why the standards of prudence demanded of non-bank DTIs could not be made comparable with those demanded of banks. In this context the role of deposit insurance might have received greater attention for it is apparently this form of depositor protection which enables the authorities in Canada and the USA to allow non-bank participation in the clearing system. And, second, although NBFI groups in the past have generally not sought direct access but instead have campaigned for arrangements which facilitate indirect participation,[35] the likely future intensification in competition for retail financial services following financial deregulation and innovation and advances in payments technology may necessitate direct participation by NBFIs in the payments system if they are to survive in the long run (Corrigan, 1982). If this is not forthcoming there may be a need for 'secondary' regulations (Davis, 1984) to limit the ability of banks to diversify.[36]

Finally, on the subject of bank-entry controls, there is widespread unease at the prospect of a continuing lack of *effective* competition in the banking industry. Following the mergers of 1981 (see p. 3) the number of major trading banks was reduced to four, although the Australian Bank became the first new bank to open since 1945 in the same year. Latterly the apparent cause for the dearth of applications for banking licences from domestic bodies was the perception that, despite the privileges associated with access to cheque-clearing, foreign-exchange licences and official lender-of-last-resort facilities, monetary regulations placed banks at a competitive disadvantage *vis-à-vis* NBFIs. Monetary deregulation has, of course, now transformed the situation to a position where there is a strong incentive to possess a licence because of the associated prudential privileges just mentioned. The problem for potential entrants is, however, that a limit is placed on the number of licences issued for reasons other that those associated with a desire to ensure the adequacy of capital and other prudential standards. This will mean that 'supernormal'[37] profits will continue to be earned by those enjoying oligopolistic competition.[38]

The Labor party's decision (endorsed in July 1984) to admit foreign banks, despite earlier hostility from within its own ranks, will go some way to reducing these efficiency losses by increasing competition and innovation in banking. This should lead both to an improvement in services and a reduction in margins, to the benefit of the community. Moreover, through a broadening of the capital market, Australia's role as a regional financial centre should be enhanced. Strings, however, attached to the granting of a licence (see p. 67) erode somewhat the efficiency gains.

Implications of financial deregulation for monetary control

One of the first issues to examine is the likely *structural adjustment* that deregulation will induce. This can take two forms: changes in market-shares of intermediation for the various categories of institution and strategic shifts in the types of business undertaken by different types of intermediary. Both forms, actual and prospective, are discussed below.

Given that the *trading banks*, especially those subject to Federal regulation, suffered most under the old regulatory regime[39] – as Table 1.5 demonstrates, their share of total assets of all financial intermediaries fell from 32 per cent in 1953 to 23 per cent in 1963, a level maintained ever since – they are likely to be the main beneficiaries from financial deregulation.[40] Removal of quantitative controls on lending and of maturity controls and restrictions on the payment of interest on chequing accounts and call money will take business away from money-market corporations, authorised money-market dealers and other NBFI deposit-takers. Additionally trading banks may absorb at least some of the functions of their NBFI affiliates in order to reap economies of scale. And, finally, trading banks are likely to defend their position as sole, direct providers of payments services from the threat of NBFI competition by establishing national EFT/POS networks and, to augment their existing retail finance packages, by acquiring equity stakes in Australian stockbrokers[41] and establishing (subject to Reserve Bank approval) insurance operations.

Savings banks are another group clearly likely to benefit from deregulation although, in the longer term, pressures may arise for their absorption by their trading bank partners. The ability to offer chequing facilities and to take deposits, without limit, from trading or profit-making bodies together with the abolition of maturity controls on deposits will allow for more effective liability competition *vis-à-vis* both bank and non-bank deposit-taking intermediaries. Similarly, relaxation of controls on asset composition will allow the savings banks more flexibility in the management of their asset portfolios.

Largely as a result of regulatory 'straitjackets', savings banks' share of total financing declined markedly between 1953 and 1982 from 20 per cent of total assets of all financial institutions to 13 per cent. This performance contrasts sharply with that of their major competitors, the permanent building societies and credit unions. In the financial year 1982/3, however, savings banks' depositors' balances surged by over 20 per cent, the improved performance reflecting, in part, the relaxation of liability controls, but also the success of their ATMs and the effect of their 'sticky' interest rate structures on deposit growth during periods of declining market interest rates. In spite of the slowdown in deposit growth experienced during the first half of 1984, the regulatory changes introduced in August 1984 should stimulate further recovery of market-share.

The largest group of NBFIs subject to the Financial Corporations Act are the *finance companies* (and general financiers). Their share of total assets peaked at 14 per cent in 1982, foreshadowing an abysmal 1982/3 financial year due to a marked weakening in the private sector's loan credit demand. Although business improved in the latter half of 1983 and early 1984 their future remains uncertain, as the 'unshackling' of the banks is likely to induce a continuing relative decline of those which are non-bank-owned and the possible absorption of those affiliated with trading banks. Moreover, competition with merchant banks in the area of corporate finance will be intensified as the latter seek to strengthen their position in this field following the loss of short-term money-market business to the trading banks.

Permanent building societies are another group facing an uncertain future, especially if state deregulation continues to lag behind Federal deregulation. They experienced disappointing results during 1981/2 and 1982/3, largely due to their inability[42] to match rising market interest rates, but benefited from strong demand for housing finance, especially from first-time buyers (as a result of fiscal privileges granted in the 1983 budget), in 1983/4. Nevertheless, removal of controls on banks is likely to lead to an intensification of competition on both sides of the balance-sheet, and the loss of housing's status as a 'protected sector' may threaten the very *raison d'être*, the provision of mortgage finance, of societies in the long run.[43] Mindful of this and of the likely continued prohibition on NBFI direct access to the payments system[44] (a policy endorsed, perhaps surprisingly, by both the Campbell Committee and the Martin Group), the Australian Association of Permanent Building Societies and the various State Registrars are currently drafting a National Building Societies Act with a view to introducing countrywide uniform legislation. Additionally the

Table 1.5　Trends in financial intermediation by type of Australian intermediary

Type of Intermediary	1953	1963	1973	1982	1983 (annualised quarterly growth rates)		1984	
					III	IV	I	II
Trading banks: (a) total assets[1]	3 093	4 465	12 853	49 267	55 381	58 474	60 380	62 622
(b) total assets as a percentage of total assets of all financial institutions[1]	32	23	21	24.1	23.9	←	n.a.	→
(c) Annual growth rate[2]	–	5[3]	14[3]	19.7	12.4	23.1	13.0	14.8
Saving banks: (a)	1 999	4 140	10 730	27 267	32 820	←	n.a.	→
(b)	20	22	18	13.3	14.1		n.a.	
(c)	–	9[3]	10[3]	9.6	20.4	21.0[4]	8.6[4]	5.0[4]
Other banking institutions: (a)	59	128	669	2 082	2 394		n.a.	→
(b)	1	1	1	1.0	1.0		n.a.	
(c)	–	11[3]	19[3]	16.8	15.0	←	n.a.	
Permanent building societies: (a)	65	210	2 907	13 655	15 230	16 895	17 520	n.a.
(b)	1	1	5	6.7	6.6	←	n.a.	→
(c)	–	15[3]	40[3]	10.8	11.5	21.8	14.8	n.a.
Finance companies and (a)	171	1 284	7 889	28 380	28 848	30 376	31 121	n.a.
general financiers (b)	2	7	13	13.9	12.4	←	n.a.	→
(c)	–	15[3]	26[3]	17.4	1.6	6.0	9.8	n.a.
Credit co-operatives: (a)	1	13	365	2 957	3 775	3 960	4 161	n.a.
(b)	–	–	1	1.4	1.6	←	n.a.	→
(c)	–	27[3]	39[3]	15.6	27.7	25.3	22.1	n.a.
Money-market corporations: (a)	3	49	2 118	11 966	13 741	15 457	16 751	n.a.
(b)	–	–	4	5.9	5.9	←	n.a.	→
(c)	–	35[3]	69[3]	38.0	14.8	28.9	34.0	n.a.

Authorised money-market dealers: (a)	—	297	878	1 405	2 005	1 900	2 173	n.a.
(b)	—	2	1	0.7	0.9	←	n.a.	→
(c)	—	—	11[3]	− 22.4	42.7	45.7	57.4	n.a.
Cash management trusts: (a)	—	—	—	1 685	2 214	1 851	1 560	1 476
(b)	—	—	—	0.8	1.0	←	n.a.	→
(c)	—	—	—	—	31.4	− 57.6	− 62.9	− 21.5

Sources: *Bulletin Supplement*, **RBA**, May 1984, tables 1.1, 1.2 and 1.3.
Occasional Paper No. 7, **RBA**, Dec 1979, pp. 4.35, 4.36.
Bulletin, **RBA**, July 1984.

Notes: [1] As at 30 June; $m.
[2] % per annum in year to 30 June.
[3] Compound annual growth rate over previous 5 years.
[4] Annual growth in depositors' balances.
n.a. = not available.

Permanent Building Societies Association of NSW has submitted proposals (1984)[45] to the NSW government designed to ensure that the industry remains stable and that housing needs can be satisfied in an increasingly competitive era. Despite these moves the pressures for further mergers remain (the number of societies with assets exceeding $1 m. contracted from 80 to 76 during 1983/4). The increasing competition will only be met through the reaping of economies of scale (Donnelly, 1984) in funds management, marketing, advertising and the provision of automated payments services.[46]

Like the building societies the fortunes of *credit unions* would appear to depend heavily upon the pace of state deregulation.[47] Nevertheless their growth in the past has been impressive (annual growth over the ten-year period to June 1983 averaged 26 per cent) and, despite the increase in competition faced from the banks, they continued to improve their market-share during 1983/4. The agency agreement reached with the National Australia Bank in August 1984, whereby chequing accounts became available to credit-union members, is designed to sustain this momentum. Many see their future growth lying in their ability to offer a more personal service than banks, although the nature of the bonds binding membership and co-operative will always ensure a certain presence in the market. Retention of privileged tax treatment and direct access to the payments system would further help their cause (Davis, 1985).

Money-market corporations are the group most discussed in speculation concerning the likely shape of a fully deregulated financial system. This is because of their obvious vulnerability to bank penetration of their short-term deposit-taking business following the abolition of maturity controls and the uncertainty surrounding the future of those (the majority) with foreign connections.[48] The peculiar difficulties faced by the merchant banking sector have been recognised by the government which, as a quid pro quo for opening up the short-term money market to trading banks, allowed merchant banks, subject to minimum capital requirements and demonstration of competence in foreign-exchange dealing, to obtain foreign-exchange licences (40 were granted). This, however, is unlikely to provide the means of salvation as the number of players in the market itself expands, leaving many to withdraw into specialist areas of corporate and investment advice, commodities and futures dealing, foreign-exchange hedging and trade financing. Thus, merchant banks will come to rely increasingly on off-balance-sheet activities, particularly fee-earning and trading activities,[49] as their 'banking' (including

CMT) business wanes.[50] Those affiliated to local trading banks are likely to have many of their functions absorbed by the parent.[51]

In spite of all the misgivings the balance-sheets of money-market corporations exhibited very strong growth during 1983/4 and the establishment of eight new concerns during the period suggests that some at least have confidence in their ability to establish a niche in the market.

The final two NBFI groupings, the *authorised money-market dealers* (AMMDs) and *Cash Management Trusts* (CMTs), are both threatened by recent deregulatory moves but the authorities' apparent desire to preserve the former leave the latter more exposed. (Although the Reserve Bank announced on 9 November 1984 that, from January 1985, it was willing to deal in government securities of over one year to maturity with all market participants who account for more than 1 per cent of daily turnover in the bond markets.) The AMMDs will, nevertheless, undoubtedly experience higher funding costs, both as a result of the banks' recently acquired ability to pay interest on chequing accounts and call money and to take deposits for periods of less than fourteen days and as a result of fiercer competition for bill-finance business as both the trading banks and merchant banks expand operations in this area. If the UK experience is anything to go by this may result in more active dealing in short-term government securities in order to boost income, but the risks are high, as discount houses in the UK have found to their cost! CMTs, on the other hand, despite the expansion in ancillary services provided, appear to be on the decline. Total assets peaked at over $2.4 b. in the first quarter of 1983, and large negative quarterly growth rates have been recorded since the middle of 1983 as the portfolio returns achieved by the trusts have fallen in absolute and relative terms.

Perhaps the most significant structural upheaval induced by financial deregulation is due to the *entry of foreign banks*. Indeed, the trading-bank mergers of 1981, although securing important economies of scale for participants and spreading the development costs of technological advance in the provision-of-payments services (on-line terminals, ATMs, EFT, etc.) can best be seen as a defensive strategy to counter the inevitability of foreign-bank entry (Stearn and Tress, 1984). The decision to admit foreign banks was endorsed by the Labor party in July 1984 and two months later the criteria according to which licence applications would be assessed were published ('Macquarie Banking Centre', 1984). These embraced prudential requirements,[52] a desire to seek a geographical spread, taking due account of the principle of reciprocity, and proposals (against the advice of the Campbell Committee – para. 25.59) to ensure a high degree of local equity participation – the preferred local equity level was established at 50 per cent. Flexibility allows, however, the authorities to grant outright control or even complete ownership to foreign bodies in return for the provision of specialist expertise or 'other benefits'. Moreover the limited size of the local pool of equity funds available *de facto* circumscribes the authorities' ability to pursue this policy too rigidly. Multiple applications covering different proposed structures were sanctioned and the Banks (Shareholdings) Act was amended to facilitate the process of new bank entry.[53]

The granting of banking licences to foreign banks will not only inject much-needed competition into the trading-bank sector, especially in wholesale money-market operations, but will also cause a rationalisation of existing foreign interests in NBFI groups.[54] This, however, has not deterred other foreign banks from buying into NBFI operations, as the actions of the UK banks Midland (through the establishment of a joint-venture institution, Associated Midland, with the State Bank of Victoria) and County (the merchant-banking arm of National Westminster, which has established two subsidiaries in Australia) demonstrate. Finally, to the extent that the reciprocity principle is adhered to, local trading banks can be expected to diversify further into overseas operations. Their international activities expanded strongly in the USA (through IBFs), Singapore and Hong Kong in the early 1980s (RBA, 1983 (b)) and the ANZ's purchase of Grindlays Bank (UK) (announced in June 1984) will result in it becoming the first fully fledged Australian international bank.

A second general issue surrounding deregulation relates to the likely impact on the average levels and volatility of *interest rates and exchange rates*. While there is little agreement on the costs associated with volatility (e.g. some still believe that exchange-rate volatility damages trade, although the weight of empirical evidence suggests otherwise) there is a general consensus that more volatility will result. As Bilson (1982) notes, the floating of the Australian dollar and dismantling of exchange control will enhance the interdependence between Australia and other countries, causing, in all likelihood, greater volatility in both rates. Australian interest rates will become linked to world interest rates through the interest-rate parity condition (resulting from covered arbitrage), although a flexible exchange rate will help to insulate domestic interest rates by allowing fluctuations in forward discounts/premia. With respect to exchange-rate volatility the present phenomenon of 'overshooting' is likely to continue, in line with predictions of the asset market approach to exchange-rate determination which asserts that exchange-rate changes are *not* closely associated with movements in differential inflation rates in the short run as prices adjust to economic conditions more gradually than asset prices (for the collapse of the purchasing-power-parity condition see Frenkel, 1981).

In practice the authorities may have to choose between greater variability in the exchange rate and greater interest-rate volatility stemming from international instability. An obvious example relates to the impact of US policies, where a monetary tightening in the US would force the Australian authorities either to accept the inflationary implications of a depreciating exchange rate or the deflationary implications of raising domestic interest rates to hold the exchange rate. The authorities' tactics will, of course, depend upon their subjective estimate of the optimal, short-run inflation/unemployment trade-off, but it could be argued that foreign-exchange operators are better equipped to deal with volatility (through the forward and hedge markets) than the generality of investors (Valentine, 1983).

On the question of the impact of deregulation on interest rates both the abolition of ceilings on loan rates and the ending of the prohibition of payment of interest on short-term deposits have to be considered. Ceilings abolition, in so far as ceilings were made low enough to 'bite', will obviously tend to raise both the average level of loan rates and their volatility. The effect of deregulating deposit rates is more subtle, however. As Davis and Lewis (1983) point out, in a competitive world with flexible deposit rates the achievement of a particular change in *relative* yields (say between government security yields and bank deposit rates) necessary to induce the desired change in the money stock will require a larger change in *absolute* yields than was necessary when deposit rates were controlled. This is because within a deregulated, competitive financial system the higher market yields will be passed on to depositors so that the 'own' rate on money will rise, thereby narrowing the interest differential created by a given change in government security yields.[55] Hence deregulation is likely to make interest rates in Australia both more volatile[56] and higher on average relative to the recent past.

The final general area of concern relates to the use of monetary targets. Reintermediation (Reserve Bank of Australia, 1985), financial innovation, the abolition of exchange control and less interest-sensitive demand for money functions, both wholesale and retail, as current accounts increasingly come to offer market-related interest rates and payment facilities, will all pose problems for *monetary targeting*,[57] at least during transitional periods.[58] For, while it is true that the relationships between different monetary aggregates will become more stable once the transition to a deregulated environment has been made, in the intervening period interpretation of movements in the targeted aggregate (M_3)[59] will become more problematic.[60] While this may be played down by the authorities, who have, for a number of years, indicated that policy judgements are not made on the basis of movements in a single indicator, others, and especially the money and foreign exchange-market operators, may continue to judge policy in accordance with the (government's) record in achieving the monetary 'projections'.

Leaving aside the general, yet crucial, issue of whether or not monetary aggregates are demand-determined (Valentine, 1984; Davis and Lewis, 1983), a number of practical difficulties will therefore have to be dealt with in the short to medium term. Reintermediation will cause a surge in M_3, both in absolute terms and relative to broader aggregates, the problem being to predict the magnitude and timing of the shift of business back to banks (and especially savings banks). Similarly, financial innovation, although apparently causing few problems to date in the unsettling of demand for money relationships (Thurloe and Valentine, 1984), is likely to complicate interpretation of movements in transactions-based aggregates (e.g. M_1),[61] as NBFIs increasingly offer more payments facilities with their 'deposit' accounts, banks extend their range of interest-bearing chequing accounts and developments in electronic funds transfer reduce the demand for cash and chequing facilities. By permitting residents to hold foreign currencies and allowing non-'official' overseas holdings of Australian dollar deposits without limit, the dismantling of exchange control will further complicate matters.

Summary and conclusions

Financial deregulation in Australia will, in all likelihood, lead to greater exchange-rate and interest-rate volatility, causing the average level of interest rates to rise in the process. Monetary management, especially while it is conducted through a framework of targeted monetary aggregate growth, will be complicated by ensuing structural adjustment and financial innovation, and the authorities would be wise to retain some form of direct control for possible use in the future. The operational difficulties facing the authorities are just as acute on the prudential front, where considerations of competitive equity and efficiency have to be balanced against depositor protection and stability concerns. It remains to be seen if an 'appropriate' balance can be struck.

1.4 ADDENDUM

Since this chapter was written the Reserve Bank has announced (May 1985) that the LGS convention is to be phased out and replaced by a *prime assets ratio* (PAR). The new requirement is for a minimum of 12 per cent of each trading bank's total Australian dollar deposit liabilities to be held in notes and coin, balances with the Reserve Bank, Treasury notes and other Commonwealth securities, and loans to authorised money-market dealers secured against Commonwealth government securities. SRDs held at the Reserve Bank will be counted as prime assets for the purposes of the PAR up to a maximum of 3 per cent of Australian dollar deposit liabilities. Arrangements whereby the trading banks are allowed to borrow from the Reserve Bank to maintain the minimum LGS ratio will no longer apply.

2 The UK Financial System

2.1 STRUCTURE: CLASSIFICATION SYSTEMS

In seeking to classify the different types of financial intermediary that operate in the UK a number of different approaches may be taken (see Table 2.1). First, one could classify intermediaries according to the nature of their *liabilities*. For example, a 'bank' could be defined as an institution whose liabilities perform a *medium-of-exchange-and-payment* function. According to this defintion 'banking' status would be conferred on the clearing banks, Northern Ireland banks, the Banking Department of the Bank of England, the National Girobank and Trustee Savings Banks. A second approach would be to classify according to the nature of the operations conducted – the so-called *functional* approach. According to this system the above list for 'banks' would need to be extended to include accepting houses, 'secondary'[1] banks and discount houses, a grouping which is close to the old 'banking sector' definition used in official statistics.[2] The remaining institutions would make up the 'non-bank financial intermediaries' (NBFI) sector, which would comprise building societies, finance houses, insurance companies, pension funds, investment trusts, unit trusts and investment agencies. Further, the NBFIs could be split into deposit- and non-deposit-taking intermediaries (see Table 2.2).

Business operations of the major deposit-taking financial intermediaries (DTIs)

Given the purpose of this text it is inappropriate to spend much time covering the operations of domestic DTIs other than the Bank of England. Accordingly, readers are recommended to consult a number of other texts (for example, the Wilson Report (1980); Carter and Partington (2nd ed. 1981); Bain (1981); Wilson (1983); Boleat (1982);

Table 2.1   'Bank' classification systems used in official UK statistics

	UK banks	Banking sector	Monetary sector[6]
Bank of England:			
Issue Department	x	x	x
Banking Department	x	/	/
London clearing banks	/	/	/
Scottish clearing banks	/	/	/
N.I. banks	/	/	/
Accepting houses	/	/	/
'Other' British banks	/	/	/
Overseas banks	/	/	/ if recognised
Consortium banks	/	/	/
Discount market[1]	x	/	/
TSB[2]	x	x	/
NSB[3]	x	x	x
National Girobank	/[4]	/[5]	/

Notes:

x = excluded.

/ = included.

[1] Discount houses belonging to the London Discount Market Association plus (until November 1981) certain 'discount brokers' and bank 'money-trading departments'.

[2] From the 3rd quarter 1979 until November 1981 the TSBs were classified within the 'other financial institutions' category but, prior to this, the 'ordinary' department (as distinct from the 'special investment' department) was included in public-sector accounts as part of central government.

[3] Until 1st quarter 1981 the NSB 'investment account' had been categorised within the 'other financial institutions' sector, but, since then, along with ordinary departments (formerly the POSB) has been regarded as part of central government.

[4] From October 1978.

[5] From October 1968.

[6] From September 1983 a new 'retail banks' group was defined to comprise London and Scottish clearing banks, NI banks, the National Girobank, the Co-operative Bank, the Yorkshire Bank and the Banking Department of the Bank of England.

and Drury (1982)) at this point to familiarise themselves with the activities undertaken by each type of intermediary. To act as an update, however, recent developments are surveyed below.

Central banking. The Bank of England was established as a joint-stock company in 1694 by an Act of Parliament and it was not until 1946 that it was nationalised under the Bank of England Act. Its

Table 2.2   NBFI classification system for the UK[1]

Deposit-taking:	Building societies
	Finance houses
Non-deposit-taking:	Insurance companies
	Pension funds
	'Portfolio' institutions – unit trusts
	investment trusts
	Special Investment Agencies, e.g. Finance for
	Industry, the National Enterprise Board, etc.

Note:
[1] Ignoring public-sector institutions and bodies, such as the NSB and local authorities.

managing body is the Court of Directors, consisting of the Governor, the Deputy Governor, four full-time Executive Directors and twelve part-time Directors. All are appointed by the Crown (in practice, by the Prime Minister). The Governor and Deputy Governor hold office, in the first instance, for five years and the Directors for four, four of them retiring each year (although they are eligible for reappointment). Members of the House of Commons, Ministers of the Crown, civil servants and aliens are ineligible for selection.

Under Clause 4 of the 1946 Act the Treasury was given formal power to give 'directions' to the Bank, indicating clearly that the chain of command is designed to run from Ministers to the Treasury and thence to the Bank of England. Although the Governor has a statutory right to be consulted prior to the issue of a direction, he has no power to veto it. In practice this formal power to issue directions has never been used, the Treasury and the Bank working closely together in the formulation of policy (see ch. 25 of the Wilson Report for a deeper discussion of the accountability of the Bank). The same clause also provides the Bank with a statutory power to issue directions to the commercial banks although, again, in practice this has not proved necessary.

The functions performed by the Bank of England embrace the following: the issue of notes (responsibility is vested with the Issue Department)[3]; the provision of advice to the government on and the implementation of monetary policy, involving intervention in financial markets to secure the government's financial and economic goals; banker to the government, commercial banks, overseas central banks, international organisations and a few private-sector customers and staff; provision of a 'lender-of-last-resort' facility to avert financial crises; responsibility for the prudential regulation and supervision of the banking system (according to powers assumed under the 1979 Banking Act) and the supervision of the wider financial system (e.g. the securities and other financial markets); various miscellaneous duties such as overseeing the clearing system, management of the country's gold and foreign-exchange reserves, registrar of government stock and, until its abolition in October, administration of exchange control.

Recent developments in the operations performed by other DTIs

Clearing banks. In order to secure a more stable deposit base the clearing banks, over the last two years, have finally ended their neglect of the retail depositor and have entered the competitive fray with other banks, building societies, the government (via National Savings instruments), local authorities, money-market mutual funds and 'moneyshops'. Through aggressive marketing of new competitive savings schemes, many of which are targeted at particular customer profiles (e.g. the very young or the high net worth customer), the clearers have already begun to reverse the trend decline in their share of the personal savings market. Following the mixed success achieved with international, sovereign and corporate lending, the clearers are also courting the retail (personal sector) borrower. A determination to boost market-share (in aggregate, it amounted to around 25 per cent at the end of 1985) in the provision of mortgages and the dramatic rise in unsecured lending to the personal sector are testament to this. Again, however, existing competition is intense and likely to become much fiercer.[4]

Other developments include the provision of 'retail financial packages' (e.g. comprising insurance underwriting, sharebroking, estate agency and travel-agency services, money-transmission services, etc.)[5] to meet perceived customer demand and, it is hoped to allow for the achievement of economies of scale and scope, the undertaking of activities designed to boost fee and trading income (e.g. underwriting, foreign exchange, 'including futures, options, swaps, etc.', and, after 'Big Bang',[6] share-broking and dealing) as a means of boosting return on capital employed,[7] and the development of new payments and delivery systems (e.g. more sophisticated Automated Teller Machines and electronic 'point-of-sale' systems). The main motivation for the last set of activities is to cut staff and branching costs by slowing down the growth in the paper-based clearing system and providing automated delivery systems, many of which can be located away from the branch.

Finally the relative importance of leasing operations to the clearing banks will decline after 1986, both as a result of the tax and allowance changes instituted in the 1984 Budget[8] and of the improved profitability of the corporate sector (which would obviate, for many firms, the need to use financial intermediaries in this capacity).[9]

Merchant banks. Despite the announcement of generally good results for 1985,[10] merchant banks have been forced to reappraise strategies in the light of a general downturn in traditional banking profits (as competition in corporate banking intensified and the trend towards 'securitisation' increasingly brought head-on confrontation with commercial banks (*BEQB*, Sep 1985)) and the opportunities offered by the securities market revolution in the UK. Most have responded by trying to boost fee, commission (new issue and mergers and acquisitions business was very profitable in 1985) and trading income, in much the same way as the clearing banks, and the largest have built up integrated securities operations, in the style of US investment banks, to enable them to offer a worldwide issuing, dealing, broking and distribution service. For example, Morgan Grenfell has bought into the stock exchange member firms Pember & Boyle and Pinchin, Denny and expects to fully integrate them into its securities operations by mid-1986, while Kleinwort Benson and S. G. Warburg have similarly established integrated financial services groups. Even for these, though, lack of capital may prove a hindrance in the securities market, an argument certainly accepted by Morgan Grenfell, whose merger with money broker Exco International was vetoed by the Bank in February 1986. The industry, however, has become more polarised, with smaller merchant banks developing more specialist roles. For example, Lazards intend to become a money broker in the reshaped gilts market, resisting the temptation to acquire exchange member firms at what it regards as extortionate sums (because of the 'goodwill' element), Schroders specialise in the energy sector, County Bank plays a major role in corporate activity among investment trusts, Robert Fleming makes a market outside the stock exchange for electrical and pharmaceutical shares and Hambros intends to develop its retail financial services following its link with Bairstow Eve, the estate agency and financial services group, in November 1985.[11]

Discount houses. Following the mergers of recent years,[12] largely necessitated by a market requirement for greater size,[13] many believe discount houses are an endangered species. Certainly, the planned demise of the 'club money' arrangements (see p. 82), the very fine be-profit margins to be earned on bill trading, the extreme volatility of securities' trading profits and the imminent changes in the UK securities market are putting intense pressure on the houses but the outlook, at least in the short term, is not so black.

Most of the recent developments result from the opportunities perceived to exist in the newly structured UK securities market. Mercantile House, a financial conglomerate, for example, acquired two discount houses – the merged Jessel Toynbee/Gillett Brothers house and Alexanders – in 1984 to gain experience in gilt trading before the new market gets under way, within which it will operate as a primary gilt dealer. Similarly, Citicorp, the US banking group, following its acquisition of Seccombe Marshall & Campion in 1985, will act as a primary dealer in the new gilt market, although the acquisition was seen by many as a means of getting closer to the Bank at a time when it was pushing strongly to join the UK clearing system. Banque Belge was yet another outside body to buy into the industry with its purchase of Gerald, Quin, Cope & Co. and, as at end-March 1986, two further bids were being considered – a full takeover of Clive Discount by Prudential Bache, a US securities firm which already owned a third stake and plans to operate as a primary dealer in the new gilt market, and a bid by Irving Trust, a US banking group, for Smith St Aubyn.

In most of the above cases the incentive for the discount house to sell out was a belief or recognition that 'small' (the director of Smith St Aubyn would argue that that meant reserves of under £15 m.) houses would not survive in their own right in the brave new world of deregulated securities markets. Lacking the capital to go it alone in the securities markets the houses could of course have attempted to diversify into other areas of operation, but their experience in the late 1970s with money-broking and gilt-fund management and in the 1980s with gilt-trading[14] did not foster great optimism. Some, how-ever, are attempting diversification through dealing in currency and interest-rate futures and, in the case of Cater Allen, through purchase of a Lloyds underwriting agency, but, generally speaking, it is the large independents which are able to be innovative. This innovation, though, is largely directed at the securities market.

Union Discount bought its way into the new-style gilt market by taking a 14.9 per cent stake (eventually it hopes to take full control) in the Glasgow gilt jobber Aitken Campbell & Co., which has been approved by the Bank as a primary gilt dealer. A rights issue was made in June 1985 to help finance the acquisition – approximately £20 m. of capital is believed to be required. Gerrard & National, the largest discount house, and Cater Allen also intend to act as primary gilt dealers. The last independent, King & Shaxson, is content to operate as a money broker in the new gilt market because of its limited size.

The largest houses, then, would appear to be confident in their ability to survive as independents in the brave new world and, at least for the time being, they will retain, like the other houses, the unique privilege of being able to borrow from the Bank against the security of eligible bills, whereas recognised primary gilt dealers will be restricted to borrowing against longer-dated securities. But this position may not endure for long if official money-market operations are extended to embrace more fully longer-dated securities (see Hall, 1986).

Building societies. Even without the powers to be conferred upon them by the new Building Societies Act (see Exhibit 2.2, p. 144), societies during the 1980s have gradually sought to extend their operations within the confines of existing legislation. This led them, for example, to offer novel forms of mortgages (e.g. index-linked mortgages), to increase the funds lent for home improvement, to offer housing-related insurance broking services and to develop links with banks (see p. 101) to enable them to offer payments system services to their customers. Some societies also took advantage of the latest technology in the shape of the provision of networks of ATMs and in the development of EFT/POS systems (see p. 101) in attempts to contain costs and increase penetration of the retail deposit market. On the liabilities side, too, with the blessing of the Chief Registrar, the largest societies have diversified their deposit base through limited recourse to the wholesale money markets. Sterling CDs, yearling bonds, index-linked stock and Eurosterling floating-rate notes have all been issued and large time deposits and syndicated loans have also been taken.

Despite these developments the operations performed by societies have not undergone substantial change, nor will they at the individual level, as a result of the implementation of the government's proposals for deregulation outlined in the Building Societies Bill. Nevertheless the limited diversification opportunities to be granted are likely to be warmly embraced and the following new activities can be expected to be undertaken: the provision of unsecured loans, cheque books and cheque guarantee cards; the ownership of land and property; investment in estate agencies, insurance brokers and other subsidiary activities; the provision of new forms of secured loans, such as local authority indemnity and equity mortgages and loans secured on a second mortgage; personal pensions business; the provision of agency and (subject to restrictions) conveyancing services and discount broking facilities; and greater use of the wholesale money markets.

Statistics. Tables 2.3 and 2.4 provide, respectively, indication of the relative importance of different intermediaries and their changing fortunes over the last fifteen years as recipients of short-term loans from the personal sector. Among other things, the tables show that despite the fact that monetary sector (formerly banking sector) institutions still dwarf building societies in absolute terms, they have proved less successful in boosting their share of personal sector liquid investments. Indeed, their share actually declined between 1970 and 1985 from 35 per cent to 30 per cent. To what extent this trend is reversed as a result of the banks' recent conscious efforts to woo the personal investor remains to be seen, but, with the opportunities created by deregulation (see pp. 101–3), the societies are unlikely to concede market-share without a fight.

Table 2.3   The size of UK DTIs at the end of 1985

Type of DTI	*Assets outstanding at end-December 1985 (£m.)*
Monetary sector institutions	587 692
Banking department of the Bank of England	2 328*
Discount market	8 457*
Non-monetary sector consumer credit companies	4 648
Building societies	120 896

* As at 11 December 1985.

Sources: Financial Statistics, Apr 1986, tables 6.1, 6.3, 6.5, 7.4 and 7.7.

Table 2.4   Selected liquid assets of the personal sector: 1970–85

Selected liquid assets	*Amounts outstanding and shares of total identified holdings at end period*							
		1970		*1975*		*1980*		*1985*
	£m	*%*	*£m*	*%*	*£m*	*%*	*£m*	*%*
National Savings instruments	8 362	29	7 977	15	12 101	11	30 445	14
Deposits with monetary (banking) sector institutions	10 062	35	19 377	37	37 407	35	63 704	30
Deposits with building societies	10 059	35	22 477	42	49 617	46	102 000*	48
Total identified	29 085	100	53 023	100	107 370	100	213 205*	100

* Estimate.

Sources: Financial Statistics, Dec 1974, table 89.
      Dec 1979, table 10.4.
      Apr 1986, table 9.5.

2.2　THE REGULATION OF DEPOSIT-TAKING FINANCIAL INTERMEDIARIES

Monetary controls

Since the abolition of hire-purchase terms control in July 1982 (see Table 2.5, p. 98), banks (including LDTs) have been free of direct monetary controls. In this sense equity *vis-à-vis* building societies has been secured. The only balance-sheet ratios (special deposits (Hall, 1983, ch. 4) remain in the authorities' armoury but are currently in abeyance) imposed on banks comprise the $\frac{1}{2}$ per cent of eligible liabilities 'cash ratio' and the 'club money' arrangements, the former representing an implicit tax and the latter a device for preserving the market-making roles of discount houses (Hall, 1986). Once the new-look UK securities market gets under way after 'Big Bang' (*BEQB*, Dec 1985) the latter requirement is likely to disappear. Monetary policy objectives will then be secured purely through open-market operations, primarily in gilts, although sales of National Savings instruments and public assets (under the 'privatisation' plan) will also continue to play a part. Discount houses, presumably, will remain subject to the 'undefined assets multiple' (see note 65) as long as official money-market management continues in the present vein (Hall, 1986).

Prudential controls

(i)　On 'banks'

The present statutory framework for the supervision of 'banking' institutions (i.e. *recognised banks* and *licensed deposit-taking institutions* (LDTs)) was established with the enactment of the Banking Act in 1979. Before discussing this framework in detail, however, it is worth while tracing how this system evolved.

The evolution of the supervisory framework. Since the Second World War the Bank of England had followed the tradition of largely allowing the City of London to regulate itself. Accordingly the Bank exercised the supervisory powers vested in it by the Bank of England Act of 1946 with respect to the 'banking system'[15] informally by means of recommendations and requests rather than, as empowered (with Treasury approval), through directives. However, over time statutory regulation acquired a more significant role, especially as a result of the passing of the Exchange Control Act of 1947, the Companies Acts of 1948 (Schedule 8) and 1967 (Section 123) and the Protection of Depositors Act of 1963 (as amended by section 127 of the Companies Act of 1967). The 1947 Exchange Control Act confined the provision of a full range of foreign-exchange services to *authorised dealers*, Schedule 8[16] of the 1948 Companies Act empowered the Board of Trade to exempt[17] *recognised banking* or *discount companies* from certain disclosure provisions (notably in respect of hidden reserves) pertaining to the drafting of the company's balance-sheet, and the 1963 Protection of Depositors Act imposed restrictions on advertising by DTIs (they first had to provide the Board of Trade with information in a specified form) other than those exempted by the Board of Trade under Section 127 of the 1967 Companies Act.[18] Finally, Section 123 of the 1967 Companies Act empowered the Board of Trade to issue certificates to those deemed bona fide carrying on the business of banking for the purposes of the Moneylenders Acts 1900 to 1927.[19]

The effect of these statutes impinging upon 'banking' activity was to establish a 'status ladder, with a series of rungs represented by individual recognitions, up which companies could progress as their reputation and expertise developed' (*BEQB*, Sep 1978, p. 383). Not surprisingly, however, given the complexity of the legal provisions and the potentially conflicting criteria[20] applied in determining the different 'recognitions', the general public (and indeed, more sophisticated investors) found great difficulty in distinguishing the standing of one DTI from another. Moreover, only those regarded as fully recognised 'banks' by the Bank of England (i.e. those having acquired the highest recognitions)[21] were brought within the supervisory umbrella where, perversely, the degree of supervision exercised was at its greatest for those having achieved the highest 'recognitions'. Thus for the discount and accepting houses annual discussions with senior management were held concerning past performance (as revealed in the annual balance-sheet) and future plans; for the clearing banks regular and close contact was maintained with senior management, but the balance-sheet was not specifically discussed; for other UK-registered 'banks' annual balance-sheets were analysed and interviews with management usually followed, but for the remaining DTIs no supervision was exercised. In the 1960s, however, there was little pressure for an enlarged or more formalised supervisory system as the balance-sheets of DTIs were, typically, of a similar make-up, thereby facilitating the use of ratio analysis within the areas of capital (through the 'gearing' ratio[22]) and liquidity (through the 'quick-assets' ratio[23]) adequacy for 'peer group' assessment. Additionally, monetary-control provisions tended to limit the risks, at least in the short run, incurred by both 'primary' and some secondary banks.[24]

In the early 1970s a number of circumstances combined to abruptly change opinion. On the monetary front the advent of Competition and Credit Control meant sweeping deregulation – lending ceilings, the clearing banks' interest rate cartel and hire-purchase terms control (at least for the time being) were all abolished.[25] Greater competition was actively promoted as the means for improving resource allocation, the efficiency of the financial system and consumer welfare. This obviously raised 'banking' risks, but, to a limited degree, the threats to the stability of the deposit-taking sector as a whole might be ameliorated to the extent that business returned to the 'primary' sector.[26] Disclosure of (relevant) information remained, however, the basis for depositor protection.

Complacency on the prudential front was short-lived. In the winter of 1973 a number of 'fringe' banks (the first was London and County Securities, which held a Section 123 certificate) experienced difficulty in renewing deposits from the money markets. The Bank were quick to act:

> The Bank thus found themselves confronted with the imminent collapse of several deposit-taking institutions, and with the clear danger of a rapidly escalating crisis of confidence. This threatened other deposit-taking institutions and, if left unchecked, would have quickly passed into parts of the banking system proper. While the UK clearing banks still appeared secure from the domestic effects of any run . . . their international exposure was such that the risk to external confidence was a matter of concern for themselves as well as for the Bank. . . . In the circumstances . . . the Bank felt it essential to meet their responsibility for fully-recognised banks by mounting a rescue operation for the benefit of the depositors of a group of institutions which were not fully-recognised banks, but whose otherwise inevitable collapse would have threatened the well-being of some recognised banks. (*BEQB*, June 1978, p. 233)

Thus was born the 'lifeboat', a rescue operation co-ordinated by a Committee consisting of senior representatives of the Bank of England and the English and Scottish clearing banks under the chairmanship of the Deputy Governor of the Bank (see pp. 115–16).

The immediate causes of the fringe banking crisis (see Reid, 1982, for a more detailed discussion) were over-exposure in property on the assets side of the balance-sheet, undue reliance on the wholesale money markets as a funding source, maturity mismatching of assets and liabilities and abrupt changes in government policy with respect to monetary policy and rent controls. Given the prospective rates of return envisaged on property development in the early 1970s on the expectation of a continued shortage of property (especially office property) and sharp rises in negotiated rentals it is easy to see the attraction for fringe banks of investing in property-related areas.[27] Moreover, competition from the 'primary' banking sector for such loans was reduced in August 1972 following the reimposition of lending guidelines designed to reserve 'primary' bank credit for the expected upsurge in industrial loan demands. The fringe banks (mainly those with Section 123 certificates) funded the bulk of this medium-term lending from money-market loans, the ambiguities created by the various 'recognitions' deriving from 'banking' legislation allowing money to be taken at interest rates only fractionally above those paid by 'primary' banks. This, however, resulted in many institutions running significantly mismatched books, with short-term (say up to three months) deposits (largely interbank deposits) financing medium- to long-term loans. Moreover, where collateral was taken much was in a property-related form, further raising the fringe banks' exposure to the vagaries of the property market. The stage was set for a classic liquidity crisis and this duly appeared with the government's switch to a 'tight money' policy in the latter part of 1973. This caused a doubling of nominal short-term interest rates in the second half of 1973, the squeeze being at its most intense in November, the month London and County Securities got into difficulties. The sudden and sustained rise in interest rates meant that many of the fringe banks' loans were running at a loss. Their problems were compounded by the government-imposed freeze on business rents in December 1972 and the threatened imposition of a land-development tax, factors which foreshadowed the collapse of property values in the Spring of 1974, and the subsequent slump in the stock market. Once the 'primary' banks and others realised the extent of the fringe banks' exposure to potential losses, inter-bank deposits and other wholesale deposits were withdrawn,[28] precipitating a liquidity crisis for the 'secondary' (i.e. fringe) banking sector.

The immediate outcome of the crisis was the recognition by the

Bank, especially in view of the increased contagion made possible through the development of wholesale money markets, that the supervisory system required overhauling. Accordingly an enlarged and more intensive system was introduced in the Summer of 1974. All UK-registered banks (excluding clearing banks and British overseas banks) were required to submit quarterly returns to the Bank and to subsequently attend interviews at the Bank to discuss the returns. Similar requirements were imposed on 'large' non-bank DTIs (numbering 60 in total), including members of the Finance Houses Association. The returns had to include information identifying balance-sheet components, the maturity structure of assets and liabilities in both sterling and other currencies, 'large' deposits and loans, deposits/ loans made by or to others with whom the company or its directors are connected, bad loan provisions and the geographical spread and purpose of international loans. Together with details on profitability the information was then analysed, with the results of ratio analysis in the areas of capital and liquidity adequacy and maturity mismatching used as the basis for subsequent discussions with senior management. These interviews were seen as the *cornerstone* of the supervisory system, enabling the Bank to assess managerial competence. As for the clearing banks and British overseas banks, annual reviews were decided upon, and the statistics collected were more detailed than for other banks. Several interviews a year, each dealing with particular aspects of business operations, were planned and greater emphasis was placed on the examination of control systems and reporting and auditing procedures. Finally, with respect to foreign concerns operating in the UK, letters of comfort were sought in September 1974 with a view to obtaining moral commitments, additional to any legal liabilities, to support associates or subsidiaries operating in the UK if they got into financial difficulties. Discussions with the management of the London branches of foreign banks were also initiated with the purpose of enhancing the Bank's understanding of their operations. These discussions complemented the previously operated reporting requirements relating to transactions in the London foreign-exchange and Eurocurrency markets.

This was not the end of the matter. The Bank accepted the need for a single body to regulate all deposit-taking institutions (bar building societies) so as to end the confusion over what actually constitutes a 'bank'. In addition the UK's entry into the EEC required observance of the proposed harmonisation of banking law (the First Banking Directive was adopted in December 1977), which would involve the establishment of formal licensing procedures for deposit taking companies in the UK. And finally, the government acknowledged the growing public demands for measures to enhance consumer protection which, in financial markets, translated into depositor protection. As a result of these pressures, and following publication of the White Paper on 'The Licensing and Supervision of Deposit-taking Institutions' in 1976, a new statutory framework for supervision emerged (operational from October 1979) under the 1979 Banking Act.

The 1979 Banking Act. The core element of this legislation was that any company wishing to take deposits in the UK had either to be *authorised* by the Bank or specifically exempted, as was then the case for building societies, local authorities, the National Girobank, National and Trustee Savings Banks and the Bank of England. A distinction was drawn between recognised banks and 'licensed' deposit taking institutions, mainly on the basis of the range of services offered, although this implied no distinction in standing in the eyes of the Bank. Supervision itself centred on the measurement and assessment of liquidity and capital adequacy and foreign currency exposure, and ratio analysis provided the starting-point for subsequent discussions with management with a view to implementing prudential controls in a flexible manner. A formal deposit protection scheme was also introduced. The Bank's system of supervision thus remained a flexible one despite the new statutory powers, with a wide measure of discretion remaining in the interpretation and application of the authorisation procedures and with the assessment of the adequacy of prudential standards carried out on an individual basis (although 'peer group' analysis is taken into account). The management interviews that follow the statistical analysis of the returns also remain the cornerstone of the system. For UK-incorporated institutions these discussions normally take place quarterly, but for the clearing banks and UK branches of overseas companies they are held roughly every six and nine months respectively.[29,30]

Before moving on to consider the key elements of the new system in more detail it is pertinent to emphasise the importance of the auditing process to the success of a system that does not involve an examination procedure (unlike in the US and elsewhere) nor insist upon the auditing of prudential returns.[31] The task of the auditor is to assess the authenticity of the facts (e.g. the valuation of assets, liabilities and reserves) as presented in the companies' accounts by the directors. Thus his first duty is to shareholders, although the reports are available to third parties, including banking supervisors. In some countries, such as Switzerland, banking law imposes a requirement upon auditors to convey any information they think relevant to banking supervisors but this is not the case in the UK where such action would represent a breach of confidentiality. Indeed, the only action an auditor can take, if he feels suitably concerned, to alert supervisors to impending problems is to qualify the accounts, but this is an extreme measure, given the risk of precipitating a run on the bank, and a path rarely chosen. Effective supervision in the UK therefore relies heavily on the expertise of auditors, a situation that has only recently been called into question following the Johnson Matthey débâcle (see pp. 114–19).

Returning to the *authorisation procedures*, the first stage of the process is for applicants to complete questionnaires asking for details of the nature of the applicant's business or proposed business and for information about its managers, controllers and directors.[32] Subsequent to this, discussions between the Bank and senior management of applicant institutions are usually held to provide a deeper insight into the nature of the institution's business. Finally, applications are assessed in the light of statutory criteria laid down for authorisation in the Banking Act. Those companies refused authorisation have a right of appeal to the Chancellor of the Exchequer (under Section 11 of the Act), who is required to refer them to an independent body acting under the Tribunal and Enquiries Act 1971.

The Bank has considerable discretion in the interpretation and application of the statutory criteria laid down for authorisation. For example, in determining whether an applicant should be classified as a recognised bank or a licensed deposit-taker the Bank will base its decision mainly[33] upon a review of the detailed information demanded in respect of each of the five categories of service set out in Schedule 2 of the Act, namely the provision of: (i) current and deposit account facilities or the acceptance of wholesale money-market funds; (ii) overdraft and loan facilities or the lending of funds in the wholesale money markets; (iii) foreign-exchange services; (iv) finance through bills of exchange and promissory notes and for foreign trade; and (v) financial advice or investment management services and services in the securities area. In general the 'recognition' categorisation will only be conferred upon those deemed to provide an adequate level of service in each of the five areas or a highly specialised banking service (such as provided by discount houses), but this requirement can be waived in exceptional cases. Similarly, the Bank has to make subjective judgements in the interpretation of the criteria relating to authorisation as a licensed deposit-taker, which, briefly, involve requirements that directors, controllers and managers are 'fit and proper persons', that at least two individuals effectively direct the business (as is also the case for a recognised bank) and that the business is conducted in a 'prudent manner'. The last requirement involves an institution in meeting certain specific demands relating to the adequacy of capital, liquidity and provisions for bad and doubtful debts, but also some undefined requirements. For the benefit of prospective applicants, these, and the approach used by the Bank to interpret the other criteria, are set out in a 'Guide for Intending Applicants' (see also the Bank's 1984 *Annual Report* (pp. 41–4)).

Capital Adequacy. Central to the supervisory process is the assessment and measurement of capital and liquidity adequacy. The question of *capital adequacy* was first addressed by the Bank in 1974 through the establishment of a Joint Working Party with the London and Scottish clearing banks. This duly reported in 1975 (*BEQB*, Sep 1975, p. 240) recommending the use of two ratios, the *'free resources'* ratio (i.e. the *'gearing ratio'*) and the *'risk-asset'* ratio, in the assessment of capital adequacy. The first ratio related current, non-capital liabilities to an adjusted capital base (premises, equipment and other fixed assets, goodwill, investments in subsidiaries and associated companies and trade investments, unquoted investments and connected lending were all deducted)[34] and was taken to represent the acceptability of an institution's capital to its depositors and other creditors. Accordingly a priority was placed on constructing it on the basis of published information (although the inclusion of inner reserves and general bad-debt provisions within the definition of capital militates against this). The second ratio was used as a measure of the adequacy of capital in relation to an institution's exposure to risk of losses and related the risk of losses to the capital available to absorb such losses. It was (and still is) this second measure which was regarded as the more relevant for supervisory purposes, although no norms were laid down for individual companies or groups of companies on the grounds that this would be inappropriate considering the great diversity of business operations between deposit-taking institutions.

These guiding principles were reviewed during 1979 by the Bank and, following circulation of a consultative document with the banking system, the present system of assessment was established (*BEQB*, Sep 1980, p. 324). The Bank's approach remains a flexible one, with assessment conducted on a case-by-case basis, and pays due attention both to the interests of depositors with individual institutions and to the need to preserve confidence in the overall system. It also reflects the acknowledged division of responsibilities (as determined within the Basle *Concordat*–see pp. 163–8) among international supervisory authorities. This led the Bank to assess the capital adequacy of UK-incorporated DTIs on a consolidated basis[35] (i.e. including the operations of all branches and wholly- or majority-owned subsidiaries) and to ensure that subsidiary companies authorised under the Banking Act were adequately capitalised in their own right. Although the gearing and risk-asset ratios were retained for the same purposes as before, modifications and extensions were introduced, notably in respect of the definition of the adjusted capital base (for both ratios) and the grading of risks incurred for the purpose of calculating the risk-asset ratio. This quantitative approach complements the Bank's qualitative judgements on such issues as the quality of capital, management strengths, profitability and business prospects and the spread of business in the assessment of capital adequacy.

For the *gearing ratio* the same deductions to the capital base[36] are made as before, except for unquoted investments and connected lending. Expressing this adjusted capital base figure as a percentage of deposits and non-capital liabilities (excluding contingent liabilities[37] and subordinated loan stock) yields the gearing ratio. Except for the exclusion of premises, identical deductions from the capital base apply for the *risk-asset ratio*, which expresses the adjusted capital base as a percentage of the adjusted total of risk assets. The novelty of the new approach to this concept lies in the calculation of this *adjusted total of risk assets* which is obtained by multiplying each balance-sheet asset by an arbitrarily chosen weight (see Specimen 2B on pp. 134–5). These weights are chosen to represent the differing degrees of susceptibility of different types of asset to three[38] specific types of risk, credit, investment and forced-sale risk,[39] with commercial advances being used as a benchmark and given a weight of unity. As for the gearing ratio, the Bank's assessment of an institution's position on the risk-asset-ratio front is flexible, taking due account of the institution's individualistic business make-up, its exposure to other risks, 'peer group' analysis and ratio trends, although the ratio is not expected to fall below an agreed level.

Liquidity adequacy. The Bank's approach to *liquidity adequacy* was set out in a Bank paper issued on 20 July 1982 (*BEQB*, Sep 1982) which represented the final version of papers previously circulated in March 1980, March 1981 and the summer of 1981.[40] The main objective of the Bank was, and remains, to ensure that banks[41] are able to meet their obligations (both deposit withdrawals and lending commitments) on the due dates. (Individual banks' liquidity requirements must generally be capable of dealing with *any* net shortfall in cash inflow, anticipated or otherwise.) To this end the Bank seeks to satisfy itself that individual bank management teams adopt a 'prudent mix'[42] of liquidity forms (cash, readily liquefiable assets, especially important for clearing banks, asset maturity moneys, and a diversified deposit base) appropriate to their individual circumstances and have monitoring and control systems in operation that will ensure that such a policy is followed continuously. Across-the-board liquidity norms are not applied. The Bank looks at the liquidity of a bank's total business undifferentiated as to currency denomination, although, in certain circumstances, it may be deemed appropriate to assess liquidity adequacy by currency denomination also (especially sterling).

The liquidity measure adopted by the Bank and used as a first step in the qualitative assessment of liquidity adequacy for an individual bank[43] is based upon a cash-flow approach,[44] with assets and liabilities (combined, irrespective of currency denomination) being placed in a 'maturity ladder', with the net positions in each time period being accumulated. The time scale analysed is up to one year, but particular attention is paid to the period up to one month. The Bank describes the measure as 'a series of accumulating net mismatch positions in successive time bands' (see Specimen 2c on pp. 136–7). Lending commitments are taken into account through their inclusion as liabilities in the appropriate time band, or as otherwise agreed,[45] and the differing degrees of marketability [46] of assets (placed at the start of the ladder and not according to their maturity date) is recognised by applying varying discounts[47] against the (normally market) value of the assets (ibid.). The treatment of loans only nominally repayable on demand (e.g. overdrafts) has to be agreed individually with the Bank and assets of a doubtful value are excluded or otherwise treated on a case-by-case basis. Contractual standby facilities negotiated with other banks are treated as sight assets, taking into account their remaining term and likelihood of renewal. Finally, on the liabilities side, deposits are included according to their earliest maturity, although account will be taken of the stability and diversification of the deposit base in establishing guidelines. Non-deposit liabilities maturing within one year are included, but contingent liabilities, unless they are thought likely to materialise, are not.

With regard to the division of supervisory responsibilities between parent and host supervisors, the Bank notes that parental responsibilities for the liquidity of affiliates (i.e. subsidiaries and participations) operating mainly in the UK may require the seeking of additional information from individual banks in order to allow for effective monitoring. In the case of affiliates (or indeed branches) operating abroad, the Bank might wish to examine the internal arrangements of the parent bank for monitoring and controlling its worldwide liquidity needs. Finally, the Bank determined to monitor the liquidity position, especially in sterling, of UK branches of foreign banks more closely,[48] taking due account of the relationship between the branch and its head office.

Deposit insurance. Another component of UK banking supervision is *deposit insurance*. The Deposit Protection Board,[49] chaired by the Governor of the Bank of England, was set up by the 1979 Banking Act to administer the Deposit Protection Scheme, which came into effect in February 1982. Under the scheme, 75 per cent of the first £10 000 of a depositor's sterling deposits with any one subject institution is guaranteed. The fund is financed by a levy on all authorised institutions in proportion to their deposit base, the initial contributions being limited to a minimum of £2500 and a maximum of £300 000. The initial target for contributions was set at between £5 m. and £6 m., but, if necessary, further sums can be called for. The scheme covers both corporate and personal depositors (but not those of persons associated with the institution), although the bulk of the former will probably not derive much satisfaction from the application of the *caveat emptor* principle above the £10 000 mark. Overseas institutions operating in the UK may be exempted by the Treasury from the scheme[50] if they can demonstrate that deposit protection arrangements provided by their home authorities guarantee as good a level of protection as that offered by the scheme to deposits taken by their UK offices. The purpose of limiting the cover offered to 'small' depositors to only 75 per cent of their investment was to ensure that prospective investors retained an incentive to act prudently in their selection of investments.[51] Although Trustee Savings Banks (TSBs), the National Savings Bank and the National Girobank are not covered by the scheme, because they are excluded from the provisions of the Banking Act, the TSB will eventually be brought into the scheme as the National Girobank has been.

Exchange rate risk. The measurement, monitoring and control of 'banks' (i.e. authorised banks and LDTs) *exposure to movements in exchange rates* is a further aspect of UK banking supervision. The Bank accepts (*BEQB*, June 1981, p. 235) that the primary responsibility for the control of exposures arising from foreign-currency operations rests with the bank's own management, but, to discharge its supervisory responsibilities, seeks to ensure that internal control procedures are adequate (see Specimen 2D on pp. 138–9)[52] and to ascertain the extent of each bank's exposure with a view to relating it to other risks incurred and to its capital base.

The Bank's concern relates to all exposures arising from any uncovered foreign-currency position (including, since April 1984, those incurred through the writing of options business) in any currency. Net positions in single currencies (including sterling) are considered alongside the aggregate net position in all currencies. In agreeing, individually with each bank, dealing position guidelines, the Bank accepts the market distinction drawn between 'structural' (i.e. those creating exposures of a longer-term nature) and 'dealing' positions (i.e. those creating exposures as a result of 'normal', day-to-day operations) and, accordingly, excludes structural positions from consideration.[53] Additionally the institution's particular circumstances and expertise in foreign-exchange operations will be taken into account before guidelines are formulated. UK-incorporated banks experienced in foreign exchange can generally expect to agree guidelines limiting the net 'open'[54] dealing position in any one currency to 10 per cent of the 'adjusted capital base'[55] and the net 'short'[56] open dealing positions of all currencies taken together[57] to 15 per cent of the adjusted capital base.[58] The same arrangements apply to the operation of all UK banks' branches at home and abroad, and, eventually, subsidiaries will be included to provide a consolidated assessment for capital adequacy purposes of banks' foreign-currency exposures. In respect of the UK branches of foreign banks the Bank requires monthly returns[59] and imposes dealing guidelines except when dealing operations are minimal.

Large loan exposures and ownership controls. The final two strands of banking supervision relate to the control of *large loan exposures*[60] and *ownership controls.* At present[61] the Bank operates a guideline whereby banks are expected to notify and justify to the Bank any individual exposure to non-banks amounting to more than 10 per cent of its capital base. In considering the acceptability of exposures the Bank will take into account the standing of the borrower, the nature of the bank's relationship with the borrower, the nature and extent of security taken and the bank's expertise in the area of lending undertaken. Exposures to borrowers connected with the bank will receive particularly close attention and, generally speaking, the greater the number of 'large' exposures the greater will be the required capital ratios. Limits are not placed on inter-bank, country[62] or sectoral exposures, but, again, all exposures of more than 10 per cent of the capital base are subject to examination and may necessitate a higher capital coverage, especially where there is a high concentration of large exposures or where the risks are conspicuously high.[63]

Finally, with respect to ownership controls, banks are restricted to a maximum 10 per cent (raised from 5 per cent in September 1984) stake in money brokers and other understandings exist between the Bank and the relevant government departments (e.g. the Department of Trade in respect of links with insurance companies) governing the permissible degree of interlocking ownership with non-bank financial institutions. These guidelines and practices, however, which are designed to limit the risks associated with connected lending and cross-contamination, are likely to be altered as the pace of diversification quickens, a fact exemplified by the Bank's willingness to allow a bank purchase of a discount house[64] during 1985 in preparation for trading in the revamped UK securities markets (although it is interesting to note that the Bank refused to allow the merchant bank Morgan Grenfell to merge with Exco International, one of the big four UK money-broking groups, in 1986).

Discount houses. Discount houses enjoy a different supervisory regime because of the special role they play as market-makers in short-term securities and conduit between the Bank and other commercial banks. Various multipliers and controls were applied for varying reasons during the 1970s,[65] but it was not until June 1982 (*BEQB*, June 1982, pp. 209–11) that formal prudential arrangements were first promulgated.[66] A different measure to that applied to other banks and LDTs in the assessment of capital adequacy through the construction of a risk-assets ratio is necessitated by virtue of the fact that credit risks only feature to a modest degree in the houses' business (e.g. in trade bills and unsecured loans). Nevertheless, a similar approach, relating capital requirements to the size and composition of the balance-sheet, is amenable to adoption, the relative weights appropriate to different assets being dependent upon the volatility of their prices.

The approach adopted by the Bank is to specify two multipliers which are set in relation to each house's capital base. One limits a house's 'adjusted total book' (total value of assets *plus* total 'net additions' (see below) to 40 times its capital base,[67] while the second, subsidiary, multiplier limits net additions to 15 times the capital base.[68] The arrangements allow houses running 'low-risk' books to operate a larger total book than those running 'high-risk' books. Flexibility on the part of the Bank allows some exceptions to the rule, providing competitive equity is upheld.

In computing the above ratios the item 'net additions' is of paramount importance. This represents the total, for three classes of 'added risk', of the product of a risk weight (see Specimen 2E on pp. 140–1) times the values of assets (less deductions) in the class. The risk weight for a particular type of asset reflects the fact that investment risk tends to increase with the term to maturity of the asset and that forced sale risk is lowest, for a given maturity, for gilt holdings. The broadness of the markets heavily influences the degree of forced sale risk run on other security holdings. Deductions are allowed against the total value of assets in computing net additions to reflect the fact that maturity matching, by reducing interest-rate risk, reduces the overall risk associated with asset holdings. Accordingly, for each risk class, the amount of fixed-term deposits of appropriate maturity is an allowable deduction.

(ii) On building societies

Prudential supervision of building societies is achieved almost entirely by statutory means under the oversight of the Chief Registrar of Friendly Societies. The main legislative framework is provided in the 1962 Building Societies Act, which circumscribes the operation of building societies in the following ways: (i) they are to be 'mutual' bodies (i.e. owned by their share investors and borrowers); (ii) their main operation must be to raise funds from members to lend to members on the security of a first mortgage of freehold or leasehold estate; (iii) the terms of their lending and the disposition of any liquid funds[69] (they are held mainly in bank deposits and public sector securities) are closely controlled; and (iv) lending in large amounts and to corporate bodies is limited to a specified maximum – currently such 'special advances', for amounts greater than £60 000 or of any amount to corporate bodies, are limited, in aggregate, to 10 per cent of total advances.

In addition to these constraints, covering *permissible business activities, lending limits* and *liquidity rules*, societies are also subject to *capital requirements* (in order to gain 'trustee status' for their borrowings), 'registration' and 'authorisation' procedures (first introduced in 1981), and a deposit protection scheme. Under the Building Societies' (Designation for Trustee Investments) Regulations, SI 1972, no. 1577, as amended by SI 1977, no. 1207, the requirements are that a 'designated' society must have funds of at least £10 m. and must possess reserves equivalent to $2\frac{1}{2}$ per cent of total assets in the case of smaller societies (i.e. with total assets not exceeding £100 m.), reducing by steps to $1\frac{1}{4}$ per cent for the largest (i.e. with total assets exceeding £100 m.).[70] *Registration* procedures require a new building society to register with the Registrar[71] (a civil servant appointed by the Treasury) before commencing business and to satisfy him that it meets the requirements of the 1962 Act.[72] *Authorisation* procedures, which took full effect in June 1983, give effect to the European Community First Banking Co-ordination Directive (adopted in December 1977) by requiring positive authorisation of building societies by the Chief Registrar. This will only be granted where the business is deemed to be 'effectively directed' by at least two individuals who 'are of sufficiently good repute and sufficient experience to perform their duties' and to have adequate own funds (deferred shares and/or reserves). The last provision effectively increased the minimum investment required of founder members from £5000 to £50 000. No minimum reserve or liquidity ratios are specified (although the intention is to move towards the establishment of commonly observed ratios)[73] and, by itself, the directive does not allow British societies to act on the Continent.[74]

Proposals for a *deposit protection* scheme, under discussion since the collapse of Gray's Building Society in 1977 (Boleat, 1982, ch. 12), came to fruition in the Spring of 1982. Signatories, controlling over 99 per cent of all building-society assets, to a voluntary declaration of intent to contribute to a protection fund should the need ever arise effectively guarantee up to 90 per cent of an investor's capital (75 per cent for a member of a non-contributing society), irrespective of the size of the amount. Contributions to the fund are limited to 0.3 per cent of total assets. As is the case for the banks' scheme, less than 100 per cent coverage is provided to (share) investors in order to avoid the moral hazard of investors disregarding risk considerations when choosing to apportion their investible funds.[75]

2.3 FINANCIAL DEREGULATION IN THE UK

The programme of financial deregulation since 1971

The major deregulatory moves are presented in Table 2.5, covering the phasing out of direct monetary controls, the floating of sterling, the abolition of exchange control, reform of the London Stock Exchange and the deregulation of building societies. The rationale for and implications of the first three events are well-established in the UK literature (e.g. see Hall, 1983) and, as such, little is to be gained from rehearsing the arguments here. Moreover, the issue of the reform of securities markets is too specialist for this text (see Hall, forthcoming 1987). Thus, the analysis will concentrate upon the deregulation of building societies, especially the ramifications for the conduct of monetary and prudential policy.

Deregulation of building societies

Although the discourse presented on pp. 95–6 still relates to present-day prudential regulation and supervision of building societies, the legislative environment and supervisory approach are about to change radically, with the blessing of the Building Societies Association (BSA) and the government. The BSA's case for new, enabling legislation, was based on the following premises: (i) the current size of societies makes current legislation cumbersome; (ii) societies need greater powers if they are to compete effectively, on equal terms, in the more competitive world of the future; (iii) societies should be allowed to play a larger role in the housing field, but current legislation inhibits this (e.g. societies can only lend on a first mortgage, cannot directly offer index-linked or equity-sharing mortgages, etc.); (iv) societies should be able to operate throughout the EEC.

Embracing the principle that additional powers should only be incidental to the primary objectives of financing home ownership and offering financial services to members, the BSA (1984), after due consideration of the *Spalding Report* (1983), thus sought a number of new powers for building societies. These comprised: (i) a power to hold freehold or leasehold reversion in homes being purchased under shared ownership schemes, to own the rented share of dwellings and to offer index-linked and equity-sharing mortgages; (ii) a power to hold land for the purpose of housing development; (iii) powers

Table 2.5   The programme of financial deregulation in the UK since 1971

Date of announcement	Details
(a) *Monetary controls**	
October 1971	Under *Competition and Credit Control* the following events occurred: the clearing banks' interest-rate cartel was abolished; the 8 per cent cash ratio and the 28 per cent minimum liquid assets ratio, both imposed upon the clearing banks alone, were replaced by a *minimum* ($12\frac{1}{2}$ per cent of 'eligible liabilities') *reserve assets ratio*, to be applied to clearing banks, secondary banks and 'large' (deposits totalling at least £5 m.) finance houses (for the last group of intermediaries the minimum ratio was set at 10 per cent of eligible liabilities); a *minimum* $1\frac{1}{2}$ per cent of eligible liabilities '*cash ratio*' was imposed upon the clearing banks; clearing and secondary banks became liable to a *special deposits ratio*; hire-purchase terms controls and lending ceilings were abolished; the collective tender for Treasury bills by the Discount House Syndicate was discontinued; discount houses were asked to hold a minimum of 50 per cent of their 'borrowed funds' in defined categories of public-sector debt (the '*public sector lending ratio*').
October 1972	Bank rate, the Bank's traditional rediscount rate, was replaced by a market-determined *minimum lending rate* (MLR).
July 1973	The discount houses' public-sector lending ratio was replaced by an 'undefined assets multiple'
September 1973	An interest-rate ceiling ($9\frac{1}{2}$ per cent) was imposed on the amount banks could pay on sterling deposits of less than £10 000 (removed in February 1975).
December 1973	Hire-purchase terms control was reintroduced and the 'supplementary special deposit scheme' (the *corset*) was introduced.
May 1978	MLR was set by administrative action, i.e. the market-related formula was scrapped.
June 1980	The *corset* was abolished.
May 1981	The 'undefined assets multiple' was raised from 20 to 25 (and later 30) times capital and reserves.

*See Hall (1983) for further details.

Table 2.5 — continued

Date of announcement	Details
August 1981	A new monetary control regime was implemented which incorporated: the imposition of a $\frac{1}{2}$ per cent of 'eligible liabilities' non-operational, *cash ratio* requirement on all 'monetary sector' institutions with liabilities averaging at least £10 m. over a selected period; monetary sector institutions agreeing to maintain at least 6 per cent of their 'eligible liabilities' on average (subject to a minimum of 4 per cent) in the form of secured call money with the London Discount Market Association if they wish their acceptances to be 'eligible' for rediscount at the Bank – the 'club money' arrangement; the abolition of the minimum reserve assets ratio and the $1\frac{1}{2}$ per cent cash ratio imposed upon the clearing banks; the suspension of MLR (it reappeared for one day in January 1985).
July 1982	Hire-purchase terms control was abolished.
August 1983	The 'club money' arrangements were revised. Henceforth, the restrictions on average and minimum holdings of secured money at call with the London Discount Market Association were to be 5 per cent and $2\frac{1}{2}$ per cent of eligible liabilities respectively.

(b) *Other*

Date of announcement	Details
June 1972	Sterling was floated.
October 1979	Exchange control was abolished.
October 1986	'Big Bang' at the London Stock Exchange – see Exhibit 2.1 on pp. 142–3.
January 1987	The new legislation governing the operations of building societies comes into force.

allowing societies to offer housing-related services, such as estate agency, structural surveys, conveyancing and insurance broking; (iv) relaxation of the restriction on lending on first mortgage only; (v) powers enabling societies to offer more retail banking services, such as the provision of personal loans and hire-purchase finance;[76] (vi) a power to allow the offering of insurance direct; and (vii) a power allowing societies to act as collecting and payment agencies.

The arguments put forward can be seen as an attempt to deal with the existing and potential 'threats' facing building societies through alleviation of the constraints under which they operate while, at the same, allowing them to embrace the opportunities afforded by technological advance in the provision of payments services.

The threats faced by societies embraced both an intensification in competition on both sides of the balance-sheet and a possible decline in future mortgage demand. On the liabilities side of the balance-sheet the societies already faced strong competition for retail savers from the government, as recipient of the proceeds from sales of National Savings instruments, and from the clearing banks in the shape of interest-bearing cheque accounts. Money-market funds posed a lesser threat, but both the Trustee Savings Bank and the National Girobank had transformed themselves into fully fledged banks, while retailers (e.g. Debenhams and Great Universal Stores) and unit trusts (e.g. the Britannia, M & G, Save and Prosper and Henderson groups) had demonstrated their determination to carve out a niche for themselves in the market. Competition for housing loans was no less severe; the clearing banks had settled at a 25 per cent market-share by 1984 (following the abandonment of direct monetary controls in 1981), a number of foreign banks had come to dominate the large loans market and insurance companies (e.g. Confederation Life and the Prudential Assurance Company) had ventured into the market in a determined fashion. With the simultaneous erosion of alleged fiscal advantages,[77] this competition posed a formidable challenge to the building society movement. To add to their problems serious concerns about the future level of mortgage demand were being widely expressed and justification for this viewpoint was not hard to come by. For example: (i) owner-occupation was already at a high level (covering roughly 60 per cent of dwellings) and the stock of public-sector houses remaining to be sold had been substantially reduced; (ii) an inelastic supply of building land and economic uncertainty had slowed the growth in housing starts; (iii) fiscal changes (e.g. erosion of the real value of the £30 000 limit on mortgage interest tax relief and indexation of the tax-free allowance given against capital gains tax) had served to reduce the attractiveness of owner-occupied property as an investment; (iv) the prospect of a continuation of low inflation rates meant that future mortgage demand might be curtailed both as a result of high real mortgage interest rates and the fact that borrowers would no longer be able to rely on inflation to erode the real value of their liabilities; (v) there appeared little scope for the personal sector to increase its income gearing (i.e. debt-service payments as a proportion of income) as it remained little short of the peak level (5 per cent of personal disposable income) experienced in 1982. In the light of these pressures the BSA was right to press for the widest possible flexibility in the anticipated 'enabling' legislation and to seek the right of incorporation for those societies wishing to diversify into areas necessitating a rapid build-up of capital.[78] Finally, as a means of matching the competitive challenge deriving from the banks' ability to provide packages of retail financial services, incorporating, among other things, payments services and of countering the threat posed by the banks' attempts to construct barriers to entry to electronic funds transfer at point of sale (EFT/POS),[79] the BSA wisely determined to seek powers to broaden the range of money transmission services societies are able to offer direct[80] to customers.

The Green Paper. The response of the government to the call for an amendment to building society legislation came in the shape of a Green Paper ('Building Societies: A New Framework', Cmnd 9316) published in July 1984. With respect to the provision of new financial services, and subject to the general principle of ensuring 'that the building societies continue primarily in their traditional roles ... while loosening the legal restraints under which they have operated ... so that they can develop in other fields', the following points were made. First, new activities would be subject to the following broad limits (other balance-sheet constraints were also suggested and subsequently confirmed in the Building Societies Bill – see Exhibit 2.2 on p. 144): (a) at least 90 per cent of 'commercial assets' (i.e. total assets less liquid assets and fixed assets) should be in the form of advances to individual members secured by first mortgage on residential property which the borrower occupies; (b) liquid-asset holdings should be sufficient to cover conceivable fluctuations in cash flow, but should be no greater than $33\frac{1}{3}$ per cent of total assets; and (c) at least 80 per cent of funds should be raised from individual members (at least 50 per cent of borrowed funds being raised in the form of shares rather than loans or deposits), allowing up to 20 per cent from the money markets and other sources. Second, on the specific question of money transmission services, the government asserted that building societies should be able to offer a fuller range of personal banking and money transmission services to their members if they so wish. It proposed giving societies an unsecured lending power (individual loans to be subject to a ceiling of £5000) to overcome the problems of underwriting payments to third parties (which arise through the use of cheque guarantee cards and could arise with new electronic money transmission systems, e.g. 'point-of-sale' terminals or Automated Teller Machines (ATMs)), but also considered a possible amendment to legislation to provide an explicit power for all societies to guarantee certain categories of payment, with a power to require a member to make good, within a specified period, any debt arising from a call on that guarantee. A limit of £1500 on the guarantees societies are able to give would enable effective competition to develop with banks' chequebook-issuing activities. The government also canvassed the idea of passing legislation to enable building societies to enter into reciprocal payment arrangements with other societies or financial institutions (e.g. to provide an encashment and paying service for each other's customers). For building societies undertaking banking business 'appropriate' cheque-clearing arrangements would have to be made. Those societies seeking to play a wider role in banking than that envisaged in the Green Paper would be allowed to convert into a company and apply for a deposit-taking licence under the 1979 Banking Act. Granting of a licence would crucially depend on the new company possessing the requisite capital, liquidity and management skills for the business it was contemplating. Third, on the provision of other financial services the following views were expressed. With respect to integrated house-buying services, the BSA's proposal that societies should be able to offer a package of services to house-buyers (e.g. estate agency, conveyancing and structural surveys) is subject to the problem of how to increase competition and improve consumer choice yet avoid possible conflicts of interest. The government resolved to consider these issues further before making a decision (in the event the offering of conveyancing services by a society to its own borrowers was prohibited unless provided through a subsidiary in which a minority stake is held). On the provision of agency services (the BSA proposed that societies should have a power to act as paying and collecting agents for other organisations (e.g. to collect local authority rent and rates and bills for public utilities) in order to make fuller use of their branch offices), the government was inclined to the view 'that the societies should be able to provide certain services on an agency basis for a defined list of bodies'. In reply to the BSA's proposal that societies should be able to undertake the full range of insurance broking or agency services, the government pointed out that the extension of activities beyond mortgage protection policies, house insurance and endowment mortgages (where societies act as intermediaries, introducing the business to insurance companies for a commission) 'would need to be subject to proper standards of prudence and investor protection'. Finally, on the subject of stock market services, the government accepted that this could help societies to make better use of existing branch networks and encourage the individual rather than institutional holding of shares. Risk and staffing questions would need careful consideration, however.

The Green Paper also touched upon the question of prudential supervision. Apart from the balance-sheet constraints already mentioned, the government envisaged:[81]

(i) a redefined series of duties for boards to undertake (covering capital and liquidity adequacy and the adequacy of management plans, internal control and inspection procedures, arrangements for independent valuation of mortgaged property and reporting requirements);

(ii) strengthened monitoring arrangements for the Registry and more systematic arrangements allowing for discussions between the Registry and societies about their future plans;

(iii) replacement of the voluntary investor protection scheme with a compulsory, statutory scheme similar to that operated by the banks and LDTs. Compulsory contributions would be limited to 0.3 per cent of total assets, coverage would only extend to deposits of up to £10 000, and shareholders and depositors would receive a minimum of 75 per cent and 100 per cent cover respectively (societies could, however, if willing, pay to raise the degree of protection offered to the former);

(iv) the repeal of the current special advances limit once the proposed constraints on assets and liabilities are introduced (the BSA wanted the limit replaced by an obligation to report to the Chief Registrar all loans to bodies corporate and the amount of all loans to individuals exceeding a certain limit);

(v) new-entry criteria. '*Authorisation*' would depend upon a society satisfying the Chief Registrar of its management (consisting of at least two persons) competence and integrity, and meeting a minimum capital requirement which, as now, could be met for an initial period by 'deferred shares'. A new society would have to build up its 'free reserves' to £1 m. and satisfy the Chief Registrar as to its ability to maintain such reserve before it gained 'trustee designation' status. 'Designation' status of societies already designated but failing to meet such criteria should be revoked.

The BSA's response to the Green Paper was published in September 1984 and, in brief, embodied the following:

(i) there should be more flexibility in the amount a society can advance to individuals in the form of 'unsecured lending' – the £5000 ceiling is too restrictive;

(ii) the 20 per cent limit on the amount societies can raise in the wholesale markets should be raised to 30 per cent;

(iii) it would be better for estate-agency (like insurance underwriting) activities to be carried out through a subsidiary rather than as a general branch office activity; and

(iv) disappointment at the lack of government resolve to enable societies to operate in EEC countries.

Some of these points were subsequently taken on board by the government in the drafting of the Building Societies Bill (see pp. 122–5).

Implications for the conduct of monetary policy. How the reform of the legislative framework governing the operations of building societies impacts upon monetary policy will depend primarily on how successful societies are in exploiting the new opportunities open to them. For many societies the freedoms sought were a defensive action against the threats and challenges posed by the market-place rather than a means of launching an offensive attack on new markets. For example, societies will in the future be able, in principle, to match the challenge posed by banks in the offering of retail financial packages. Nevertheless, to the extent that the new legislation allows societies to increase, rather than arrest the decline, in market-share on existing service fronts and provides them with the opportunity to enter into new markets, e.g. unsecured lending (see Johnson, 1986, for estimates of the likely aggregate penetration of the market), societies might actually take business away from the banks. Even if this does not prove to be the case, however, the statistical 'fog' surrounding broad money-supply data ($£M_3$, PSL_2) will still be thickened as extrapolation of past trends will prove unreliable owing to the uncertainty of future market-shares of intermediation services. To the extent that $£M_3$ returned as a target aggregate in the 1986 budget, this might prove troublesome, but with a target range of 11–15 per cent and inflation predicted to fall towards 3 per cent during the financial year few outside analysts are likely to be concerned at deviations from target. Indeed, at the time of writing, strong pressures were building up, yet again, for the UK to participate in the exchange-rate mechanism of the European Monetary System, a move that would formalise the (perceived) present policy of loose 'targeting' of the exchange rate (especially the sterling index). If this comes to fruition the debate on monetary targeting will become largely sterile.

Prudential regulation—outstanding issues

(i) Banking supervision[82]

Capital adequacy. The first and indeed the most basic issue arising on the capital adequacy front is the *definition of capital* itself. The Bank's approach has already been outlined in brief, but more detailed justification for this is now called for. A major problem facing supervisory authorities around the world in recent years has been the reconciliation of a desire to improve the capital ratios of banks,[83] at a time when the perceived risks of banking, especially on the international front, have risen appreciably (Group of Thirty, 1982 (a), and 1982 (b)), with the need to ensure adequate provisioning against bad and doubtful debts. The problem is compounded by fiscal considerations, which favour both subordinated debt at the expense of equity capital by allowing tax relief on interest payments but not dividends and specific against general provisions by confining tax deductibility to the former. Moreover, fiscal changes can sometimes necessitate sudden revisions to banks' policies on deferred tax provisioning. (The significance of this for banks operating in the UK became only too clear with the 1984 Budget amendments to the systems governing the availability of capital allowances and liability to corporation tax.[84] For the English clearing banks alone this prompted a £2 b. transfer from reserves.)[85] Finally, profitability considerations influence the banks' ability to boost capital through both equity issues and retained earnings.

The response of the UK clearing banks to these pressures has been fairly uniform[86] and, to a large degree, determined by the Bank's approach to defining capital. Of particular significance here is the official line taken on subordinated loan capital and debt-provisioning.

The Bank's treatment of *loan stock* issues in its 1980 paper (op. cit.) differs from that which obtained since 1975. Its former view was that the function of loan stock (which had to be subordinated and medium to long term) was to finance part of the infrastructure of the business and *not* to provide a cushion against losses. This view rested on the observation that, unlike shareholders' funds, loan stocks are impermanent, do not offer flexibility with respect to servicing costs and are not available to absorb losses without precipitating a liquidation. This observation, of course, still held true in 1980, but the Bank was by then more conciliatory, emphasising that, in spite of the drawbacks, fully-subordinated medium- to long-term loan stocks might reduce the threat to creditors' confidence in the event of an institution experiencing difficulties and so enhance its ability to servive. Moreover, where the loan stocks were long term and denominated in foreign currency, maturity and currency mismatches might be reduced. In the light of these considerations the Bank decided to allow the inclusion of fully-subordinated loan stock, up to a maximum of one-third, within the capital base provided that they were of a minimum initial period to maturity of five years, did not incorporate restrictive covenants triggering early repayments, and were subject to an amortisation factor once passing within the five years remaining to maturity threshold. This last stipulation was designed to 'discourage unduly short initial terms, soften the impact on capital ratios when loan stocks mature and are not replaced, and reflect the diminishing comfort afforded'. Finally, the Bank demonstrated its determination to prevent an illusory boosting of capital for the banking system as a whole, in recognition of the fact that the bulk of bank issues are held by other banks, by insisting that all banks operating in the UK[87] deduct their holdings of other banks' issues in calculating the size of their capital base. In so doing the risk of a domino-style collapse of the banking system is reduced. (Reminders of the ruling were issued in May 1984.)

The Bank's limited seal of approval for subordinated loan-stock issues was eagerly seized upon by the clearing banks in the early 1980s, but by the end of 1984 most were near to or up against the stipulated ceiling. Accordingly different means had to be found for raising capital ratios (all four English clearing banks suffered a decline in their gearing ratios during 1984 – see Table 2.6) to levels expected by investors and supervisors alike.[88] To a limited degree, improvement was sought by restraining balance-sheet growth[89] and/or raising the quality of loans and the level of commission income for a given sized balance-sheet, but the major contribution still had to come from new capital raising activities. Barclays broke the ice in March 1985 with a £513 m. rights issue, but the other clearing banks did not follow

Table 2.6 Gearing ratios of the English clearing banks: 1982–5

| | *Gearing ratio (%)* | | | |
Bank	*end-'82*	*end-'83*	*end-'84*	*end-May '85*
Barclays	3.9	4.6	4.1	5.5
Lloyds	4.4	5.2	5.0	6.3
Midland	3.9	4.5	4.4	5.0
National Westminster	4.6	4.9	4.5	6.0

Source: Published accounts and (for end-May '85) estimates.

suit. Instead they opted for perpetual floating-rate note (FRN) issues after Lloyds's pioneering $750 m. May 1985 issue which, for the first time,[90] the Bank accepted as *'primary'* capital.[91] (In June 1985 Barclays also made a $250 m., five-year term, fixed-rate Eurodollar bond issue, which ranked as senior subordinated debt, and National Westminster announced a ten-year Swiss Franc 300m. bond-with-equity-warrants issue, which qualified as subordinated capital.)

The Bank's earlier treatment of undated/perpetual FRNs was explained in a note circulated in November 1984 to members of the British Bankers' Association containing new proposals for measuring capital adequacy in the light of recent capital market innovations. A maximum of a half of primary capital could be held in FRN form provided that: (i) the issue never has to be repaid, except in case of liquidation; (ii) the issue converts automatically into equity if the issuing bank gets into financial difficulties; and (iii) no cross-default clauses, negative pledges or clauses which trigger early repayment of the moneys raised are contained in the terms of the issue. The market's initial reaction to the Bank's ruling was that the market in perpetual FRNs would collapse as anyone prepared to buy the notes in the form demanded by the Bank as an alternative to pure equity would probably demand a substantial discount, thereby making the issue prohibitively expensive for the banks. In the event the market could not have been more wrong for the May 1985 issues,[92] admittedly in slightly different form from that initially demanded by the Bank, were snapped up by investors at very fine margins ($\frac{1}{8}$ per cent to $\frac{1}{4}$ per cent above LIBOR). Given that a very high proportion of FRN issues ends up in bank hands (perhaps as much as 80 per cent), the (bank) purchasers were presumably of the view that the collapse of an English clearing bank was an extremely remote possibility and one which, at any rate, would only likely occur after their own demise!

The collapse of Continental Illinois in the US in 1984 and the practice of central banks bailing out depositors *not* shareholders of individual banks should caution against complacency however. Indeed, the 'triple − B +' rating given to Midland Bank's issue by Standard & Poor's, the US credit rating agency, suggests a more reasoned investor approach has now set in following the initial euphoria.

The important feature of the Lloyds' FRN issue enabling it to be classified as primary capital was that interest payments could be suspended if no dividend was declared on common stock and that, in the event of Lloyds going into liquidation, note holders would be deemed to be preference shareholders ranking behind all bar ordinary shareholders for repayment. The apparent softening in the Bank's approach (it had earlier insisted upon automatic conversion to *pure* equity should the issuing bank get into difficulties) was played down by Bank officials, who insisted that there had been no climbdown: 'the issues "did not represent ... any diminution in practice in the standards the Bank originally set out to achieve" and were "sufficiently close to equity in terms of the protection afforded to depositors to rank *pari passu* with equity for capital adequacy measurement purposes"'.[93] From the ordinary shareholder's point of view the Bank's action had, in effect, raised the riskiness of their investment, but the countervailing impact of higher capital ratios held bank share prices up. For the issuing bank, investors and supervisors were placated with healthier capital ratios, the money had been raised more cheaply than an equity issue would have allowed,[94] and the dollar denomination of the notes would provide a buffer against future exchange-rate fluctuations, thereby facilitating an expansion in foreign-currency business without damaging capital ratios. The only nagging doubts about the affair relate to the impact on the international supervisory system. For although the UK authorities insist that, for the institutions they regulate, holdings of another bank's FRNs must be deducted from the holder's capital base before computing capital ratios, supervisory authorities elsewhere (e.g. in the US and Japan) are unlikely to act with such rectitude. If this proves to be the case a further illusory expansion in global bank capital will have been sanctioned. Moreover, even for the Bank of England, the inbuilt reluctance to let a major financial intermediary fail may unfortunately be strengthened by virtue of the fact that the vast bulk of bank FRNs will end up in bank hands, thereby increasing the risk of a domino collapse should one bank get into serious difficulties.

Moving on to an assessment of the Bank's treatment of *debt-*

provisioning, the justification for including only general bad debt provisions (this was *not* the case before 1980 when specific provisions were included also) in the capital base is that provisions set aside for likely losses that have already been identified are not available to cushion future unidentified losses. This ruling, making allowance for the tax deductibility of specific reserves (including, since January 1983, those made against sovereign loans), favours general rather than specific provisioning for all except the relatively well-capitalised banks, which the English clearing banks certainly were not in the early 1980s (see Table 2.6). Accordingly only modest specific provisions (especially against 'international lending') were made by the clearing banks during the 1983/4 financial year. For the whole of 1984, however, the policy was reversed, with the bulk of the increase (£500 m. on 1983) in bad-debt provisions being made in specific form. As Table 2.7 indicates, this approach was adopted by each of the English clearing banks (although Midland's 'non-Crocker' specific provisions fell relative to the figure recorded in 1983).

Table 2.7   1984 debt provisions of English clearing banks (£m.)

Provisions		*Barclays*	*Lloyds*	*Midland*	*National Westminster*
Specific:	domestic	178	103	471	104
	international	267	101		137
General:	domestic	80	65	145	110
	international				
Total		525	269	616[1]	351

Source: Published accounts.

Note: [1]Of this total, £456 m. was attributable to losses experienced by Midland's subsidiary Crocker National Bank. If the influence of Crocker National Bank is excluded from the figures, specific provisions total £150 m. (down £38 m. on the 1983 figure) and the general provision amounts to zero.

An explanation for this change in clearing-bank policy on debt-provisioning, in the face of continuing pressures to improve capital ratios, may lie in the banks' desire to boost recorded profits and hence maintain dividend payments in real terms,[95] perhaps as a precursor to future rights issues (perpetual FRNs had not, at this stage, been accepted as primary capital by the Bank). This highlights the problem facing bank supervisors in assessing the adequacy of debt provisions, for the final decision of an individual bank will, subject to meeting the requirements of the 1981 Companies Act, always reflect a compromise between adequately reflecting the risk of losses likely to arise (and hence satisfying auditors, regulators and the long-term interests of shareholders), recording profits that are thought politically acceptable to the incumbent political administration (i.e. levels which will dissuade the Treasury from mounting new revenue-raising exercises), satisfying the short-run desires of shareholders and possibly facilitating the imminent fund-raising activities of the bank itself by declaring adequate dividends. The Bank faces an unenviable task in reconciling and weighting the often conflicting requirements of interested parties and coming to a conclusion on the adequacy of provisions made by banks.

A problem subsidiary to that of defining capital is how to take account of banks' *off-balance-sheet activities* within the assessment and measurement of capital adequacy. The recent rapid surge in such activities has demonstrated, yet again, that prudential control, like monetary control, is not immune to disintermediation, but supervisory authorities are only just beginning to come to grips with the problem. The response of the Bank to what the Governor has termed the 'securitisation' of lending (i.e. the switch from making normal loans to trading in and underwriting security issues) and the mushrooming of activity in new markets (options, futures, interest-rate swaps, forward-rate agreements and interest-rate protection packages) has been to advise caution. With respect to the latter set of activities the Bank has expressed fears about the competence of management to exercise adequate internal control over the use of highly sophisticated computer programming techniques and a review is currently being held to inquire into the risks that can arise from the acceptance of contingent liabilities through these mediums.[96] On the 'securitisation' of lending, the Bank has already acted (Apr 1985), demanding that 'note-issuance facilities' (NIFs) and 'revolving underwriting facilities' (RUFs),[97] whether or not they have been drawn down, be treated as contingent liabilities for the purpose of calculating risk-asset ratios (i.e. bearing a weight of 0.5, half the amount allotted to a normal loan) and that the risks[98] arising from the sale by banks of packages of assets be taken into account in the assessment of capital adequacy. For a bank underwriting the commercial issue of short-term paper the risk is that it might find itself, in adverse conditions, holding a worthless investment. Although participating banks do attempt to minimise their likely exposure to losses by confining facilities to borrowers with a high credit rating[99] (e.g. banks, 'blue-chip' companies and governments), and do charge commitment fees (commonly in the range $\frac{1}{24}$ to $\frac{1}{32}$per cent),[100] these are regarded as inadequate[101] by the authorities to cover the risks involved.

A further problem relates to the assessment of capital adequacy for banks or *banking groups* engaged in a wide range offinancial, and even non-financial, activities. One approach, and one which the Bank takes towards 'primary' gilt market-makers, is to insist that part of business capital be dedicated or ascribed to particular areas of operation, but this raises a number of issues. For example, to what extent do different business operations require separate incorporation rather than a simple earmarking of capital, and how should 'banking' status, with its attendant privileges and responsibilities, affect the attitude of regulators in their assessment of capital adequacy for conglomerates incorporating 'banking' operations? Finally, how should the adequacy of capital be assessed for a securities trading operation, an area in which banks are becoming heavily involved?[102]

The final major issue outstanding on the capital adequacy front is the need, despite the risk of impairing flexibility (see p. 113 and Dale (1982), pp. 25–9), for *greater harmonisation* of the regulatory treatment adopted by supervisors around the world. This would prove beneficial on the following counts: (i) it would improve global resource allocation by allowing investors to make sensible comparisons of banks' capital positions whatever the banks' country of incorporation or place of operation;[103] (ii) it would reduce competitive inequalities faced by banks operating in an international market;[104] and (iii) it would improve the stability of the international banking system.[105]

Liquidity adequacy.   The flexible approach taken by the Bank to the assessment of liquidity adequacy has effectively dealt with most of the criticisms of previous liquidity controls. These embraced the arbitrariness of designating a certain class of assets as 'liquid', with the associated distortive effects on relative yields, the impracticability of applying norms to the whole banking community, the illogic of specifying requirements in the form of specific rather than average levels of liquid-asset holdings and the potential dangers associated with an overlap with monetary policy.[106] Additionally, most concede that the Bank, as guardian of the stability of the whole financial system, has the right to ensure that internal control and monitoring procedures at least are adequate. Moreover, the existence of deposit protection schemes does not obviate the need for liquidity controls as the former protect only the nominal value and not the liquidity of deposits.[107]

If any criticisms are to be made of the liquidity arrangements, perhaps the most valid concerns the lack of any explicit 'cost-benefit' analysis, a feature common to the other strands of banking supervision. Of particular concern are the disintermediation incentives provided (e.g. for business to move off-balance-sheet or offshore) and the competitive inequities introduced, especially between locally-incorporated and foreign banks. Although there is a tendency to exaggerate the extent of the problem supervisors, whatever their achievements and aspirations with respect to international supervisory harmonisation, should be less dismissive of the problem than is their occasional wont. Finally, banks and supervisors alike must remain alert to increasing depositor sensitivity to interest-rate and service differentials, a process accelerated by rapid technological advance, with concomitant ramifications for deposit stability.

Deposit insurance. The most basic, yet continuing, controversy on the deposit insurance front relates to the very need for such arrangements. Arguments in favour embrace the following: (i) that they help preserve the stability of the financial system by promoting investor confidence; (ii) that the protection of the nominal value of some monetary assets is a communal benefit (Santomero and Watson, 1977); (iii) that it is necessary to provide a safety haven for the small, and by implication, unsophisticated investor; (iv) that it is preferable for banks to pay explicitly for deposit protection rather than to receive it through government largesse in the form of an implicit government guarantee.[108] Opponents, however, would emphasise the following: (i) 'moral hazards' may be created by discouraging the investing public from undertaking adequate appraisal of prospective risk-adjusted rates of return and by encouraging bank management to take higher risks for a given pattern of expected rates of return;[109] (ii) the provision of an adequate risk-return spectrum of investment opportunity may be impaired; (iii) the costs incurred, in terms of funding and administering deposit insurance schemes, might outweigh the benefits which, at any rate, might be achieved by alternative means.[110]

Despite the initial reluctance of the clearing banks, which argued that the introduction of deposit insurance would reduce the level of competition in financial markets and underwrote the unfortunate principle of the more efficient subsidising the less efficient/prudent,[111] the Deposit Protection Scheme was eventually introduced with features designed to minimise the moral hazard dangers and overcome some of the other objections. For example, coverage is limited to a relatively low value of deposits (£10 000) and only 75 per cent protection is provided.[112] The failure, however, to link the premium payable to the level of risk incurred by the insured institution (which might, for example, be readily obtained by standardising the risk-assets ratio computed for capital adequacy purposes) detracts somewhat from these efforts. Moreover, it is not clear to what extent, if any, the existence of the scheme has allowed for an offsetting reduction in supervisory effort elsewhere.

International operations. On the international front the banks have grudgingly accepted the principle of the Bank setting specific limits on exchange exposure,[113] despite the competitive inequities introduced *vis-à-vis* non-UK-incorporated banks, but welcomed the flexible approach taken by the Bank to the monitoring/control of international loan exposures. Although in stark contrast to the more detailed involvement sought by regulators elsewhere (e.g. in the US), the moral suasion exercised through discussions with bank management appears, to date, to have contained the problems posed by debt-rescheduling and other risks incurred on international loans.[114] There is little room for complacency, however, as the OECD has pointed out (1983, ch. IV), improvements being required on the following fronts: (i) the quality of information obtained by supervisors and the scope of statistical coverage; (ii) convergence in countries' reporting requirements, accounting practices and supervisory systems generally to limit the competitive inequalities created; (iv) a wider adoption of the consolidation principle and a greater consensus on the division of supervisory responsibilites between parent and host supervisors (despite the existence of the Basle Concordat, as revised in 1983). Additional concerns relate to the risks created by the growth in the international interbank market (BIS, 1983, pp. 32–40) and the dangers posed by disparities in national deposit insurance and lender-of-last-resort operations (Dale, op. cit. 1982).

Technological advance. Technological developments in the provision of payments and other financial services hold a number of important ramifications for banking supervision. First, as indicated directly above, they can alter the competitive balance between bank and non-bank DTIs by reducing the entry cost to banking. Alternatively the net result may be the exact opposite, namely the barring of non-bank DTIs from the effective use of EFT developments because of the banks' determination to ensure that the very high initial start-up and developmental costs, together with their vast distribution network (i.e. branches), are used to erect an effective barrier to entry. The good offices of the Bank may well be necessary to ensure that the general public's best interests are served by these developments. Second, developments which facilitate the provision of a greater proliferation of interest-bearing transaction balances, by eroding the 'endowment' element of profits arising from low-cost retail balances in an era of high and rising interest rates, will raise the riskiness of banking, *ceteris paribus*. And finally, a number of operating risks are substantially raised as operations become more mechanised. For example, failure of power supply or hardware, loss of file records and computer fraud all pose acute problems for both individual banks and, given the ever-increasing degree of interdependence induced by computer linkages, the system as a whole.

Lender-of-last-resort facilities. The problems posed by the exercise of lender-of-last-resort facilities, which are necessary in addition to liquidity controls to deal with runs on sound and viable institutions resulting from circumstances beyond their control (e.g. unfounded rumours), were vividly illustrated in the rescue of Johnson Matthey Bankers (JMB) in October 1984. To fully appreciate them, however, it is necessary to fill in some of the background.

The Johnson Matthey Bankers Affair. In October 1984, following an approach from the directors of Johnson Matthey plc, who believed that the establishment of the necessary loan provisions adequately to cover anticipated losses arising from the lending activities of their banking arm JMB would threaten the whole group, the Bank of England bought JMB and its subsidiaries for a nominal sum (£1) and wrote-off a large chunk of their assets. Under the rescue plan Johnson Matthey was required to put up £50 m. to allow JMB to continue trading (Charter Consolidated, a substantial investor in Johnson Matthey – it held 27.9 per cent of its shares at the time of the rescue – contributed £25 m.). On 7 November, after much dispute, and, given the uncertainty of eventual provisions, a fruitless search for an outright purchaser of the company (or its loan book) and additional minority shareholders, an agreed package of indemnities was announced to cover the possibility that JMB's eventual loan losses might exceed its original £120 m. capital base.[115] The package was necessary to keep JMB's lines of credit open and involved the participation of banks (the clearing banks, much to their annoyance, being required to contribute the bulk of the banks' share, set at

£35 m.), the other four members of the Gold Ring[116] (£30 m.), accepting houses which are not members of the 'Gold Ring' (£10 m.) and the Bank of England (£75 m.).[117] Calls below these limits were to be met in the same proportions. The indemnities relate solely to JMB's commercial loan portfolio and participating banks will share in any 'profits' made on the eventual return of JMB to the private sector. Finally, on 22 November the Bank made a further loan, in the form of a deposit,[118] of £100 m. to provide additional working funds.

Perhaps the most far-reaching issue raised by the JMB affair concerns a consideration of the criteria upon which a bank rescue may be justified. In deciding whether or not to rescue an insolvent institution[119] a central bank must weigh the requirement to preserve the stability of the financial system against the resource misallocation, welfare losses and *moral hazard* implications likely to result from interfering with the workings of the market-place. Even for a market not characterised by the full requirements of 'perfect competition', welfare optimisation demands minimal interference with the process of entry to and exit from the industry (Baumol, 1982).

The rescue of JMB is the first 'lifeboat' to be launched since the much grander operation mounted during the 1974/5 'fringe banking crisis' (Reid, 1982), when resources of up to £2.5 b. or so were marshalled. On that occasion the Bank's intervention was justified in the following way:

> The Bank thus found themselves confronted with the imminent collapse of several deposit-taking institutions and with the clear danger of a rapidly escalating crisis of confidence. This threatened other deposit-taking institutions and, if left unchecked, would have quickly passed into parts of the banking system proper. While the UK clearing banks still appeared secure from the domestic effects of any run . . . their international exposure was such that the risk to external confidence was a matter of concern for themselves as well as for the Bank. The problem was to avoid a widening circle of collapse through the contagion of fear. (*BEQB*, June 1978, p. 233, para. 25)

Similar arguments, especially relating to the likely damaging effect on external confidence, were advanced to justify the JMB rescue. First and foremost, the Bank argued (Bank of England, 1985) that a number of special factors contributed to rendering a liquidation of JMB (an option which was considered, but rejected)[120] unacceptable because of the potential consequences for the banking system as a whole. The Bank felt that it would be unable to convince the market in the early days of the crisis that Johnson Matthey's bullion business was trouble-free, with the result that JMB's failure *might* have precipitated liquidity problems for the remaining four members of the London 'Gold Ring'. In turn the crisis of confidence *might* have spread to other British banks at home and abroad,[121] for the former, because of both a domestic and international[122] lack of confidence in the 'recognised bank' sector and, for the latter, because of the 'fragility' of international markets due to continuing sovereign debt problems and banking scares. Of particular importance on this last front was the rescue by the US authorities of Continental Illinois, an event which appears to have had considerable impact on the Bank's reaction to its own problem supervisees. Indeed, the US experience of a drift of international funds away from their banks in the wake of the Continental Illinois crisis is seen as indicative of the likely response to a collapse of JMB. To the extent that this would have involved a switch out of sterling, exchange-rate pressures would also have been intensified. The second strand of the case for rescuing JMB is the more obvious one, namely a desire to preserve London as the major international bullion market. Failure of JMB would almost certainly have precipitated the collapse of Johnson Matthey plc, carrying the risk that London's position would have suffered irreparable damage[123] thereby threatening a reduction in future invisible earnings.

The main difficulty for an 'outsider', in trying to compare the two events, lies in assessing the scale of the problem present on the two occasions. For, while the risk of further 'contagion' was self-evident in the 1974/5 crisis, with the potential to threaten even the clearing banks (National Westminster was at one stage moved to publicly deny that it would require lifeboat support itself), as the Bank even conceded it is not, at first glance, obvious why the collapse of JMB, engaged to only a comparatively minor degree in commercial banking activities, should have raised a similar spectre of large-scale financial collapse.[124] Second, the principles guiding the style of rescue were not explicitly stated in the latest event.[125] Nevertheless, Charter Consolidated, the largest shareholder at the time of the rescue, was brought into the rescue and Johnson Matthey was asked to contribute an amount judged to be the maximum that could be made without seriously impairing its own creditworthiness.[126] Unlike the Slater Walker Ltd support package of 1975/7, however, no longer-term claim on the parent's assets/profits was taken, partly as a result of the

Bank accepting Charter Consolidated's participation on the latter's terms, namely that it was conditional on Johnson Matthey not incurring an open-ended commitment to JMB.

Whether or not the Bank exaggerated the potential dangers of a JMB collapse, a dangerous *moral hazard* has been created. For although JMB's original shareholder – JM plc – lost its investment and certain key executives were replaced, others, wholly or partly engaged in the provision of 'banking' services, might be encouraged to act less prudently than circumstances would otherwise dictate.[127] The authorities are patently aware of this danger,[128] but no amount of exhortation is likely to persuade market operators to ignore their actual deeds in the market-place. Despite the existence of the banks' deposit insurance scheme, which might act to reduce the degree of 'automaticity' apparent in the Bank's response to difficulties experienced by 'banking' institutions, the Bank's inclusion of (net) holdings of banks' perpetual floating rate notes within a bank's capital base, given that the bulk will end up in bank hands, compounds the moral hazard problem by reinforcing the Bank's reluctance to let *any* 'banking' institution fail. Finally, as the Bank's actions suggest, if blanket protection of 'small' depositors is to be assured, then the benefits accruing from offering only limited coverage to depositors under the Deposit Protection Scheme will be nullified.[129]

Other issues raised by the JMB affair concern the adequacy of existing authorisation procedures and the subsequent surveillance of banks' operations through quarterly discussions with management, the role played by auditors in the supervisory process and the implications for the regulation of diversified financial conglomerates.[130]

The fundamental weakness in existing authorisation procedures, whereby recognised banks are supervised less rigorously than LDTs, was highlighted by the JMB affair. Admittedly, until this case, little evidence had emerged to call this aspect of banking supervision into question,[131] but this does not necessarily mean that all other recognised banks have been adequately supervised. Rather it may be the case that the scale of any problems existing elsewhere have, to date, been contained. Second, the appalling catalogue of incompetence unearthed by the Bank[132] (no prima facie evidence of fraud has yet been discovered, although the City of London police were called in to investigate on 17 July 1985) calls into question the Bank's application of part of the authorisation procedures. For, by its own admission, the Bank has positively vetted individuals for the purpose of running a banking operation who have subsequently been found guilty of gross ineptitude in virtually every area of commercial banking practice. (Staff changes obviously complicate the situation.) Surveillance practices, subsequent to authorisation, are also called into question, given the extreme incompetence displayed by JMB management over which the Bank has presided, the Bank's inability to ensure adequate loan diversification despite the existence of a 10 per cent of capital 'guideline',[133,134] and the Department of Trade and Industry's willingness to tolerate late filing of accounts.[135]

Auditors occupy an awkward position within the supervisory process. Under the Companies Act they are required to report to the shareholders whether or not the accounts prepared by a bank's directors provide the required 'true and fair view'. In coming to a conclusion they will review the bank's systems material to its accounts (e.g. internal audit and inspection systems) and examine transactions on a sample basis to validate the authenticity of the records (Fowle, 1985). They will then consider the judgements made by the directors in highly sensitive areas (e.g. in making provisions against bad and doubtful debts), discuss problem loans, loan provisioning, etc., with senior management and, finally, report back to the directors, with recommendations where appropriate. If, at that stage, the auditors cannot agree with the directors that the accounts present a 'true and fair view', and fail to be appeased, they can either resign or qualify the accounts, either of which risks precipitating a run on the bank. Without the client's permission the auditor is unable, at any stage, to express his/her fears to banking supervisors. Whether or not JMB's auditors noticed the internal control and managerial deficiencies and accounting misrepresentations then is not the only relevant point, for, assuming they did, how strongly did they register their dissatisfaction with JMB's directors and were they right in signing an unqualified audit report? If the auditors are to be criticised by the Bank[136] the criticism must rest largely on the first two points, for the qualification of the audit would, in all likelihood, only have resulted in a sudden and haphazard collapse of the bank, thereby complicating any subsequent 'lifeboat' operation. The carefully orchestrated rescue operation of the Bank that actually took place is obviously to be preferred.

The role of the auditor leads conveniently into the next issue, namely the desirability of continuing with a supervisory system that depends so heavily on the auditing process for its effectiveness. In the UK banking supervision is carried out according to the legislation embodied within the 1979 Banking Act. Despite this statutory element, governing authorisation procedures and deposit protection, the Bank's system of supervision is still a flexible one, with a wide measure of discretion remaining in the interpretation and application of the authorisation procedures and with the assessment of the adequacy of prudential standards (e.g. relating to capital, liquidity and exposure to exchange-rate risk). The cornerstone of the system remains the management interviews (quarterly for UK-incorporated, non-clearing banks) that follow the Bank's statistical analysis of the required returns, with no requirement that the latter be audited. This approach contrasts sharply with that taken by bank supervisors in other countries which adopt a policy of formal bank inspections. But even there the system is not infallible (witness the collapse of Continental Illinois in the US in 1984) so, taking account of the Bank's previous track record, calls for the abandonment of the current, flexible approach in favour of a more formalised, inspection-based system are unlikely to be entertained. Nevertheless, the weak links of the present system should be strengthened (see below).

The final issue raised by the JMB affair concerns the appropriate regulatory treatment of financial conglomerates, the current fashion in financial markets. Will the offering of 'banking' services effectively guarantee the survival (though perhaps with different shareholders and managers/directors) of the group? How will equity be maintained if the 'underwritten' groups branch out into activities engaged in by non-banks, outside the sphere of banking supervision and hence beyond the benevolence of the central bank through its support operations?[137] (Perhaps limits to diversification are in order?) And how will the supervisory functions exercised by different regulatory agencies (e.g. those responsible for commodity trading, securities trading, insurance broking, etc.) be co-ordinated? All these questions, posing awkward issues for the regulatory authorities, require to be resolved.

UK banking supervision after the Johnson Matthey affair

An important consequence of the JMB 'lifeboat' operation was the establishment of a committee (the 'Review Committee'), involving Treasury and Bank officials and an outside expert, to review banking supervisory procedures to see if any changes were necessary. In particular the committee was asked to look at the relationship between bank auditor and supervisor, the handling of risk concentration and assessment of asset quality, the statistical requirements imposed on subject institutions and the adequacy of existing staff resources and training programmes in the Bank's supervisory department. The committee was asked to report to the Chancellor by Spring 1985.

The Review Committee eventually came up with the following recommendations (Cmnd 9550, June 1985): (i) the replacement of the existing two-tier system of authorisation with a single, Bank authorisation to take deposits; (ii) that legislative steps be taken to dismantle the barriers presently preventing discussions taking place between auditors and supervisors, with a view to allowing for a regular dialogue between the two parties; (iii) that exposure to a single non-bank borrower or interconnected group of borrowers should not exceed 25 per cent of a bank's capital; (iv) that banks set up audit committees and appoint finance directors; (v) that internal control and reporting requirements be strengthened;[138] (vi) that the number of staff (especially accountants) engaged in the supervision department at the Bank be increased and given commercial banking experience; (vii) that the ceiling for deposit protection granted under the Deposit Protection Scheme be raised from £10 000 to £20 000.

Recommendations (i), (ii), (v) and (vi) are all straightforward yet necessary amendments and, as such, merit no further discussion. Item (iv) represents an attempt to improve upon the internal auditing process, but stops short of requiring a full audit of prudential returns (although more random audits, on a spot-check basis, were recommended). Moves towards the Canadian system, whereby the authorities 'authorise' accounting firms for bank audit purposes and require frequent change in the auditing firms employed by individual banks, might also usefully be considered. These measures would provide a means of improving audit standards and of reducing the risk of 'moral hazards' arising from the establishment of close affinities between banks and auditors respectively. Items (iii) and (vii) merit further consideration.

The suggestion that the large exposure guideline be changed to 25 per cent of a bank's capital, with no legislative support, is curious to say the least in that JMB's problems are recognised to have largely arisen as a result of breaches of the old 10 per cent guideline. The Bank has admitted that breaches of this guideline by other banks are commonplace but a relaxation of the guideline to a 25 per cent level, even if *de facto* it becomes more of a ceiling, can hardly represent a tightening up of loan exposure control. Admittedly the Bank still expects to be notified of any single, non-bank exposure amounting to over 10 per cent of a bank's capital and, under normal circumstances, will probably insist on an appropriate capital cover, but, nevertheless, the ruling appears excessively generous (although not by international standards).

The final recommendation, that the maximum cover available to a depositor under the banks' Deposit Protection Scheme be doubled to £20 000, appears irrelevant to the JMB affair, although indexing (but in this case over-indexing) of the cover is presumably justified in its own right. For, even with the higher figure, the necessity for a 'lifeboat' for JMB, as perceived by the Bank, would not have been reduced as the problem was a fear of a contagious liquidity crisis rather than an isolated bank collapse. Assuming, then, that the purpose of the proposal is to improve the Deposit Protection Scheme, one would have liked to have seen proposed more radical reform that would have linked the contributor's premium to the degree of risk incurred through its operations.

Concluding comments on banking supervision

The recommendations of the Supervision 'Review Committee', if implemented[139] (most were included in the 'Banking Supervision' White Paper published in December 1985 – see Exhibit 2.3), will plug some of the supervisory 'gaps' evident in the wake of the JMB affair, but do not go far enough in improving the standards of prudential supervision in the UK. Bearing in mind the principles that should underlie any system of prudential controls,[140] the following measures might usefully be considered for adoption with a view to improving the system's cost-effectiveness: (i) full auditing of prudential returns; (ii) the 'authorisation' of bank auditors; (iii) a review of existing authorisation procedures, additional to the ending of the two-tier system; (iv) linking a contributor's 'premium' under the Deposit Protection Scheme to the degree of risk incurred; (v) providing legislative backing to tighter loan exposure 'rules' (the sanction of de-authorisation appears a weak deterrent given it is rarely exercised); (vi) a raising of the weighting (currently 0.2) given to 'market loans with listed banks' within the computation of a bank's risk-assets ratio, in order to reduce the risk of a domino-style collapse arising from interbank exposures and thus, it is hoped, making it easier for the

Bank, under certain circumstances, to allow 'banking' institutions to fail; (vii) limiting the diversification opportunities open to banks. While the adoption of these measures risks impairment of the flexibility of prudential supervision, it would go some way to reassuring investors that self-regulation of financial markets will only persist as long as market operators demonstrate their ability to regulate themselves in a manner which satisfies the expectations of investors and supervisors alike. The recent Lloyds underwriting scandals and now the JMB fiasco both suggest that a reaffirmation of a desire for *effective* deposit/investor protection is in order.

(ii)   The prudential regulation and supervision of building societies

As Exhibit 2.4 demonstrates, the *Building Societies Bill* incorporated a number of important proposals for the amendment of the supervisory system governing the operations of building societies. These proposals embrace the following: (i) the establishment of a 'Commission' with wider powers than possessed by the Chief Registrar; (ii) the introduction of a statutory investor protection scheme along the lines of the scheme applied to 'banks'; (iii) an extension in the role played by auditors within the supervisory process, including a requirement for auditors to consult with the 'Commission', even without their client's consent where investor's capital is held to be at risk; (iv) the introduction of new authorisation procedures; (v) a broadening of the scope of supervision to include formal assessment of the adequacy of capital, liquidity, management plans, and internal control and inspection procedures. The broad aims of the proposed amendments are to ensure that the new risks created through the diversification opportunities granted in the Bill will be both identified and contained and that, despite the harsh limits to diversification, some convergence in the depositor protection schemes applying to banks and building societies will be achieved.

The *Commission* is to comprise not less than four and no more than ten (this can be increased at the discretion of the Treasury) members to be appointed by the Treasury. Its general functions shall be: (a) to promote the protection by each building society of the investments of its shareholders and depositors; (b) to promote the financial stability of building societies generally; (c) to ensure that the principal purpose of building societies remains that of raising, primarily from their members, funds for making advances to members secured upon land for their residential use; (d) to administer the system of regulation of building societies provided for by or under this Act; and (e) to advise and make recommendations to the Treasury or other government departments on any matter relating to building societies. More specifically the Act will confer a number of other functions on it which will provide powers to: impose conditions on or, in the extreme, revoke authorisations; petition for a winding-up of a society's operations; control advertising; impose limitations on the acceptance of deposits or making of advances; require alteration in the conduct of business (e.g. to ensure requirements, such as those relating to asset and liability structure, are met); remove any director or other officers; determine a society's power (i.e. what a society is able to do under the Act); prevent association with other bodies; obtain information and documents; launch investigations.

Under the Act the duties of *auditors* will be to carry out investigations to enable them to form an opinion on whether proper accounting records have been kept, whether a society has maintained satisfactory systems of control of its business and records and of inspection and report, and whether a society's annual accounts are in agreement with the accounting records. To this end the annual accounts (which must give a 'true and fair view' of income and expenditure during the financial year, the financial position at the end of the financial year and the sources and uses of funds during the financial year) and the directors' annual business statement, the report to the societies' annual general meeting and the summary financial statement for members and depositors are subject to an annual auditor's report. This must be carried out within three months of the end of the financial year and a copy must be sent to the Commission. Furthermore, in exceptional circumstances, auditors may pass information to the Commission 'notwithstanding any duty of confidentiality owed to a society'.

The new *authorisation procedures* proposed to replace the Building Societies (Authorisation) Regulations 1981 will require societies to be authorised before they can raise funds or borrow money. This will normally be granted provided that the following conditions are met: (i) a society has 'qualifying capital' of at least £100 000; (ii) the chairman of the board of directors, the executive directors, the chief executive and managers are all deemed 'fit and proper' persons; (iii) the Commission is satisfied that the society's affairs will be conducted 'prudently' and that the investments of shareholders and depositors will be adequately protected.

A critique. At the philosophical level the guiding principle of the suggested reform is that the prudential regulation of societies should assimilate more closely to that employed with respect to 'banks' yet should remain simpler because of the more homogeneous nature of societies' activities. This proposition, however, is based on the authorities' unwillingness to allow societies any more than limited diversification opportunities.[141] While this might be justified on the grounds that evolution is to be preferred to revolution, the authorities' willingness, under certain circumstances, to allow societies to convert from mutual to corporate status and the general desirability of achieving fiscal and regulatory 'neutrality'[142] militate against such limitations. Moreover the proposals present a serious impediment to the authorities' avowed intention of regulating by function rather than by type of intermediary. The logical solution is surely to remove (gradually if preferred) all restrictions and apply a uniform system of supervision to all deposit-taking financial intermediaries.

In respect of the specific reform proposals, amendments to the deposit protection scheme should, in order to reduce the incidence of moral hazard, ideally incorporate a measure to link the premium paid by an insured intermediary to the degree of risk incurred in the course of its operations. To this end the Commission might consider incorporating within the more detailed capital adequacy requirements promised a simplified form of risk-assets ratio (*BEQB*, Sep 1980, p. 329), analoguous to that required of banks, to facilitate calculation of the required premiums. On the question of extending the powers of the Registrar, only some of the concerns raised in the Wilson Report (ch. 24) appear to have been answered. Most notably the provision of (unaudited)[143] monthly cash-flow statements is to remain voluntary (although the adoption of a cash-flow approach to liquidity adequacy would largely overcome the dangers – at the moment the Act will require only that an 'adequate' proportion of liquid assets are kept, having regard to the range and scale of its business and the character and composition of its assets and liabilities) and the Registrar will still lack the power to enforce (he can only petition to the courts) a winding-up of a society. The delay in closing New Cross illustrated only too well the impotence of the Registrar in this respect.[144]

Finally, the impediments placed in the way of 'hostile' mergers and conversion to company status militate against optimal resource allocation. In respect of hostile take-over bids by another society the government has watered down its original (Green Paper) proposal to allow the 'predator' (appellant) society to appeal directly to the membership of the 'target' (respondent) society and to facilitate this by allowing the former access to the latter society's membership list. Under the Bill the following restrictions will apply: (i) the appellant society will have to wait three months before asking the Commission to grant access to the list; (ii) even then it will be denied access if the respondent society agrees to circulate the merger proposals to its own members; (iii) when the appellant society is more than eight times the size of the respondent society, at least 20 per cent of the latter society's members must approve the merger proposal. As a safeguard for 'depositors'' interests, the proposals appear unnecessarily restrictive, a remark which is equally applicable to the procedures suggested (in a consultative document that accompanied publication of the Bill) for the conversion to company status. For, under the proposals, conversion would require the approval of a 75 per cent majority of voting investors, 50 per cent of voting borrowers and at least 20 per cent of all investors,[145] figures most unlikely to be attained if the present levels of turnout at publicised merger proposals are anything to go by!

Concluding comments on building society supervision

Only time will tell if the proposed supervisory framework – much detail has yet to be filled in – matches up to expectations (*re* the identification and containment of risks and the strengthening of investor protection), but the determination of the Chief Registrar (who will become head of the Commission) to boost societies' capital[146] and improve management skills,[147] and the extended role to be played by auditors, should certainly contribute towards this. As it stands, however, the detailed restrictions envisaged undermine the cost-effectiveness of supervision through the impairment of societies' ability to respond flexibly to changing circumstances (e.g. as a result of the restriction on access to the wholesale markets),[148] and through the creation of competitive inequities and a misallocation of resources. Moreover, the suggested approach will delay further movement towards the adoption of a common supervisory approach to all deposit-taking financial intermediaries, a move that is both logical and desirable.

Specimen 2A

List of institutions recognised or licensed by the Bank of England at 28 February 1985

1 Recognised banks

A P Bank Ltd
Alexanders Discount plc
Algemene Bank Nederland N.V.
Allied Arab Bank Ltd
Allied Bank International
Allied Bank of Pakistan Ltd
Allied Irish Banks plc
Allied Irish Investment Bank Ltd
American Express International
  Banking Corporation
American National Bank and Trust
  Company of Chicago
Amsterdam–Rotterdam Bank N.V.
Anglo-Romanian Bank Ltd
Henry Ansbacher & Co. Ltd
Arab Bank Ltd
Arbuthnot Latham Bank Ltd
Associated Japanese Bank
  (International) Ltd
Atlantic International Bank Ltd
Australia & New Zealand Banking
  Group Ltd

Banca Commerciale Italiana
Banca Nazionale del Lavoro
Banco Central, S.A.
Banco de Bilbao S.A.
Banco de la Nación Argentina
Banco de Santander, S.A.
Banco de Vizcaya, S.A.
Banco di Roma S.p.A.
Banco di Sicilia
Banco do Brasil S.A.
Banco do Estado de São Paulo S.A.
Banco Espirito Santo e Comercial
  de Lisboa
Banco Exterior—UK S.A.
Banco Mercantil de São Paulo S.A.
Banco Nacional de Mexico S.N.C.
Banco Português do Atlântico
Banco Real S.A.
Banco Totta & Açores E.P.

Banco Urquijo Hispano Americano
  Ltd
Bancomer, S.N.C.
Bangkok Bank Ltd
Bank Julius Baer & Co. Ltd
Bank Bumiputra Malaysia Berhad
Bank für Gemeinwirschaft A.G.
Bank Hapoalim B.M.
Bank Leumi (UK) plc
Bank Mellat
Bank Melli Iran
Bank of America International Ltd
Bank of America N.T. & S.A.
Bank of Baroda
The Bank of California N.A.
Bank of Ceylon
Bank of China
Bank of Cyprus (London) Ltd
Bank of India
The Bank of Ireland
Bank of London & South America
  Ltd
Bank of Montreal
The Bank of New York
Bank of New Zealand
The Bank of Nova Scotia
Bank of Scotland
The Bank of Tokyo Ltd
Bank of Tokyo International Ltd
The Bank of Tokyo Trust Company
The Bank of Yokohama Ltd
Bank Saderat Iran
Bank Sepah
Bankers Trust Company
Banque Belge Ltd
Banque Belgo-Zaïroise S.A.
Banque Bruxelles Lambert S.A.
Banque Française du Commerce
  Extérieur
Banque Indosuez
Banque Nationale de Paris plc
Banque Paribas
Barclays Bank plc
Barclays Merchant Bank Ltd

Baring Brothers & Co. Ltd
Bayerische Hypotheken—und
  Wechsel—Bank A.G.
Bayerische Landesbank
  Girozentrale
Bayerische Vereinsbank
Berliner Bank A.G.
The British Bank of the Middle
  East
The British Linen Bank Ltd
Brown, Shipley & Co. Ltd

CIC—Union Européenne,
  International et Cie
Canadian Imperial Bank of
  Commerce
Carolina Bank Ltd
Cassa di Risparmio delle Provincie
  Lombarde
Cater Allen Ltd
Central Bank of India
Central Trustee Savings Bank Ltd
Charterhouse Japhet plc
Chase Bank (Ireland) Ltd
The Chase Manhattan Bank, N.A.
Chase Manhattan Ltd
Chemical Bank
Chemical Bank International Ltd
The Cho-Heung Bank Ltd
The Chuo Trust & Banking
  Company Ltd
Citibank N.A.
Citicorp International Bank Ltd
Clive Discount Company Ltd
Clydesdale Bank plc
Comerica Bank—Detroit
Commercial Bank of Korea Ltd
The Commercial Bank of the Near
  East plc
Commercial Bank of Wales plc
Commerzbank A.G.
Commonwealth Bank of Australia
Continental Illinois National Bank
  and Trust Company of Chicago
Co-operative Bank plc
County Bank Ltd
Coutts & Co.
Crédit Lyonnais
Crédit Lyonnais Bank Nederland

N.V.
Crédit Suisse
Credit Suisse First Boston Ltd
Creditanstalt-Bankverein
Credito Italiano
Crocker National Bank
The Cyprus Popular Bank

The Dai-Ichi Kangyo Bank Ltd
The Daiwa Bank Ltd
Deutsche Bank A.G.
Discount Bank (Overseas) Ltd
Dresdner Bank A.G.

Euro-Latinamerican Bank Ltd
European Arab Bank Ltd
European Banking Company Ltd
European Brazilian Bank Ltd

Fidelity Bank N.A.
First City National Bank of
  Houston
First Interstate Bank of California
First Interstate Ltd
The First National Bank of Boston
The First National Bank of
  Chicago
First National Bank of Maryland
First National Bank of Minneapolis
First Pennsylvania Bank N.A.
First Wisconsin National Bank of
  Milwaukee
Robert Fleming & Co. Ltd
French Bank of Southern Africa
  Ltd
The Fuji Bank Ltd

Gerrard & National plc
Ghana Commercial Bank
Girozentrale und Bank der
  österreichischen Sparkassen A.G.
Grindlay Brandts Ltd
Grindlays Bank plc
Guinness Mahon & Co. Ltd
Gulf International Bank B.S.C.

Habib Bank A.G. Zürich
Habib Bank Ltd
Hambros Bank Ltd

Hanil Bank
Havana International Bank Ltd
Hessische Landesbank-Girozentrale
Hill Samuel & Co. Ltd
C. Hoare & Co.
The Hokkaido Takushoku Bank
 Ltd
The Hongkong and Shanghai
 Banking Corporation
Hungarian International Bank Ltd

The Industrial Bank of Japan Ltd
InterFirst Bank Dallas N.A.
International Commercial Bank plc
International Energy Bank Ltd
International Mexican Bank Ltd
International Westminster Bank plc
Irving Trust Company
Istituto Bancario San Paolo di
 Torino
Italian International Bank plc

Japan International Bank Ltd
Jessel, Toynbee & Gillett plc
Johnson Matthey Bankers Ltd
Leopold Joseph & Sons Ltd

King & Shaxson plc
Kleinwort, Benson Ltd
Korea Exchange Bank
Korea First Bank
The Kyowa Bank Ltd

Lazard Brothers & Co. Ltd
Libra Bank plc
Lloyds Bank plc
Lloyds Bank International Ltd
Lloyds Bank International (France)
 Ltd
London & Continental Bankers Ltd
London Interstate Bank Ltd
The Long-term Credit Bank of
 Japan Ltd

Malayan Banking Berhad
Manufacturers Hanover Ltd
Manufacturers Hanover Trust
 Company
Marine Midland Bank N.A.

Mellon Bank, N.A.
Mercantile Bank Ltd
Merrill Lynch International Bank
 Ltd
Midland Bank plc
The Mitsubishi Bank Ltd
The Mitsubishi Trust and Banking
 Corporation
The Mitsui Bank Ltd
The Mitsui Trust & Banking
 Company Ltd
Samuel Montagu & Co. Ltd
Morgan Grenfell & Co. Ltd
Morgan Guaranty Trust Company
 of New York
Moscow Narodny Bank Ltd

NCNB National Bank of North
 Carolina
National Australia Bank Ltd
National Bank of Abu Dhabi
National Bank of Canada
National Bank of Detroit
National Bank of Greece S.A.
The National Bank of New Zealand
 Ltd
National Bank of Pakistan
National Westminster Bank plc
Nedbank Ltd
Nederlandsche Middenstandsbank
 N.V.
The Nippon Credit Bank Ltd
Noble Grossart Ltd
Nordic Bank plc
Northern Bank Ltd
The Northern Trust Company

Orion Royal Bank Ltd
Oversea-Chinese Banking
 Corporation Ltd
Overseas Union Bank Ltd

PK Christiania Bank (UK) Ltd
Philippine National Bank
Postipankki (UK) Ltd
Privatbanken Ltd
Punjab National Bank

Qatar National Bank, S.A.Q.

Gerald Quin, Cope & Co. Ltd

Rafidain Bank
Rea Brothers plc
P. S. Refson & Co. Ltd
Republic Bank Dallas, N.A.
Reserve Bank of Australia
The Riggs National Bank of
  Washington, D.C.
N. M. Rothschild & Sons Ltd
The Royal Bank of Canada
The Royal Bank of Scotland plc
The Royal Trust Company of
  Canada

The Saitama Bank Ltd
The Sanwa Bank Ltd
Saudi International Bank (Al-Bank
  Al-Saudi Al-Alami Ltd)
Scandinavian Bank Ltd
J. Henry Schroder Wagg & Co. Ltd
Seccombe Marshall & Campion plc
Security Pacific National Bank
Shanghai Commercial Bank Ltd
Singer & Friedlander Ltd
Smith St Aubyn & Co. Ltd
Société de Banque Occidentale
Société Générale
Société Générale Merchant Bank
  Ltd
Somali Bank
Standard Chartered Bank
Standard Chartered Bank Africa
  plc
Standard Chartered Merchant Bank
  Ltd
Standard Chartered plc
State Bank of India
The Sumitomo Bank Ltd
The Sumitomo Trust and Banking
  Company Ltd
Swiss Bank Corporation
Syndicate Bank

The Taiyo Kobe Bank Ltd
Texas Commerce Bank N.A.
The Thai Farmers Bank Ltd
The Tokai Bank Ltd
The Toronto-Dominion Bank

The Toyo Trust & Banking
  Company Ltd

UBAF Bank Ltd
Ulster Bank Ltd
Ulster Investment Bank Ltd
Union Bank of Switzerland
The Union Discount Company of
  London plc
United Bank Ltd
The United Bank of Kuwait Ltd
United Commercial Bank
United Overseas Bank Ltd

S. G. Warburg & Co. Ltd
Wardley London Ltd
Wells Fargo Bank N.A.
Westdeutsche Landesbank
  Girozentrale
Westpac Banking Corporation
Williams & Glyn's Bank plc
Wintrust Securities Ltd
Württembergische Kommunale
  Landesbank Girozentrale

The Yasuda Trust and Banking Co.
  Ltd
Yorkshire Bank plc

Zambia National Commercial Bank
  Ltd
Zivnostenská Banka National
  Corporation

2 Licensed deposit-taking institutions

A1 (Investment) Ltd
Abbey Finance Co. Ltd
Adam & Company plc
Afghan National Credit & Finance
  Ltd
African Continental Bank Ltd
Aitken Hume Ltd
Ak International Ltd
Al Baraka International Ltd
Al Saudi Banque S.A.
The Alliance Trust plc

Allied Banking Corporation
Allied Irish Finance Co. Ltd
Altajir Ltd
Anglo-Yugoslav (LDT) Ltd
Arab African International Bank
Arab Bank Investment Co. Ltd
Arab Banking Corporation B.S.C.
Armada Investments Ltd
Armco Trust Ltd
Assemblies of God Property Trust
Associated Credits Ltd
Associates Capital Corporation Ltd
Auban Finance Ltd
Avant Overseas Finance Ltd
Avco Trust Ltd

B.A.I.I. plc
B.C.F. Finance Co Ltd.
BMI (Hampshire) Ltd
Badische Kommunale Landesbank
  Girozentrale
Banca Nazionale dell'Agricoltura
  SpA
Banca Serfin S.N.C.
Banco di Santo Spirito
Bank Handlowy w Warszawie S.A.
Bank Mees & Hope N.V.
Bank of Credit and Commerce
  International S.A.
Bank of Ireland Finance Ltd
Bank of Ireland Finance (N.I.) Ltd
Bank of New England N.A.
The Bank of Nova Scotia Trust
  Company (United Kingdom) Ltd
Bank of Oman Ltd
Bank of Seoul
Bank of Tejarat
Bankers Trust International Ltd
Banque du Liban et d'Outre-Mer
Banque Internationale pour
  l'Afrique Occidentale S.A.
The Baptist Union Corporation Ltd
Barbados National Bank
Barclays Bank Trust Company Ltd
Barclays Bank UK Ltd
Thomas Barlow & Bros Ltd
Barrie Vanger & Co Ltd
Beaver Guarantee Ltd
Beirut Riyad Bank S.A.L.

Beneficial Trust Ltd
Boston Trust & Savings Ltd
Bradford Investments
Bridgeover Ltd
Bridgeway Finance Ltd
British Credit Trust Ltd
Brook Securities & Co. Ltd
Buchanan Securities Ltd
Bucks Land & Building Co. Ltd
Bunge & Co. Ltd
Burns-Anderson Trust Company
  Ltd
Business Mortgages Trust plc
Byblos Bank S.A.I.

Caisse Nationale de Credit Agricole
Calculus Finance plc
Canada Permanent Mortgage
  Corporation (UK) Ltd
Canara Bank
Castle Phillips Finance Co. Ltd
Cattles Holdings Finance Ltd
Cayzer Ltd
Cedar Holdings Ltd
Century Factors Ltd
Chancery Securities plc
Charter Consolidated Financial
  Services Ltd
Chartered Trust plc
Charterhouse Japhet Credit Ltd
Chesterfield Street Trust Ltd
Citibank Trust Ltd
City Trust Ltd
Close Brothers Ltd
Clydesdale Bank Finance
  Corporation Ltd
CE Coates & Co. Ltd
Cobnar Finance Co Ltd
Combined Capital Ltd
Commercial Credit Services Ltd
Commonwealth Savings Bank of
  Australia
Consolidated Credits & Discounts
  Ltd
Consumer Credit Investments Ltd
The Continental Trust Ltd
Co-operative Bank (Commercial)
  Ltd
Copenhagen Handelsbank A.S.

Coutts Finance Co.
Craneheath Securities Ltd
Crédit Commercial de France
Crédit du Nord
Credito Italiano International Ltd
Cue & Co.
Cyprus Credit Bank Ltd
Cyprus Finance Corporation
 (London) Ltd

Dalbeattie Finance Co. Ltd
Darlington Merchant Credits Ltd
Dartington & Co. Ltd
Den Danske Bank of 1871
 Aktieselskab
Deutsche Genossenschaftsbank
The Development Bank of
 Singapore Ltd
The Dorset, Somerset & Wilts
 Investment Society Ltd
Dryfield Finance Ltd
Dunbar & Co. Ltd
Duncan Lawrie Ltd
Dunsterville Allen plc

E.T. Trust Ltd
Eagil Trust Co. Ltd
East Anglian Securities Trust Ltd
East Midlands Finance Co. Ltd
Eccles Savings and Loans Ltd
The English Association Trust Ltd
Ensign Discount Co. Ltd
Enskilda Securities-Skandinaviska
 Enskilda Ltd
Equatorial Trust Corporation Ltd
Everett Chettle Associates
Exeter Trust Ltd

FIBI Financial Trust Ltd
Fairmount Trust Ltd
Family Finance Ltd
Farmers (WCF) Finance Ltd
Federated Trust Corporation Ltd
FennoScandia Ltd
Financial and General Securities
 Ltd
James Finlay Corporation Ltd
Finova Finance Ltd
First Bank of Nigeria Ltd

First Commercial Bank
First Co-operative Finance Ltd
First Indemnity Credit Ltd
First National Boston Ltd
First National Securities Ltd
Fleet National Bank
Ford Financial Trust Ltd
Ford Motor Credit Co. Ltd
Foreign & Colonial Management
 Ltd
Forward Trust Ltd
Robert Fraser & Partners Ltd

Gillespie Bros. & Company Ltd
Goldman Sachs Ltd
Goode Durrant Trust plc
Gota (UK) Ltd
Granville Finance Ltd
H. T. Greenwood Ltd
Greetwell Finance Ltd
Gresham Trust plc
Greyhound Guaranty Ltd
Grindlays Humberclyde Ltd
Grindlays Industrial Finance Ltd
Grosvenor Acceptances Ltd
Gulf Guarantee Trust Ltd

HFC Trust & Savings Ltd
H. J. Finance Co. (Midlands) Ltd
Habibsons Trust and Finance Ltd

The Hardware Federation Finance
 Co. Ltd
Harris Trust and Savings Bank
Harrods Trust Ltd
Harton Securities Ltd
The Heritable & General Trust Ltd
Holdenhurst Securities Ltd
Houston Financial Services Ltd

IBJ International Ltd
Industrial Finance and Investment
 Corporation plc
Industrial Funding Trust Ltd
The Investment Bank of Ireland
 Ltd
Investment Trustees Ltd
Investors in Industry plc
Investors in Industry Group plc

Iran Overseas Investment
  Corporation Ltd
ItaB Group Ltd

Jabac Finances Ltd
Jordan Finance Consortium plc

Kansallis-Osake-Pankki
Keesler Federal Credit Union
Knowsley & Co. Ltd
Kredietbank N.V.

Liechtenstein (UK) Ltd
Little Lakes Finance Ltd
Lloyds & Scottish plc
Lloyds Bank (LABCO) Ltd
Lloyds Bowmaker Ltd
Lodhi Finance Ltd
Lombard Acceptances Ltd
Lombard & Ulster Ltd
Lombard North Central plc
Lombard Street Investment Trust
  Co. Ltd
London and Arab Investments Ltd
London Law Securities Ltd
London Scottish Finance
  Corporation plc
Lordsvale Finance Ltd

McNeill Pearson Ltd
Mallinhall Ltd
Manchester Exchange Trust Ltd
W. M. Mann & Co. (Investments)
  Ltd
Edward Manson & Co. Ltd
Manufacturers Hanover Export
  Finance Ltd
Manufacturers Hanover Finance
  Ltd
The Mardun Investment Co. Ltd
Matheson Trust Co. Ltd
Medens Trust Ltd
Meghraj & Sons Ltd
Mercantile Credit Company Ltd
Mercury Provident Society Ltd
Merseyside Finance Ltd
The Methodist Chapel Aid
  Association Ltd
Middle East Bank Ltd

Midland Bank Equity Holdings Ltd
Midland Bank Finance Corporation
  Ltd
Midland Bank Trust Company Ltd
Milford Mutual Facilities Ltd
Minster Trust Ltd
Moneycare Ltd
Moorgate Mercantile Holdings plc
Mount Credit Corporation Ltd
Multibanco Comermex S.N.C.
Muslim Commercial Bank Ltd
Mynshul Trust Ltd

N.I.I.B. Group Ltd
National Bank of Egypt
National Bank of Fort Sam
  Houston
The National Bank of Kuwait
  S.A.K.
National Bank of Nigeria Ltd
National Commercial & Glyns Ltd
National Guardian Finance
  Corporation Ltd
New Nigeria Bank Ltd
Norddeutsche Landesbank
  Girozentrale
The North of Scotland Finance Co.
  Ltd
North West Securities Ltd
Northern Bank Development
  Corporation Ltd
Northern Bank Executor & Trustee
  Company Ltd
Norwich General Trust Ltd

Omega Trust Co. Ltd
Oppenheimer Money Management
  Ltd
Oriental Credit Ltd
Overseas Trust Bank Ltd

PL Investments & Savings Ltd
Park Street Securities Ltd
The People's Trust & Savings Ltd
Phibrobank A.G.
Philadelphia National Bank
Pointon York Ltd
Prestwick Investment Trust plc
Provincial Trust Ltd

Punjab & Sind Bank

Ralli Investment Company Ltd
R. Raphael & Sons plc
Rathbone Bros. & Co.
Reliance Trust Ltd
Republic National Bank of New
   York
Rhône Trust Ltd
Riyad Bank
Roxburghe Guarantee Corporation
   Ltd
The Rural and Industries Bank of
   Western Australia

S.P. Finance Ltd
St Margaret's Trust Ltd
Schroder Leasing Ltd
Scottish Amicable Money Managers
   Ltd
Seattle–First National Bank
Security Pacific Trust Ltd
Shawlands Securities Ltd
The Siam Commercial Bank, Ltd
Smith & Williamson Securities
South Notts Finance Ltd
Southsea Mortgage & Investment
   Co. Ltd
Spring Gardens Securities plc
Spry Finance Ltd
Standard Credit Services Ltd
Standard Property Investment plc
State Bank of New South Wales
State Bank of South Australia
State Bank of Victoria
State Street Bank and Trust
   Company
Sterling Trust Ltd
Svenska International Ltd
Swiss Bank Corporation
   International Ltd

TCB Ltd
The Teachers & General Investment
   Co. Ltd
Thames Trust Ltd
Thorncliffe Finance Ltd
Trade Development Bank
Treloan Ltd
Trucanda Trusts Ltd
The Trust Bank of Africa Ltd
Tullett and Riley Money
   Management Ltd
Turkish Bank Ltd
Türkiye Iş Bankasi A.Ş.
Tyndall & Co.

Ulster Bank Trust Company
Union Bank of Finland Ltd
Union Bank of India
Union Bank of Nigeria Ltd
United Dominions Trust Ltd
United Mizrahi Bank Ltd
Unity Trust Ltd
Universal Credit Ltd

Venture Finance Ltd
Vernons Trust Corporation
Volkskas Ltd

Wagon Finance Ltd
Wallace, Smith Trust Co. Ltd
Welbeck Finance plc
West Riding Securities Ltd
Western Trust & Savings Ltd
Whiteaway Laidlaw & Co. Ltd
Wimbledon & South West Finance
   Co. Ltd
N. H. Woolley & Co. Ltd

Yorkshire Bank Finance Ltd
H. F. Young & Co. Ltd

Source: 'Bank of England: Report and accounts for the year ended 28
February 1985'.

Specimen 2B

Classification of assets (and risk weights) held by UK offices of reporting banks for the purpose of calculating risk-asset ratios

(i) Nil weight

Bank of England notes and UK coin
Other sterling notes
Balances with Bank of England
Special deposits with Bank of England
Debits in course of collection on banks in the UK
Balances with overseas offices of the reporting bank
Lending under special schemes for exports and shipbuilding
Certificates of tax deposit
Items in suspense
Refinanced lending at fixed rates
Gold physically held in own vaults
Gold held elsewhere on an allocated basis

(ii) 0.1 weight

Foreign currency notes and coin
UK and Northern Ireland Treasury bills

(iii) 0.2 weight

Debit items in course of collection on overseas banks
Market loans with listed banks, discount market, etc.
Market loans to UK local authorities and public corporations
Balances with banks overseas with a maximum term of up to one year (including claims in gold)
Bills other than UK and Northern Ireland Treasury bills
Other loans and advances to Northern Ireland government, UK local authorities, public corporations and other public sector
British government stocks with up to eighteen months to final maturity
Acceptances drawn on UK and overseas banks and UK public sector
Claims in gold on UK banks and members of the London Gold Market

(iv) 0.5 weight	British government stocks with over eighteen months to final maturity Northern Ireland government stocks UK local authority and other public sector stocks and bonds Acceptances drawn on other UK and overseas residents Guarantees and other contingent liabilities
(v) 1.0 weight	Market loans placed with other UK residents Other loans and advances, net of specific provisions for bad debts, but excluding connected lending Assets leased to customers Working capital provided for overseas offices of the reporting bank, both in the form of deposits and in other forms Balances with banks overseas with a term of one year or over (including claims in gold) Claims in gold on non-banks Aggregate foreign-currency position (to be defined in the Bank's paper on 'Foreign Currency Exposure') Other assets 'other', e.g. silver, commodities and other goods beneficially owned by the reporting bank Other quoted investments, not connected
(vi) 1.5 weight	Connected lending (to be looked at case by case and to exclude market-type lending where this can be separately identified) Unquoted investments (subject to case-by-case treatment)
(vii) 2.0 weight	Property (includes all land and premises beneficially owned by the reporting bank)
Items to be deducted from capital	Plant and equipment Intangible assets Investments in subsidiary and associated companies and trade investments

Source: *BEQB*, Sep 1980, p. 329.

Specimen 2C

Procedures adopted in the assessment of liquidity adequacy in the UK

Annex 1   Discounts applied to sterling assets

Nil discount	Treasury, eligible local authority and eligible bank bills.
	Government and government-guaranteed marketable securities with less than twelve months remaining term to maturity.
5 per cent discount	Other bills and certificates of deposit with less than six months remaining term to maturity.
	Other government, government-guaranteed and local authority marketable securities with less than five years remaining term to maturity or at variable rates.
10 per cent discount	Other bills, certificates of deposit and FRNs with less than five years remaining term to maturity.
	Other government, government-guaranteed and local authority marketable debt with more than five years remaining term to maturity.
Discount to be determined	All other marketable assets.

The categories of asset used in this annex approximate to those currently employed in UK statistical returns. Comparable foreign currency assets are to be included on a similar discounted basis.

Annex 2   The system of measurement

	Sight– 8 days	8 days– 1 month	1–3 months	3–6 months	6–12 months
Liabilities					
Deposits					
Commitments					

Less   **Assets**
Marketable
Non-marketable
Standby facilities available

+ / −   **Net position**
Carried forward

Net cumulative position

Source: BEQB, Sep 1982, p. 402.

Specimen 2D

Control of foreign-exchange dealing in the UK[1]

Reports of the losses suffered this year by banks in a number of countries, as a result of operations in foreign-exchange markets, will undoubtedly have caused many banks to undertake a rigorous review of their internal regulations governing procedures for foreign-exchange dealings by, and dealing and overnight and forward credit limits imposed on, individual branches and wholly-owned subsidiaries at home and abroad. Any banks which have not yet done so are urged to undertake such a review as soon as possible and to ensure in particular that authorities to deal are specific and are confined to strictly selected staff and branches.

The list that follows is not intended as an exhaustive check for conducting such a review; it merely covers points which have arisen from the Bank's discussions in a number of centres about the losses:

1 Some general managements seem to have placed their dealers in an exposed position by looking well beyond the service element of the dealing function and imposing ambitious profit targets upon them.
2 In some overseas offices, managements do not appear to have paid sufficient attention to the relations between dealers and brokers; in London, the Foreign Exchange and Currency Deposit Brokers' Association has exercised a beneficial influence in this area.

3 Dealers should never write their own outgoing
confirmations or receive incoming confirmations.
4 Forward deals should always be confirmed at once; in
particular, confirmations should not be delayed until
instructions are passed just prior to maturity.
5 There should be snap checks of dealing activities
between regular internal audits or inspections.
6 Central management should from time to time, on a
random basis, seek from correspondent banks
independent second confirmations of outstanding
forward contracts.
7 A bank should check with its correspondent's head or
main dealing office if it notices that a branch of that
bank has suddenly or appreciably expanded its
operations in the forward market.

---

1. Extract from the Bank of England circular of December 1974.

Source: *BEQB*, June 1981, p. 237.

Specimen 2E

Risk classification of assets for discount houses

Risk classification of assets			
No added risk	**Added risk classes**		
	Added risk weight = 1	*Added risk weight = 2*	*Added risk weight = 4*
Cash at bankers Deposits with Bank of England			
Eligible bills up to 3 months	Eligible bills 3–6 months		
Ineligible bank bills up to 3 months	Ineligible bank bills 3–12 months	Ineligible bank bills over 1 year	
Trade bills up to 3 months[1]	Trade bills 3–6 months[1] Other trade bills up to 3 months	Trade bills over 6 months[1] Other trade bills over 3 months	
£ CDs up to 3 months $	£ CDs 3–12 months $	£ CDs 1–3 years $	£ CDs over 3 years $
Fixed-rate BGS up to 3 months	Fixed-rate BGS 3–18 months (or short positions in such stocks)[2]	Fixed-rate BGS 1½–5 years (or short positions in such stocks)[2]	Fixed-rate BGS over 5 years (or short positions in such stocks)[2]
Variable-rate assets where rate fixed for 3 months or less	Variable-rate assets where rate fixed for 3–6 months	Variable-rate assets where rate fixed for more than 6 months	
Fixed-rate quoted assets up to 3 months	Fixed-rate quoted assets 3 months–1 year	Fixed-rate quoted assets 1–3 years	Fixed-rate quoted assets over 3 years
Fixed-rate unquoted assets up to 3 months	Fixed-rate unquoted assets 3–6 months	Fixed-rate unquoted assets 6–18 months	Fixed-rate unquoted assets over 18 months

Loans to next business day	Loans longer than to next business day	Open position in foreign currency	Equity investments (including preference shares)
	Deductions Fixed money 3–12 months	*Deductions* Fixed money 1–3 years	*Deductions* Fixed money over 3 years

1. Trade bills which are drawn and accepted by independent names, or bear one public-sector name, or are insured.
2. Where short positions in assets within a certain class exceed long positions, the added risk weight is to be applied to the short position.

Source: *BEQB*, June 1982, p. 211.

Exhibit 2.1

Timetable for Reform of the London Stock Exchange

Date	Reform announced or implemented
April 1982	The maximum permissible equity stake allowed to 'outsiders' (i.e. non-Exchange members) revised from 10 per cent (the limit introduced in 1969) to 29.9 per cent.
27 July 1983	The Secretary of State for Trade and Industry came to an agreement with the Chairman of the Stock Exchange that examination by the Office of Fair Trading of the Stock Exchange's rule book would not be allowed to proceed to the Restrictive Practices Court if the Exchange agreed to phase out fixed commissions (by the end of 1986) and to admit outsiders to the Stock Exchange Council.
December 1983	Five lay members appointed to the Stock Exchange Council.
9 April 1984	Member firms are allowed to set up international dealing subsidiaries to compete with foreign firms in overseas securities (but not in ADRs or UK equities with UK residents). Firms acting within this capacity need not adopt 'single capacity' nor charge minimum commissions and outsiders are to be allowed equity stakes of up to 49.9 per cent in the subsidiaries.
April 1984	The Stock Exchange published a discussion document outlining possible future trading systems and other recommended changes in the Exchange's rule book. The main points were:

: 'single capacity' is doomed;
: a new centralised market-making dealing system, containing 'committed market-makers', is the best alternative dealing system;
: participants ('broker-dealers') in the new dealing system will be able to act as agents or principals or both as long as the capacity in which they are acting is declared to the client;
: the limit on outsiders' equity stakes in member firms should be abolished;
: the rule that a non-member firm may not own an interest of more than 5 per cent in a member firm if it already owns a 29.9 per cent stake in another Stock Exchange broker or jobber should be relaxed;
: new firms should be admitted to the Stock Exchange, subject to payment of an entrance fee;

	: the market in gilts should be developed along the lines of the market in Treasury bonds in the US; : new supporting technical systems will be needed to effect the restructuring of the stock market.
September 1984	The Stock Exchange Council endorsed the choice of dealing system recommended in the Exchange's 1984 discussion document.
17 June 1985	The Bank of England published the names of the 29 applicants for 'primary dealerships' in the new gilt market.
24 June 1985	The Stock Exchange Council announced that outsiders are to be allowed to hold 29.9 per cent stakes in member firms irrespective of any other investments held in brokers or jobbers.
1 March 1986	Limit on equity stakes held by outsiders in member firms is to be abolished, and the moratorium, imposed in July 1984, on the creation of new member firms with outside financing is to be lifted.
27 October 1986	Fixed commissions are to be abolished and 'single capacity' ended.

Exhibit 2.2

New Powers for Building Societies: The Building Societies Bill
(6.12.85)

New activities sanctioned (from January 1987)		*Limit(s) prescribed†*
'Class 2' assets:	non-'Class 1'* wholly-secured lending (e.g. loans to bodies corporate or loans secured on non-residential property plus certain new types of loan e.g. loans secured on a second mortgage, local authority indemnity or equity mortgages.)	In aggregate Class 2 assets held must not exceed 10 per cent of a society's 'commercial assets' (i.e. total assets less fixed and 'liquid' assets).
'Class 3' assets:	unsecured lending (to be conducted 'in-house'); property and land ownership; investment in estate agencies, insurance brokers and other subsidiary activities (normally to be confined to those societies with 'free reserves' (i.e. general reserves less fixed assets) or over £3 m.	In aggregate Class 3 assets held must not exceed 5 per cent of a society's commercial assets. Unsecured loans are limited to £5000 per individual and, like the acquisition and development of land, may only be provided by societies with commercial assets of at least £100 m.

* 'Class 1' assets represent advances (including home-improvement loans and index-linked mortgages) secured on first mortgage to owner-occupiers of residential property.
† The aggregate of a society's Class 2 and Class 3 assets must not exceed 10 per cent of its total commercial assets.

Exhibit 2.3

The White Paper on 'Banking Supervision'
(Cmnd 9695, 17.12.85)

Major Proposals

1. The establishment of a 'Board of Banking Supervision' to advise the Governor on supervisory matters and oversee the implementation of the (reformed) Banking Act.
2. An end to the two-tier system of 'authorisation' by applying a single set of criteria to all 'banks'.
3. Auditors should be brought more fully into the supervisory process, preferably according to agreed guidelines but, if necessary, according to statute. The Bank is keen that, in exceptional circumstances (e.g. when fraud is suspected), auditors will contact the supervisors directly without informing the client bank's management or directors.
4. Misreporting to the Bank should become a criminal offence.
5. The Bank should have wider statutory powers to obtain information.
6. Banks should be obliged by law to report 'large' (i.e. those amounting to more than 10 per cent of the capital base) exposures to the Bank and provide prior notification of those in excess of 25 per cent of the capital base.
7. Institutions should have paid-up share capital of at least £5 m. before they can call themselves 'banks'.
8. The definition of 'deposits' should be amended to take account of new banking instruments.
9. The Bank should be allowed to pass on information obtained in its supervisory capacity to other government departments (except the Inland Revenue) where the public interest is at stake or when it would best serve the interests of depositors.

Exhibit 2.4

The Building Societies Bill
(6.12.85)

Proposed Changes in the Supervision of Building Societies

1. A 'Building Societies Commission' should take over the supervisory role of the Chief Registrar of Friendly Societies and it should be given a much wider range of powers, including the discretion to alter the provisions of the legislation through statutory instruments.
2. A statutory investor protection scheme should be introduced and administered by a new 'Building Societies Investor Protection Board'. The Board should be empowered to levy contributions from societies, up to a maximum of 0.3 per cent of the amount invested with them, and protection should be limited to 75 per cent of the first £10 000 worth of 'deposits' (although higher coverage could be provided on a voluntary basis).
3. In situations where investors' capital is at risk, auditors should be able to pass information to the Commission without the society's permission.
4. The introduction of new 'authorisation' procedures.
5. The introduction of a new set of constraints on the composition of assets and liabilities (e.g. on the proportion of total lending that can be devoted to 'new' activities and on the proportion of funds that can be taken from the wholesale money markets).
6. Supervisory arrangements should be extended to embrace the assessment of capital and liquidity adequacy and the adequacy of management plans and internal control and inspection procedures.

3 Financial Deregulation in Australia and the UK Compared

In both countries the prime motivating force behind the deregulation programmes implemented was the desire to raise the level of competition in financial markets as a means of improving efficiency. Additional considerations related to a determination to restructure the financial services industry in a manner capable of reaping the maximum possible benefits for the economy (e.g. in terms of invisible earnings, tax revenue and enhanced employment prospects) in the increasingly competitive and integrated world financial markets and, in the case of Australia, to a desire to enhance Australia's role as a regional financial centre through a broadening of its capital market.

3.1 DISMANTLING OF MONETARY CONTROLS

Following the lead given by the UK, which removed the final vestiges of direct monetary control mechanisms with the abolition of hire-purchase terms control in July 1982, and the Campbell Committee's endorsement of the view that direct monetary controls are ineffective, inefficient and inequitable, Australia embarked upon a rapid and wide-ranging dismantling of its controls during the 1982/4 period. Significantly, however, a number remain, such as the Statutory Reserve Deposits Ratio and the Prime Assets Ratio imposed upon trading banks, the minimum liquidity ratio applied to savings banks and interest-rate ceilings applying on certain 'small' loans made by both types of bank. In line with the UK though, no monetary controls are applied to non-bank DTIs (although the possibility remains should Part IV of the 1974 Financial Corporations Act be proclaimed). Together with the offering of market-related yields on public-sector debt, such deregulatory moves, nevertheless, have facilitated transition towards the use of open-market operations in Commonwealth government securities as the prime, and ultimately the only, means of securing the administration's monetary objectives. The

Australian authorities differ, however, with the UK monetary authorities as to how policy should be managed, the former emphasising the impact of open-market operations on the banks' cash base, with concomitant implications for the banks' lending capacity, while the latter emphasise the interest-rate effects of open-market operations, especially those which impact upon the demand for money and bank credit. Whatever the disagreement, any impediments to interest-rate or exchange-rate flexibility (the Australian dollar was floated in December 1983) introduced by the authorities will likely preclude their ability to attain prescribed monetary targets, which remains the proximate goal of monetary policy in both countries (although the UK is (still) seriously considering joining the 'exchange-rate mechanism' of the European Monetary System).

Targeting problems. Although the adoption of a floating exchange-rate enhances the authorities' ability to hit monetary targets by insulating the domestic money stock from international capital flows (but at the possible cost of dampening trade flows), other deregulatory moves are likely to complicate the authorities' task. Common to both countries is what one might term '*industry deregulation*', the removal of constraints on building societies' operations and deregulation of the securities markets being notable features in each country. Such deregulation will allow for the entry of building societies into unsecured lending and the entry of banks into securities trading and broking operations. (For UK details see Hall, 1986 (a).) Any resultant change in the shares of intermediation services provided by different financial institutions will complicate interpretation of movements in broad money-supply aggregates. An additional form of 'structural adjustment' also arises in the shape of '*reintermediation*', as those institutions most heavily controlled in the past retrieve market-share. In the UK this is unlikely to be a problem in the future as the abolition of direct monetary controls was completed back in 1982, but in Australia the difficulties the authorities face in trying to predict the scale and timing of reintermediation are very real, the major beneficiaries being the trading and savings banks and the likely losers the finance companies and merchant banks (although other opportunities, in the form of foreign-exchange dealing and securities broking/dealing activities, have been opened up to the latter). As a result the authorities will find it even more difficult (indeed the M_3 target was suspended early in 1985 in Australia for this reason) to interpret movements in broad monetary aggregates (the abolition of exchange controls compounds the difficulties), at least during the transitional phase. A similar problem is also faced in connection with interpretation of movements in 'narrow' money as a result of financial innovation and the payment of (market-related) interest rates on deposits.

3.2 PRUDENTIAL REFORMS: DEREGULATION OR 'REREGULATION'?

In Australia calls for the reform of supervisory arrangements governing the activities of both banks and non-bank DTIs were made by the Campbell Committee and endorsed (subject to disagreement on certain points) by the Martin Group. In the UK reform of banking supervision resulted from the collapse of Johnson Matthey Bankers in 1984, while the supervision of building societies is to be amended in the light of the diversification opportunities offered under the Building Societies Bill of 1985.

According to the Banking Supervision White Paper of 1985 'banks' operating in the UK will remain subject to authorisation procedures, the assessment of capital and liquidity adequacy and the adequacy of internal control and inspection procedures, a compulsory deposit insurance scheme, lending limits, 'agreed' foreign-exchange dealing guidelines and 'agreed' guidelines on ownership of non-bank financial intermediaries. Building societies, however, face more radical change in the shape of new authorisation procedures, new (but relaxed) constraints on asset and liability composition, formal assessment of capital and liquidity adequacy, a statutory (previously the scheme was voluntary) deposit insurance scheme and, for the first time, formal assessment of the adequacy of managerial plans and of internal control and inspection procedures.

Under the Campbell Committee's proposals the existing supervisory networks, embracing authorisation/registration procedures, gearing ratios, liquidity ratios, restrictions on business activities, lender-of-last-resort facilities and, for banks, the monitoring of loan concentration, country risk, foreign-currency exposure and internal control systems, would be replaced by five new separate regimes. Institutions would be categorised in the following manner to determine which scheme they would become subject to: banks; authorised money-market dealers; non-bank DTIs soliciting small investments from households without issuing prospectuses; institutions soliciting small investments from households through the issue of prospectuses;

and other institutions which only accept large deposits, predominantly from the business sector. The framework proposed for banks would embrace the assessment of capital and liquidity adequacy, liquidity support (i.e. last resort) facilities and risk-asset limits, while non-bank DTIs would be subject to similar but less rigorous controls under state supervision. A process of rationalisation was also called for within state-administered regimes and the recommended abolition of interest-rate controls and restrictions on business activities was intended to go some way towards offsetting the degree of 'reregulation' implied in the more formalised supervisory system called for.

In both countries it would thus appear that prudential reforms, on balance, have involved a degree of 'reregulation' in contrast to the deregulatory moves on the monetary control front. Indeed, perhaps this is only to be expected as 'industry' and monetary deregulation both possess the potential to destabilise the financial system and raise the risk of loss to individual investors. Viewed in this light, prudential 'reregulation' is a rational response to financial deregulation but, nevertheless, in the interest of efficiency, more attention might be devoted to improving the cost-effectiveness of supervisory arrangements. Given that the opportunity is ripe for reform, it would be reassuring if policy-makers returned to basics in constructing new systems rather than building on existing frameworks that had largely developed in *ad hoc* fashion in response to deficiencies revealed in periodic 'crises'. To maximise cost-effectiveness, supervisors must devise a flexible system that embraces the minimal level of regulation necessary to achieve the prudential objectives of preserving the stability of the financial system and protecting investors from loss arising from fraud or managerial incompetence. On this basis provision of a lender-of-last-resort facility (to deal with the systemic problems associated with a generalised loss of confidence or other financial 'shocks') and a mechanism for protecting the liquidity of deposits are essentials, as is formal assessment of capital adequacy. The debate, then, concerns the necessity of the remaining strands of the supervisory framework traditionally employed and the possibility of rationalisation within this group. Pressure is growing in the US and elsewhere to introduce risk-related premium deposit insurance, despite the considerable practical difficulties involved, as a means of reducing the *moral hazard* introduced by *de facto* government (via the taxpayer) guarantee of all deposits, 'large' and 'small', and of allowing for a reduction of supervisory effort elsewhere. Specifically it is hoped that it might allow central banks to be more sparing in their activation of support operations and, with the costs of 'excessive' risk-taking falling squarely on the shoulders of individual deposit-taking intermediaries, allow for the repeal or relaxation of some of the restrictions imposed on business operations.

Even should the above amendments be implemented, however, a number of prudential issues would remain, notably the urgent need for further harmonisation of national supervisory systems (e.g. in defining capital, in deciding what constitutes capital adequacy and in the treatment of off-balance-sheet activities), for the wider adoption of the consolidation principle, and for clarification of the role of auditors in the supervisory process and the indemnification they should receive under arrangements requiring direct consultation with supervisors. A piecemeal approach to the adoption of such recommendations would prove better than nothing, but implementation of a carefully-thought-out package is likely to secure much greater gains for the economy. Demonstration of a political will for reform along the lines suggested would be a starting point.

3.3   IMPLICATIONS FOR OTHER GOVERNMENTS CONTEMPLATING OR ENGAGED IN FINANCIAL DEREGULATION

The Benefits of Deregulation. The programmes of financial deregulation undertaken by both the UK and Australian governments are typical of official measures being undertaken throughout the financially developed world to raise the level of competition prevalent in financial markets. Fiscal reform often complements financial deregulation as a means of further reducing distortions in the financial system and minimising competitive inequities, while technological advances in computing systems and communications facilitate an additional intensification in competition. The perceived benefits of increased competition lie in the reduction in intermediaries' margins that result (which are likely to benefit both borrower and saver), the likely reductions in transactions and operating costs), which will raise operational efficiency), a probably improvement in resource allocation as impediments to price competition are removed and the opportunity cost of holding money (as a result of the payment of market interest rates on deposits) is reduced, thereby freeing real resources that were previously employed in economising on cash-balance holdings, and an increase in consumer choice. Costs, however, are potentially high, involving the possible destabilisation of domestic and international financial systems with concomitant implications for domestic and international supervisory systems.

'*Costs*'. Concerns about the stability of *domestic* financial systems or industries relate to fears that declining profit margins resulting from increased competition, increasingly from both domestic and international operators, may stimulate greater risk-taking, especially as a result of diversification into new areas of operation which are likely to require different management skills or to induce managerial diseconomies. Additionally there is the question of the appropriate pace at which deregulation should proceed. While few, on economic grounds, would dissent from the proposition that a greater freedom of exit (and indeed entry) from financial industries is desirable on welfare and resource allocation grounds, many question the ability of existing supervisory frameworks to handle the likely rush of casualties. For example, as things stand at the moment in the UK, restrictions imposed by the supervisory authorities militate against rationalisation within the building society industry and the authorities do not possess an effective instrument for dealing with the systemic risks associated with a failed securities arm (which is widely anticipated) of a banking group. Beyond the difficulties posed for managing exit from the industry, the individual investor is likely to require greater protection in the deregulated environment as a result of the greater proliferation of conflicts of interest, especially within emerging financial conglomerates. Effective investor protection is likely to prove costly and more thought should be given to rationalising the existing systems to raise their cost-effectiveness.

At the *international* level, doubts about the adequacy of supervisory arrangements are also widely held, first as a result of the inexorable trend towards greater integration of financial markets (both domestic and Euromarkets, as a result of the removal of exchange controls on capital transactions and of the implicit taxes on domestic operations, and credit and capital markets as a result of the 'securitisation' trend) and the apparent lack of political will to harmonise national supervisory systems, accounting practices and fiscal treatment of debt provisions and, second, because of the lack of an agreed allocation of supervisory responsibilities should the activation of international support operations ever prove necessary. Perhaps the greatest threat is that a process of competitive deregulation will result as national governments strive to maximise market-share, invisible earnings, tax revenue and employment opportunities in the face of slow growth elsewhere in the economy, thereby driving the standards of prudential regulation and supervision down to the lowest common denominator. On the securities front it would appear that London is now in the deregulation driving seat, but it is not at all clear that the prudential and supervisory framework proposed for dealing with the problems likely to arise in the new market-place will match up to expectations (Hall, op. cit. 1986 (b)).

On the *monetary policy* front the UK leads the world in eschewing direct controls in the conduct of policy. The various distortions induced by the application of direct monetary controls are widely recognised, but only in the UK have the authorities been willing to operate without even prescribed reserve ratios. This raises the question as to why others, such as the Australian Reserve Bank, have not followed the UK line in totally dispensing with such instruments, and the answer would appear to lie in remaining nagging doubts about the effectiveness of policy within such a regime, an argument which holds most substance when the proximate goal of policy is the attainment of a monetary target. Even here, however, despite the instruments' potential for facilitating the attainment of targets, one should question very closely what one has achieved; in all likelihood control of a meaningless statistic, as the use of the instrument destroys any previously stable relationship between growth in the target aggregate and nominal income! The UK authorities, however, would be forced to concede, given the reactivation of minimum lending rate for one day in January 1985 and the retention (although it remains in abeyance) of the 'special deposits' instrument within its armoury, that, on occasions, direct control devices might be useful, albeit temporarily, because of superior announcement effects as a result of their ability to secure speedier results as compared to the use of open-market operations.

Apart from the dismantling of direct monetary controls, financial deregulation, like financial innovation (which, to a degree, represents a response to the existing regulatory framework employed), has complicated the targeting policies of monetary authorities, which are widely adopted throuhout the financially developed world. In line with financial innovation and facilitated by technological developments in computing and communication systems it has contributed to the breakdown of demarcations between financial intermediaries and industries, domestic and international, thereby challenging the conventional wisdom on what constitutes 'broad' or 'narrow' money and unsettling demand for money functions, at least during 'transition' to the new deregulated environment. Unlike the complications caused by financial innovation, which represents a more enduring feature of financial development, however, it might prove technically possible to accommodate the 'structural adjustments' induced by deregulation within targeting policy by, for example, adjusting target ranges to reflect anticipated changes (e.g. in market-shares of various deposit-taking intermediaries). In practice, credible attempts to accommodate such changes will depend heavily on the monetary authorities' ability to predict the likely consequences and timing of any deregulatory moves introduced. These awesome difficulties led both the UK and Australian authorities, at least temporarily, to suspend targets for 'broad' money although, of course, the problem of when to reinstitute them (i.e. of identifying when the 'structural adjustment' has been or is likely to be completed) remains.

Finally, in connection with the conduct of monetary policy, recent experience in the UK and Australia tends to confirm the economist's prediction that, because of the reduced interest elasticity of the demand for money caused by the payment of (market-related) interest rates on demand deposits, greater interest-rate volatility will result under monetary targeting, *ceteris paribus*. Although, in itself, this is not an argument for down-grading monetary targeting within the economic policy mix (indeed, the power of monetary policy in terms of its ability to influence real income, at least in the short run, is enhanced), it does indicate the need for greater harmonisation of domestic monetary and prudential policies as greater interest-rate volatility threatens greater instability in financial markets and institutions and can impact heavily on intermediaries' capital-raising activities through its effect on profitability.

APPENDIX

The Prudential Regulation of Deposit-taking Financial Intermediaries: An Overview

A.1 THE NEED FOR CONTROLS

The necessity of prudential regulation is normally assessed in terms of the requirements of *consumer protection* and *financial stability*. Desires to protect the small or less financially sophisticated investor from the fraudulent activities or ineptitude of management has led to the introduction of deposit insurance schemes (see p. 161) and an improved flow of relevant information from those soliciting deposits to the general public. The economic benefits are perceived to lie in an improvement of the *allocative efficiency*[1] of the financial system, due to both increased investor confidence and the improvement in market informational flows. Costs, however, are potentially high, covering the areas of compliance[2] with and enforcement of regulatory requirements, resource misallocation[3] and possible reductions in consumer choice (through the imposition of restrictions on business activities) and *operational efficiency*.[4]

Preservation of financial stability is seen as a prerequisite of economic growth and accounts for the closer scrutiny of financial *vis-à-vis* non-financial enterprises. The problem for central banks arises in deciding which, if any, financial institutions be allowed to fail: the requirements of a sound financial system must be set against the virtues of the competitive market-place. In any event the legitimate liquidity needs of the system as a whole should never be threatened, a requirement that demands the provision of an official 'discount facility' (see pp. 162–3) to deal with instances of loss of public confidence and other financial 'shocks'.

Factors responsible for the proliferation and increasingly wide-spread use of prudential controls embrace: (1) the internationalisation (with attendant risks, e.g. country risk, foreign-currency exposure, maturity transformation, risk concentration and overdependence on interbank sources of funds)[5] of banking operations (OECD, 1983, ch. IV); (2) the problems caused by higher and more volatile inflation rates and more volatile capital flows and exchange-rate movements; (3) structural changes (often in response to deregulation in monetary control and of the business operations of the securities markets) in domestic financial systems creating the potential for the emergence of various kinds of 'conflict of interest' and necessitating a rethink of monetary and prudential control systems generally; and (4) an intensification in competitive pressures (due to the breakdown of demarcations in the provision of financial services and technological advance), both domestically and internationally, threatening greater instability in the financial industry.

Given acceptance of the need for prudential regulation the supervisory authorities must then decide upon the most appropriate mix of statutory and non-statutory controls[6] that satisfies prudential objectives yet minimises inequities[7] and 'costs'. In the UK self-regulation is preferred, with government exercising the necessary degree of moral suasion, with minimal back-up statutory powers, to ensure that objectives are fulfilled.[8]

A.2   TAXONOMIC APPROACH

For the purpose of drawing international comparisons in the field of prudential regulation the approach taken by Dale (Group of Thirty, 1982) is adopted. Accordingly national prudential systems are analysed under the following headings: market entry; capital adequacy; liquidity adequacy; permissible business activities; loan concentration; country risk; foreign currency exposure; deposit insurance; lender-of-last-resort facilities. Detailed analyses of national systems are contained within the 'country-specific' parts of the text, but the general principles underlying the foundation of each control and the *international* framework of arrangements and agreements that seeks to standardise national regulatory systems are outlined below. As will become evident the supervisory process can differ widely between countries reflecting, in part, fundamental disagreement on the optimal approach to be taken. Thus, at one extreme (e.g. in the USA), regular bank inspection represents the cornerstone of supervision, while in other countries (e.g. the UK) bank inspections are eschewed and supervisors rely instead on extensive consultation of management and data collection and analysis.

A.3 GENERAL PRINCIPLES

Market entry. Barriers to entry are often justified on the grounds of risk-reduction and hence stability. These putative benefits, however, must be set against the likely costs in terms of the denial of free competition and hence allocative inefficiencies and the stimulus given to the growth of less-regulated intermediaries. In practice would-be entrants are normally subject to licensing requirements, the severity of which varies substantially.[9] Likewise, treatment of foreign bank entry can differ markedly, some authorities preferring to admit *subsidiaries*, on the grounds that locally incorporated bodies are legally independent of their parents (and hence unaffected by their performance) and best supervised by host authorities while others prefer the establishment of *branches* in the expectation of full parental support in times of need.[10]

Capital adequacy. As a measure of the resources available to repay creditors, especially depositors, in the event of liquidation capital adequacy (alternatively termed *solvency*) must be judged in relation to the exposure to risk that financial intermediation involves.[11] For this reason weighted *risk-assets* ratios[12] are frequently designed to assist the supervisory authorities, although such screening devices are no substitute for assessment of loan quality and detailed surveillance of current and prospective managerial plans. These ratios normally complement *gearing ratios*, relating capital to total liabilities. The imposition of uniform requirements, however, should be avoided as the likely outcome is the stifling of innovation among the more efficient banks as protection of the depositor of the weakest banks is sought by the regulators. Moreover the supervisory authorities have to distinguish capital requirements appropriate to 'disaster' and 'going-concern' scenarios, as the relevant net worth (capital and reserves) valuations are likely to differ substantially in the two cases (Revell, 1975, ch. 2, and Colje, 1982).[13] Finally, supervisors have to weigh the benefits of maintaining confidence in banks and hence the soundness of the whole banking system against the costs of disadvantaging commercial banks *vis-à-vis* other commercial enterprises in the capital market.

International comparisons of capital adequacy are complicated by the diversity of valuation conventions and accounting procedures applied, the significance of which is readily apparent if capital is defined as total assets less total liabilities to third parties. Particular areas of disagreement concern the treatment of subordinated debt (Colje, ibid. 1982),[14] hidden reserves and provisions (Revell, 1986) and, where the principle of *consolidation* is applied, the treatment of non-wholly-owned subsidiaries and minority interests. As a general rule the regulation of capital adequacy of foreign bank subsidiaries (and, sometimes, branches) is left to the host supervisory authority (see p. 164).

The pressing concern of many supervisors at the moment is to reverse the secular decline in banks' solvency ratios (OECD, 1980, ch. 9), a situation that results from rapid growth in international business, increased competition and a concomitant fall in profit margins, inflation constraining real profitability (ibid., ch. 7) and a reluctance or inability of banks to attract new equity capital in preference to subordinated debt. The rate of decline has accelerated in recent years, at a time when the perceived risks of banking, especially on the international front, have risen appreciably (see *Risks in International Bank Lending* and *How Bankers See the World Financial Market*, Group of Thirty, New York, 1982). In practice, however, a number of problems arise. First, inadequate profits hinder both the raising of equity capital (further exacerbated if dividends are passed) and boosting of retained earnings as capital sources. Second, fiscal considerations, allowing tax relief on interest payments but not dividends, favour subordinated debt at the expense of equity capital. Third, differences in solvency requirements between countries may create pressures for a further decline in capital ratios as banks subject to stricter regulations press their supervisors to relax controls in order to allow them to compete with those subject to less stringent regulation which can operate on lower interest margins. Although adoption of the consolidation principle in supervision acts to stem the drift of business to the areas of supervisory 'laxity', it fails to deal with the competitive inequalities created by differences in national requirements. For this reason a degree of harmonisation of capital controls is desirable.

On the question of how regulatory practice should be adapted to meet the challenges of the future there is little unanimity (Heggestad and King, 1982). Ideally, minimum capital levels should be set individually for each bank, taking account of its business characteristics, management expertise, etc., and of the social cost of failure. While some supervisors (e.g. in the UK where a bank is assessed in relation to a *peer group* of similar banks of more or less the same size) tailor requirements to a high degree to the individual bank, the cost and difficulty of obtaining information on the social cost of failure excludes its consideration. While there is little doubt that the likely social costs of failure are higher for larger institutions this rarely results in the imposition of higher ratios. Rather, arrangements tend to favour the larger institutions at the expense of the small, despite the strong possibility of the former facing greater risk exposure. The main argument in favour of size-related requirements with discretion for individual tailoring is its flexibility, but the break-down of product and industry barriers as financial deregulation gathers momentum is likely to cause loss of market-share and lower profits for regulated banks, making compliance with regulatory requirements that much more difficult. Alternatives to the above system (improved, where possible, when advances in financial analysis of banks' soundness are made) are the introduction of an equal *marginal* capital requirement, which accepts the present disparity in capital levels, but moves all banks towards the same *average* level, and deregulation (Heggestad and King, ibid., 1982). The advantage of the former is that it would preserve competitive equality at the margin, but its major drawback is that the arbitrary choice of a standard requirement is likely to penalise the safer and better-managed banks. The final option, deregulation, would rely upon financial markets to establish appropriate capital ratios, but suffers from the fact that the social costs of failure would not be considered, the equity of small banks might not be actively traded and that market prices for bank stock might not adequately reflect differences in leverage.

Liquidity adequacy. Liquidity adequacy can be distinguished from capital adequacy in that it is concerned with the availability of funds in an 'on-going' business situation rather than at the point of liquidation. Like capital adequacy, however, it is concerned with ensuring that intermediaries are able to meet the risks of operation. First and foremost, liquidity is required to deal with *funding risk* or the risk that insufficient funds will be available to meet liabilities as they fall due. Under this heading, situations accounting for a shortfall in availability would encompass unexpected shortfalls in asset earnings, unexpected withdrawal of deposits or credit facilities, unanticipated expenditure (current or capital) and unexpected movements in the maturity profiles of assets and liabilities. A separate class of risk, *interest-rate risk*, arises in situations of maturity transformation when unexpected movements in interest rates occur. The classic example for institutions borrowing short on a floating or variable-rate basis and lending long on a fixed-rate basis is a sudden but lasting jump in short-term rates which not only raises the prospect of institutions making *running* losses but also the spectre of insolvency as asset values decline.

The use of ratios for prescribed liquid assets to some measure of liabilities is common practice among prudential supervisors, but differences of opinion emerge as to what assets should be prescribed for liquidity purposes,[15] what the denominator should be, whether the ratio should be specified as a minimum or an average over a given time period,[16] whether a uniform ratio should be applied to all *like* deposit-taking intermediaries and to what extent ratio analysis needs to be supplemented with further supervisory measures.[17] The last point is particularly important for, despite measurement difficulties, liquidity analysis should recognise the significance of access to credit facilities, operating flows (e.g. loan repayments) and managed liabilities[18] as alternative sources to readily marketable assets. Moreover, some notice should be taken of the degree of maturity mismatching adopted.

Permissible business activities. Regulation or prohibition of business activities is often only partially justified on prudential grounds. For example, concerns about concentration (sometimes expressed through ownership restrictions) reflect more a political judgement concerning possible abuse of power. Nevertheless, a wide range of restrictions is imposed in the name of consumer (depositor) protection or preservation of financial stability. The more popular comprise: interest-rate controls;[19] constraints on asset choice; limitations on the source and maturity of liabilities; limitations on the type of business conducted (e.g. separation of commercial and investment banking business (USA)); limitations on investment in property and equity and loans to directors; 'risk-asset limits' (see below); disclosure requirements.[20] The overriding drawback, apart from breeding inefficiency, of most of these restrictions, however, is that very often they can cause the event against which protection is sought by denying intermediaries the flexibility to deal with problems as they emerge.

Loan concentration. Concern about loan concentration normally manifests itself in the form of *risk-asset limits*, where maximum holdings of certain classes of asset[21] are specified in terms of capital proportions. Whatever the merits of the restrictions the inflexibility introduced inevitably involves economic 'costs' in the form of a reduction in consumer/lender choice and allocative inefficiency and encouragement of market imperfections.

Country risk. Following the lead taken in the USA in 1978, supervisors in most countries seek to measure and monitor exposure to country risk (that is the possibility that a country's debtors fail to meet their external commitments to debt-servicing and/or repayment for reasons beyond the normal lending risks), although not always on a fully consolidated basis. Disagreement, however, arises on what further action should be taken. Some rely heavily on formal loan limits[22] determined according to 'risk-class' analysis (as in the USA) while others are content to ensure diversification through discussions with management without specifying any 'norms'. The Basle Committee (see p. 164) produced a report in 1982 ('Management of banks' international lending: country-risk analysis and country-exposure measurement and control') specifying a set of guidelines for consideration with respect to country-risk analysis, focusing in particular on risk allocation, consolidation, the analysis of claims by borrowing country, control of country exposure and the establishment and monitoring of country-exposure limits. The broad philosophy is to allow management to take their own commercial decisions on a case-by-case basis, with supervisors ensuring that individual banks' risk analysis, ranging from qualitative assessment of political, social and economic factors at one extreme to complex computerised techniques based on multivariate discriminate analysis and logit analysis at the other, is adequate and that the necessary information required for effective monitoring and control of country exposure is available.

Foreign currency exposure. As for country risk, monitoring of exposure to foreign-currency risk (i.e. exposure to losses on an 'unmatched' book arising from unanticipated changes in exchange rates) is widespread but the extent to which formal limits are imposed on net exposure (in individual currencies or on an aggregate basis) varies considerably from one country to the next. Some supervisors choose to rely on spot examinations and/or consultation with management to ensure the adequacy of internal control procedures. Outside the USA, regulation rarely occurs on a consolidated basis. Differences in official monitoring practice largely reflect past experience, institutional idiosyncrasies and the extent of any exchange controls adopted.

Deposit insurance. Unlike other forms of insurance, deposit insurance is intended mainly to reduce the risk of the insured event (i.e.

collapse of a financial intermediary) occurring rather than as a means of compensating those who would suffer should the event actually occur. It hopes to do this by raising the public's confidence in the financial system. A typical scheme would involve intermediaries providing deposit protection up to a specified maximum sum[23,24] by contributing[25] to a self-financed, industry-run pool. Exhortations from the authorities are, however, normally required to initiate the setting up of the fund and, in some countries, government departments may play a part in financing/administering the scheme. Coverage of deposits varies, but usually embraces only those denominated in domestic currency and held with intermediaries operating within national boundaries.

The advantages of deposit insurance schemes are taken to stem from the stabilising influences imparted to the market and the possible reductions in capital requirements and overall supervisory effort that such benefits allow. The drawbacks lie in the costs of funding, administering and enforcing the schemes, factors which are likely to militate against both allocative and operational efficiency. Moreover, there is always the danger that industry-run schemes are used as an entry barrier through control of membership. Much of the current debate (Maisel, 1981) centres on the relative merits of variable-rate premium deposit insurance schemes *vis-à-vis* flat-rate premium schemes, which are the norm in the real world today.

Lender-of-last-resort facilities. It is the duty of all central banks[26] to ensure, at discount rates and penalties of their own choosing, that adequate liquidity is available to the financial system to guard against destabilisation caused by loss of confidence or other financial 'shocks'. Unfortunately, in activating the facilities, a number of policy dilemmas are bound to arise.[27] First and foremost is the need to decide how the liquidity is to be injected and which enterprises are to be supported; scarce resources may be misallocated if bodies deemed non-viable (always a subjective evaluation) in the long run nevertheless require 'rescuing' for the benefit of the system as a whole. This problem is likely to be particularly acute if adverse rumours concerning relatively large enterprises circulate (as happened with Continental Illinois, the eighth-largest US bank, in 1984), creating a further *moral hazard* issue in that size might be construed as conferring *automatic* access to lender-of-last-resort facilities under *all* prospective circumstances leading to the temptation for managers to act less prudently than circumstances would otherwise dictate.[28] Second, in restricting access to last-resort facilities to specific types of financial intermediary, preservation of *competitive neutrality* is likely to be sacrificed.[29] Finally, on the international front, controversy surrounds the division of responsibility between 'host' and 'parent' authority, as the *Basle Concordat* (see below) explicitly excludes lender-of-last-resort functions from consideration, although schemes have been suggested (e.g. an international deposit insurance fund (see Group of Thirty, 1984), a multilateral investment guarantee scheme and a privately organised international safety-net) to complement existing IMF-sponsored efforts to nurture the international banking system through troubled times.

A.4   INTERNATIONAL SUPERVISORY CO-OPERATION

Additional to the requirement (as exemplified in recent banking problems experienced in Canada, West Germany, the USA and the UK (see p. 141))[30] for a tightening of *domestic* supervisory arrangements is the need for further progress in the harmonisation of prudential control at the international level. For, despite the establishment of the *Basle Committee of Supervisors* in 1975 following the Herstatt affair,[31] and the substantial progress made since then in the area of supervisory co-operation, the Banco Ambrosiano fiasco[32] of 1982 and current disparities in the standards of national supervision leave much to be desired. Particularly important issues outstanding comprise the need for uniformity in the definition of capital and the approach taken to capital adequacy, the quest for harmonisation of accounting practice (e.g. with respect to the treatment of hidden reserves – see Colje, op. cit. (1982)) and treatment of provisions against bad and doubtful loans, and the desirability of speeding up the implementation of the principle of consolidation (see Colje, 1980). As long as regulatory disparities exist, or are perceived to exist, competitive inequalities will persist.[33] Moreover, there will remain an incentive for international business to gravitate to the more permissive areas.

The *Basle Concordat*

The wave of uncertainty that followed the Herstatt affair and other financial crises (e.g. the UK fringe banking crisis)[34] in 1974 led European central bank governors in September of that year to issue a joint statement reassuring the markets that adequate temporary liquidity support facilities were available: 'it would not be practical to lay down in advance detailed rules and procedures for the provision of temporary liquidity ... satisfied that means are available for that purpose and will be used if and when necessary'. At the same time a standing committee of bank supervisors from the Group of Ten countries plus Switzerland and Luxembourg was formed under the auspices of the Bank for International Settlements (BIS) to co-ordinate prudential supervision to achieve effective control over a rapidly changing world banking system. The Committee was named the *Committee on Banking Regulations and Supervisory Practices* and meetings were held three times a year. The first task taken on board was to consider ways of improving early-warning systems with the purpose of identifying, at an embryonic stage, domestic banking problems that were likely to have international repercussions. A decision was taken, mainly on the grounds of practicability, to continue to rely on national supervisors rather than a supranational body for both the provision of early-warning signals and, after consultation with other supervisors if necessary, implementation of the appropriate remedial action.

In December 1975 a document was drawn up outlining the committee's views on the principles that should guide the division of supervisory responsibilities between national regulators. Known as the *Basle Concordat*, it has been described by the current Chairman of the committee as 'a most important cornerstone of international supervisory cooperation' (*BEQB*, June 1981, p. 240) and, as such, merits further consideration. The principal guidelines were:

(1) The supervision of foreign banking establishments should be the joint responsibility of host and parent authorities.
(2) No foreign banking establishment should escape supervision, each country should ensure that foreign banking establishments are supervised, and supervision should be adequate as judged by both host and parent authorities.
(3) The supervision of liquidity should be the primary responsibility of host authorities since foreign establishments generally have to conform to local practices for their liquidity management and must comply with local regulations.
(4) The supervision of solvency of foreign branches should be essentially a matter for the parent authority. In the case of subsidiaries, while primary responsibility lies with the host

authority, parent authorities should take account of the exposure of their domestic banks' foreign subsidiaries and joint ventures because of the parent banks' moral commitment in this regard.

(5) Practical co-operation would be facilitated by transfers of information between host and parent authorities and by the granting of permission for inspections by or on behalf of parent authorities on the territory of the host authority. Every effort should be made to remove any legal restraints (particularly in the field of professional secrecy or national sovereignty) which might hinder these forms of co-operation.

The committee subsequently also recommended that supervision of international business be conducted on a *consolidated* basis to ensure that banks could not evade regulation by operating from areas where supervision was lax or non-existent and to allow parent supervisors to assess risk exposure on a global basis and hence to formulate adequate supervisory requirements for capital and liquidity adequacy, foreign-currency exposure, etc. The principle of consolidation was endorsed by the Group of Ten governors in 1978, but has still not yet been fully implemented.[35]

Conspicuous by its absence from the *concordat* guidelines is the question of the provision of last-resort facilities,[36] uncertainties surrounding which tend to compound confidence crises. While the architects of the *concordat* can rightly claim that they were only concerned with the *allocation of supervisory responsibility* not with the determination of how those responsibilities should be exercised in practice, this does not excuse them from seeking to ensure that adequate provisions are available in *all* financial centres and that support facilities are standardised in order to minimise the competitive inequalities that disparities create.

While accepting the painfully slow progress made on implementing the consolidation principle worldwide the committee's present Chairman, Peter Cooke, rebuffs (*BEQB*, Mar 1983) criticisms relating to the constraints imposed by bank secrecy and variations in national regulatory practice and the charges that some banks are still largely unsupervised as a result of continuing uncertainties relating to the interpretation[37] and acceptance[38] of the *concordat* guidelines. Thus, on the question of bank secrecy,[39] he asserts that few problems are experienced by supervisors in collecting the necessary aggregated data and that 'no member country considered itself barred from monitoring country risk on a consolidated basis because of banking secrecy constraints'. He continued, 'verification of data and rights of inspection may also present some problems but again, either through passing data within banking groups up to the parent entity, or by the use of external auditors, or by the host authority undertaking to pursue inquiries on behalf of the parent authority, ways can usually be found, in practice, of ensuring that supervision can be effectively conducted'.

On the problems caused by differences in national prudential control systems, Cooke believes that 'there can be a clear understanding of the nature and extent of the supervision being exercised by each authority which can be varied sensibly to meet individual circumstances'. To the charge that some international banking business escapes the supervisory net, Cooke replies that only a very few centres fail to conduct adequate supervision and, at any rate, those involved are insignificant in statistical terms and largely shunned by the banking community, leaving them no scope for undermining the system as a whole. Finally, the Banco Ambrosiano affair is dismissed as being quite exceptional (and therefore unlikely to be repeated) with no blame attaching to the *concordat*. Nevertheless, the committee saw fit in June 1983 to reaffirm and expand upon the basic principles embodied within the document, clarifying the position of 'intermediate' institutions such as bank holding companies and joint ventures.

The Revised *Concordat*

In June 1983 a revised version of the principles and understandings that should underlie the supervisory approaches adopted by both parent and host authorities with respect to banks' foreign establishments was published by the Basle committee of supervisors. The revision was prompted by a desire to incorporate agreements reached since 1975 on the principle of *consolidation* (e.g. with respect to capital adequacy and risk exposure) and to clarify and expand upon, in the light of experience, some of the points raised in the original document.

First and foremost the paper confirms the line taken in the original towards the division of responsibility for the provision of lender of last resort facilities, namely to exclude it from consideration. This is perhaps surprising given the difficulties that emerged and the uncertainty created following the collapse of Banco Ambrosiano Holdings, but probably reflects the authorities' desires not to undermine attempts being made to improve supervisory standards in certain offshore centres. Nevertheless an attempt is made to plug some of the gaps in supervision made apparent by the Banco Ambrosiano fiasco, especially those arising from inadequate supervisory standards in certain countries or as a result of the existence of holding companies and non-banking companies within banking groups. For example, when a foreign establishment is classified as a bank by the parent supervisor but not by the host authority it should be the responsibility for the parent authority to ensure that adequate supervision is exercised by the host authority, although the latter should, of course, inform the parent authority of the instances when it is unable to effect adequate supervision (in which case parental supervision should be stepped up or the bank discouraged from operating in the host's territory).[40] Should the problem be reversed and the host authority doubt the adequacy of supervision exercised over the parent institutions of foreign bank establishments operating in its territory[41] it should either discourage/prohibit such operations or impose conditions governing the conduct of such business. The problems created by the existence of holding companies and non-banking companies within banking groups are best dealt with by increased co-ordination and co-operation between the relevant bank supervisors (determined according to the place of incorporation of the banks within the group) in the former case[42] and between bank and any non-bank supervisory authorities in the latter situation. Should inadequate supervision be exercised over the non-banking activities of the group in the second scenario then bank supervisors should take formal steps to minimise the risks created for the banking business.

Generally the document stresses the need for close co-operation between host and parent supervisors and emphasises the overlapping nature of supervisory responsibilities in contrast to the original *concordat*, which was more concerned with the formal allocation of supervisory responsibilities. This is brought out in the discussions on the supervision of solvency, liquidity and foreign-exchange operations. On the issue of *solvency*, supervision, as before, is held to be primarily the responsibility of the parent authority in the case of branches (on the presumption that solvency of a foreign branch is indistinguishable from that of the parent (see Dale, 1983), but a joint responsibility[43] in the case of subsidiaries, in contrast to the primary importance ascribed to the host authority in the original *concordat*.[44] In the case of joint ventures[45] supervision should normally, for practical reasons, be primarily the responsibility of the authorities in the country of incorporation, although the pattern of shareholdings (particularly where one bank is a dominant shareholder) might occasionally dictate that responsibility become a joint concern, bringing in the parent authorities of the shareholder banks.

Similarly, on *liquidity* the revised *concordat* places more emphasis than the original (which gave primary responsibility for supervision to the host authority in all prospective circumstances) on the need for consultation between host and parent supervisors[46] although, formally, primary supervisory responsibility is given to the host authority for both branches and subsidiaries and to the authorities in the country of incorporation for joint ventures.

Finally, in respect of banks *foreign-exchange operations* (an area omitted from consideration in the original *concordat*) supervision is held to be a joint responsibility of parent and host authorities. Parent authorities need to ensure that the monitoring systems used by parent banks to assess their group's overall exposure is adequate and host authorities need to monitor the foreign-exchange exposure of foreign establishments operating in their territories and acquaint themselves with the degree of supervision exercised by parent authorities.

Other International Supervisory Committees

In addition to the *Basle Committee* of supervisors a number of other agencies are involved in international supervisory co-operation. These include the Group of Ten's *Standing Committee on Euromarkets* (established in April 1980), the *Banking Advisory Committee* to the European Commission, the *Contact Group of Supervisors* from the member states of the European Communities, *The Committee on Financial Markets* of the Organisation for Economic Co-operation and Development, the *Offshore Group of Supervisors* and the *Commission of Latin American and the Caribbean Supervisory and Inspection Organisations*. The last two groups are, respectively, concerned with promoting multilateral co-operation among member and non-member supervisory authorities and discussion of supervisory issues of mutual interest to the membership.

A.5 EEC ARRANGEMENTS

The creation of a common market in banking is provided for in the Treaty of Rome, which demands the freedom of movement of both services and capital in the Community. Progress on both fronts, however, has been disappointing. For, although the UK has no exchange control (abolished in June 1979) and capital controls in Germany and the Benelux countries are limited, restrictions in other member states are more extensive. Similarly, liberalisation of the financial services industry has been painfully slow. The right of establishment in other member states is provided for in Articles 52 and 53 of the Treaty of Rome and Articles 59 and 60 specifically endorse the principle for (financial) services. In practice, however, 'there are differences of view on the extent to which member states may maintain restrictive national rules requiring that the provider of services be authorised in the country where the service is offered before he can operate, even though he is already authorised by the authorities of his home country' (Henriksen (1983), EEC Director-General for Financial Institutions and Taxation). So far, no disputes arising in the banking area concerning the issue of 'double authorisation' have surfaced in the European Court.

In dealing with the banking sector the Community can either issue recommendations or *directives*, the latter alone carrying legal force to ensure the desired result, although the means of achievement are left to the individual member states. Experience with recommendations in non-financial areas has been disappointing and the mixed results achieved by the recommended *Code of Conduct for Security Markets* confirms this position. Close co-operation between the Commission and national regulatory authorities and the use of *directives* have, however, retrieved the situation somewhat.

The first move was made in 1971 with the setting up of the *Contact Group*, an informal club comprising member-state supervisory authorities, to provide a forum for national supervisors to exchange views on the supervisory process. It commissions its own research studies and submits reports to the *Basle Committee*, the *Banking Advisory Committee* (see below) and the EEC Commission.

The next step was taken in July 1972 with the publication of the Commission's *draft* directive on the harmonisation of regulation of banks and other credit institutions in the Community (see Revell, op. cit. (1975), ch. 6). Closely based on West German banking law it was strongly resisted by the British authorities and was subsequently withdrawn in favour of a 'step-by-step' approach to harmonisation. A revised directive, dealing with only part of the material contained in the earlier draft, was issued in January 1975 and duly adopted by member states in 1977 (see below).

Supervisory harmonisation (see ICBS (Bonnardin), 1981) is an emotive issue among supervisors, as evidenced by the comments made by the present Chairman of the Basle Committee in a recent paper (Cooke, 1982). In summary the following points were made: (1) there are more serious impediments to cross-border competitive equality than differences in supervisory practice and these obstacles should be tackled first; (2) care must be taken to ensure that harmonisation does not lead to over-regulation, damage innovative zeal, unduly interfere with commercial judgement (implying flexibility), impair the freedom of action of national authorities or wider attempts to secure the soundness of international banking or damage the competitive position of community banks active in Eurocurrency markets; (3) a less juridically-based attitude to the implementation of community initiatives is desirable (implying a bias towards *recommendations* rather than directives); and (4) continued efforts (a *Committee of Credit Associations* was established in 1980 for this purpose) should be made to find a consensus between the banking and credit industries and the regulatory authorities at both the national and Community level. On specifics, the 'desirability, practicality and relevance' of seeking to establish normative (*observation*) ratios (see below) is questioned, the wisdom of including specific aspects of the *consolidation* principle in any future directive is challenged and reservations are expressed concerning the harmonisation of prudential returns, the establishment of a Community credit information exchange and the necessity for standardised statutory winding-up procedures for banks. Finally, the possibility of a second *Banking Co-ordination Directive* is shunned as is the idea of transferring supervisory powers from national authorities to a supranational Community body.

In apparent response to this fairly wide-ranging condemnation of Community supervisory initiatives the Director-General for Financial Institutions and Taxation (Henriksen, op cit. 1983) vigorously defended the Commission's approach, seeking to allay some of the fears expressed above. Thus the Commission:

(1)	'does not pursue harmonisation for its own sake' (Tugendhat (1985) describes the commission's approach as 'negative harmonisation') and 'given a choice will put emphasis on co-ordination of national practices rather than on legal harmonisation';

(2)	'has no intention, or even ambition, of setting up supranational supervisory authorities';

(3) 'has no particular preference for one banking structure over another. It is up to the markets. . . . We endeavour to put forward proposals that are neutral in this respect';

(4) seeks to ensure that co-ordination of banking supervision does 'not lead to a monotonous increase in the administrative burden for European credit institutions and authorities';

(5) believes that 'the framework for a common market in banking in Europe must be flexible in order to meet the challenges' presented by technological advance in data processing; and

(6) takes 'an interest in the working conditions of Community banks operating or trying to operate in third countries' . . . and is 'fully aware that we cannot create a banking market among the Ten which turns its back on the rest of the world'. Whether or not this defence of EEC policy reassures critics such as the Basle Committee chairman is doubtful, however.

The *First Banking Co-ordination Directive* was adopted in December 1977 and provided for minimum authorisation criteria, the establishment of common prudential ratios (which, initially, were for *observation* purposes only and covered solvency, liquidity (for which trial calculations were suspended in 1984) and profitability – see Revell, op. cit. 1975, ch. 6) and the setting up of a *Banking Advisory Committee*[47] to assist the Commission in its co-ordination work. As a general principle the directive sought to effect the gradual shift of effective prudential supervision from the host to the parent supervisory authority (the 'home-country-control' objective), not entirely in keeping with the recommended allocatory system for supervisory responsibility adumbrated within the *Basle Concordat*, and the integration of community 'banking' through the liberalisation of the right of establishment. The latter is likely to require further harmonisation.[48] Since the 1977 Directive the Commission has drafted proposals for the standardisation of the banks' and other financial institutions' annual accounts,[49] the supervision of credit institutions holding substantial participations in other credit or financial institutions on a consolidated basis by the authority host to the head office (adopted June 1983)[50] and the co-ordination of winding-up procedures. Proposals have also been made concerning the definition of capital and the control of risk concentration.

Notes

Preface

1. *Monetary Policy Since 1971: Conduct and Performance* (Macmillan Press, 1983).

Chapter 1

1. The financial support of the British Council and the Bank of England-administered Houblon–Norman Fund and the assistance of the Reserve Bank of Australia are gratefully acknowledged.

1 The Australian Financial System

1. The Bank of New South Wales and the Commonwealth Bank of Australia Ltd merged to form Westpac Banking Corporation and the Commercial Banking Company of Sydney Ltd and the National Bank of Australasia Ltd merged to form the National Commercial Banking Corporation.
2. Comprising the Commonwealth Development Bank, the Australia Resources Development Bank and the Primary Industry Bank of Australia (see RBA, 1979, pp. 3.33–3.36, for further details).
3. Effective 29 June 1984, the Commonwealth Savings Bank became a wholly-owned subsidiary of the Commonwealth Trading Bank, which was renamed the Commonwealth Bank of Australia.
4. Members are able to make limited cash withdrawals from the offices of other credit unions ('Redi Access') can use a system of ATMs ('Redi Teller') for withdrawals and deposits outside normal trading hours and away from business offices, and are able to participate in credit-card systems ('Redicard'). Since August 1984 credit unions have also been able to offer chequing accounts through an agency agreement reached with the National Australia Bank. The agreement made by the Australian Federation of Credit Unions Ltd will initially cover only affiliated unions in NSW, Victoria, South Australia and the ACT. Direct access to the payments system is not provided, but the arrangement allows credit unions to offer personalised cheques, direct debiting of wages, salaries and social security payments and access to 'Redicard' holders to the National Australia Bank's ATM network. Additionally the plastic cards of each intermediary are to be standardised to allow joint access to EFT/POS systems being developed. The fees to be paid by the credit unions are based on the volume of transactions undertaken.

5. 'The Reserve Bank believes there will continue to be a role for a group of institutions to serve as a buffer and a conduit between the Bank and the market generally' – Governor's address to members of the Council of Authorised Money Market Dealers, Sydney, 24 February 1984.
6. Deposits with a given trading bank repayable in Australia, but excluding deposits held with that bank by the Reserve Bank or another trading bank.
7. There is a provision for applying separate SRD ratios to 'prescribed banks', as long as they are no higher than those applied to the major trading banks.
8. The SRD ratio initially proved necessary because the thinness of the bond market in the early post-war period precluded the use of open-market operations by the authorities.
9. One must be careful to distinguish the rationale for liability management for an individual bank from that for subject banks as a group. In the latter case, apart from inducing the general public to economise on cash holdings, 'success' for banks as a group in acquiring more cash reserves depends crucially on the response of the central bank in the money, capital and foreign-exchange markets which, in turn, reflects its resolve to limit cash reserve creation (Hall, 1983, ch. 3).
10. The ability of banks to manage their liabilities has been severely circumscribed until recently by various limitations imposed on the interest rates they could pay on deposits and the maturities for which they could take deposits and by the lack of a well-developed interbank market. Gradual relaxation throughout the 1970s (see Table 1.3) of interest-rate and maturity controls culminated only in 1984 in removing all regulatory impediments to liability management.
11. This was the only option open to banks before the deregulation of deposit controls during the 1970s (Macfarlane, 1984, pp. 1–2).
12. These wider effects were limited before deposit controls were relaxed.
13. It was always open to banks to withdraw short-term loans to the authorised money-market dealers in the knowledge that the latter could activate credit lines at the Reserve Bank, thereby creating cash reserves and LGS assets for the banks.
14. This may still reflect a belief in policy-making circles that restricting advances has a greater impact on final expenditures than the sale of government securities, although the effect on the money supply is the same.
15. In practice, Reserve Bank policy in relation to bank liquidity concentrated on the margin of 'free liquidity', or LGS assets held above the agreed minimum, as bank holdings of LGS assets only approached the minimum during the seasonal liquidity trough (May to August). More recently, however, as a result of the development of the interbank market and more active liability management, banks have operated with a much lower level of 'free liquidity'.
16. The Act applies to financial corporations with assets exceeding $1 m. whose sole or principal business in Australia is the borrowing of money and the provision of finance. Retail corporations with instalment credit of over three months' term exceeding $5 m. (or other prescribed amount)

are also covered. Institutions covered by separate Commonwealth legislation are excluded, as are those thought of limited significance for monetary policy purposes.

17. With the exception of building society interest rates, which may differ between states.

18. Under the 'flexible-peg' arrangements banks short of cash reserves could always obtain them by bidding funds from abroad occasioning reserve creation on the intervention of the Reserve Bank to stop/slow the appreciation of the dollar.

19. The rationale for and effectiveness of exchange controls is discussed in the Campbell Report (1981, ch. 8, part c) and in Cohen (1983).

20. Or, alternatively, following concerns raised in reports from the Auditor-General.

21. More exhaustive critiques are provided in the *Australian Economic Review* ('Campbell Symposium'), 1st Quarter, 1982 and a special edition of *Economic Papers* on the Campbell Report, Apr 1983.

22. These can, at least partially, be offset by the establishment of appropriate prudential controls.

23. Wood (1982), however, doubts the significance of externalities and other forms of market failure apparent in financial markets.

24. While the Campbell Committee duly accepted the existence of market imperfections and acknowledged the right of governments to determine social priorities they, nevertheless, regarded 'deregulation' as the route offering the greatest potential 'economic' gains. Similarly the Martin Group, while specifically required to consider the administration's social and economic goals and espousing a pragmatic, case-by-case approach, did little, by way of making recommendations, to suggest a moderation of this presumption.

25. In the event the following decisions, in accord with the recommendations contained within the Campbell (C)/Martin (M) Reports, were taken: to abolish interest-rate controls on bank deposits and controls on banks' loan rates [C (4.26); M (ch. 5, 3.16)]; to abolish maturity controls on banks [C (4.29); M (2.12, 2.16, 2.22)]; to allow the banks to pay interest on all current-account balances [C (4.26); M (2.12, 2.16)]; to abolish quantitative lending controls on banks [C (4.38); M (5.13)]; to relax the asset restrictions imposed on savings banks [C (10.60, 37.91); M (4.45, 4.46)]; to abolish the 30/20 rule imposed on pension funds and insurance companies [C (10.38); M (5.10)]; and to dismantle exchange controls [C (8.35)].

26. As an instrument of social policy lending ceilings are unlikely to achieve their objective of diverting low-cost finance to low-income borrowers. This is because the supply of housing funds available will dry up once market rates move above regulated rates, and non-price rationing techniques will tend to favour those borrowers on higher incomes.

27. The Group did, however, recommend that the 'free tranche' of assets available for investment at the savings banks' discretion be increased from 6 per cent to 10 per cent and that all interest-rate controls on trading and savings banks be abolished.

28. If a variable reserve ratio is to be used as a monetary control device (as

suggested by Campbell (4.44) in the transitional stage of deregulation and accepted by the Martin Group (4.11)), two further questions have to be answered: (a) should the requirement be mandatory or voluntary?; and (b) should market rates of interest be paid on required reserves? In coming to a conclusion on the first issue the disintermediation incentives provided by any form of mandatory reserve requirement that differs from that desired by banks will have to be weighed against the uncertainties associated with allowing banks to determine their own reserve positions. (In the UK the authorities successfully use the clearing banks' balances *voluntarily* held at the Bank of England for clearing purposes as the fulcrum for official money-market operations designed to influence short-term interest rates.) With regard to the payment of market rates on (required) reserves, the difficulties of forecasting the reintermediation effects due to the removal of an effective tax on bank intermediation (Davis and Lewis, 1983, p. 92) have to be balanced against the efficiency gains resulting from removal of distortions to the financial system (although NBFIs claim that, as direct access to the payments system is denied them, it would further accelerate their demise).

29. Although the Committee believed that the privileges granted to the authorised dealers by the Reserve Bank justified continued restrictions on their asset composition.

30. The following guiding principles were to apply: financial institutions should be allowed to fail; a liquidity safety valve should be available to intermediaries; investors should receive reasonable protection against fraud and malpractice; there should be a 'fair', well-informed market in securities – disclosure of relevant information to be ensured by the government; entry requirements should be concerned only with depositor protection; prudential requirements should be applied in a flexible manner, leaving intermediaries with maximum freedom to adjust to changing circumstances, and should aim at ensuring *competitive neutrality* among intermediaries; regulation should not impair the provision of a reasonably full spectrum of risk/return investment opportunities.

31. As Perkins (1982) has pointed out, detailed controls may be unavoidable if, in practice, the authorities are reluctant to let even weak banks fail, for without such controls banks are encouraged to act recklessly.

32. This mode of implementing and enforcing the controls has also been criticised as an inconsistency, given the Committee's strong dislike of the use of moral suasion on the monetary policy front.

33. The Campbell Committee went even further and recommended that only banks be granted the authority to issue cheques.

34. No figures were offered as estimates of the extent to which cheque-based transactions would be displaced by transactions undertaken through electronic transfer systems.

35. Indirect participation by the issue of third-party cheques has generally not been resisted by banks, but agency arrangements (see Martin Report, pp. 182–3) have, on the grounds that banks would lose their competitive advantage of being able to offer superior cheque account facilities. Frequently this resistance takes the form of bank demands for unrealistically high fees.

36. By limiting the number of new banking licences the authorities are effectively ruling out the option of conserving competitive equity through the provision of perfect freedom of entry to 'banking'.
37. I.e. profit greater than that necessary to persuade the banks to remain in the industry (or product area).
38. Similarly, past experience suggests that exit from the industry will be far from 'free', a problem which might have been overcome if deposit insurance had been introduced (Wood, op. cit.).
39. They did, however, compete through affiliations with finance companies and general financiers and with money-market corporations (subject to a maximum equity interest of 60 per cent) – at end-December 1978 the Reserve Bank estimated that equity stakes held by Australian banks in the two institutional groupings stood at 42 per cent and 12 per cent respectively. More recently, affiliations with Cash Management Trusts have been used to meet the competition experienced from this quarter, in the face of a Reserve Bank prohibition on the management or sponsorship of cash management trusts by banks or their wholly-owned subsidiaries.
40. The award of foreign-exchange dealing licences to merchant banks in 1984, against the recommendation of the Campbell Committee, was one of the few moves that disadvantaged trading banks. Foreign bank entry was another.
41. Westpac Banking Corporation has acquired the maximum allowable 50 per cent stake in Ord Minnet, the National Australia Bank has acquired a half-share in A. C. Goode and ANZ has linked up with McCaughan Dyson.
42. Interest rates are regulated in NSW, Queensland, Victoria and South Australia. In NSW and Queensland the maximum rates of interest paid on shares and deposits are stipulated; in Victoria and South Australia the maximum rates on housing loans can be stipulated (although the power has not yet been exercised). In Victoria there is an agreement to keep mortgage rates within an agreed limit and, on occasions, other states have sought the co-operation of societies operating within their boundaries on interest-rate matters.
43. The incentive for a building society to become a bank (as provided for in the Campbell Report) is discussed in Glover (1983).
44. To mitigate this disadvantage societies have established clearing houses in every state and associated companies to deal with ATMs and other EFT developments. Additionally national networks of societies exist in which customers from one state can receive reciprocal facilities in others. Finally, and perhaps a precursor to wider future developments, the Compass Building Society in Victoria reached an agreement with the National Australia Bank in September 1984 enabling it to write its own cheques.
45. The proposals incorporate the following:
    (i) that societies be required to ensure that at least 60 per cent of their new lending and existing loans is for owner-occupied housing or housing-related purposes – this will allow some scope for housing-associated personal loans and similar unsecured lending;

   (ii) that societies should be able to borrow funds domestically and from abroad in any commercially accepted manner, e.g. through the issue of promissory notes and bills of exchange or by way of deposits and subordinated debt or through participation in a secondary mortgage market (or the issue of debt securities linked to a package of mortgages);

  (iii) that capital requirements be specified by the Minister according to the risks involved in various operations undertaken;

  (iv) that societies be allowed to enter into insurance and liquidity arrangements (e.g. to allow membership of the Australian Building Societies' Share and Deposit Insurance Corporation (ABSSDIC)) to increase the security of societies and so enhance the attractiveness of their 'deposit' liabilities (it was acknowledged that variable liquidity controls might prove necessary to deal with maturity transformation);

   (v) that societies be allowed to diversify their asset portfolios in Australia, e.g. to act as estate agents, to own property, to undertake conveyancing, to make unsecured loans and secured non-housing loans, to invest in shares and money-market instruments, etc.;

  (vi) abolition of the 'special loans' category (see Table 1.2) as a variable capital requirement would render it superfluous;

 (vii) that within-state and inter-state lending between societies be allowed;

(viii) that interest-rate controls be abolished.

46. The St George permanent building society has formed a consortium of six of the major inter-state societies to benefit from a pooling of surplus resources (thereby obtaining better money-market rates) and reduced computer developmental and operating costs.

47. Legislation, variable between states, covers liquidity ratios, reserve requirements, size and type of loan, permissible investments, establishment and supervision, disclosure and (in some) deposit protection schemes.

48. At the end of 1978 the Reserve Bank estimated that foreigners (mainly foreign banks) owned 62 per cent of the equity in money market corporations. In September 1984 the foreign-investment controls on merchant banks were relaxed for 12 months to allow the industry time to conduct a much-needed shareholder rationalisation exercise to deal with the challenge of the future.

49. Some have moved into sharebroking. Wardley Australia, the local merchant banking arm of the Hongkong and Shanghai Banking Corporation, joined forces with Mr Rene Rivkin in 1984 to form the first incorporated sharebroking firm in Australia. This was followed by the wholly UK-owned Morgan Grenfell Australia acquiring an interest in Hordern UTZ and Bode and Kleinwort Benson Australia announcing plans to form a link with Hattersley and Maxwell.

50. The relative attractions of bank status, in terms of lower funding costs (mainly due to the prudential privileges accorded them) and larger trading and funding limits, are substantial. This led Hill Samuel (UK) to

seek transformation into a bank – the Macquarie Bank – which started trading in March 1985.

51. Since the abolition, in August 1984, of the restriction on a bank's equity interest in a money-market corporation, Westpac has achieved full ownership of its affiliate Partnership Pacific Ltd.

52. A general requirement to operate within the framework of prudential concerns established by the Reserve Bank – covering capital and liquidity adequacy, managerial competence, adequacy of managerial control and monitoring systems for limiting risk exposure, and equity links with non-banks and other banks – will be written into new banking authorities. More specifically, a minimum paid up capital of $25 m., local incorporation and detailed analyses of proposed business plans and managerial control systems are required. And finally, applicants (42 in total) had to indicate the extent of the financial responsibility they would accept with regard to their proposed banking operation in Australia.

53. The basic threshold on individual shareholdings was lifted from 10 per cent to 15 per cent for new banks (and for existing banks with the Treasurer's approval) and exemptions to the threshold were permitted on 'national interest' considerations.

54. At the end of 1978 the Reserve Bank estimated the degree of foreign ownership of institutional groupings subject to the Financial Corporations Act to be as follows: money-market corporations, 62 per cent; authorised money-market dealers, 22 per cent; finance companies and general financiers, 34 per cent; and pastoral finance companies, 28 per cent. In addition, foreign banks can establish a presence through representative offices, which totalled 105 in number at end-June 1984.

55. The reduced interest-rate sensitivity of the demand for money implies that, within the general equilibrium IS/LM paradigm: (i) a given change in the money supply will lead to a larger change in real income and interest rates (i.e. interest rates and nominal income are likely to become more sensitive to disturbances in financial markets); (ii) the effects on economic activity of disturbances in the real sector of the economy (e.g. due to discretionary changes in fiscal policy), for a given money stock, will be reduced.

56. As the Bank of England has pointed out (1983, p. 362), financial innovation may also make interest rates more volatile because it tends to render monetary aggregates less interest-sensitive. The problem has already appeared in the UK and arises because a large part of credit provision occurs on a floating-rate basis (e.g. overdrafts, mortgage loans) with the result that increases in interest rates may have a smaller impact on the demand for credit because the incentive to wait for lower rates is reduced (as the borrower is not locking himself in to fixed rates).

57. The arguments for and against the use of monetary aggregates as intermediate targets of policy were not adequately covered in the Campbell Report. For an overview of the issues involved see Hall, 1983, ch. 4.

58. Benefits, however, result from the floating of the Australian dollar which, making due allowance for short-term 'smoothing' and limited official intervention to 'test' the market, effectively insulates the domestic money stock from capital flows. This removes a major impediment to the

successful conduct of monetary policy since, under the old 'flexible-peg' arrangements, banks short of cash reserves could always obtain them by bidding funds from abroad, occasioning reserve creation on the intervention of the Reserve Bank to stop/slow the appreciation of the Australian dollar. By changing the environment in which liability management takes place the authorities may, however, create transitional problems in the interpretation of financial data as the correlation between M_3 and bank advances may be weakened and the cyclical behaviour of M_3 modified.

59. M_3 is defined as currency in circulation plus total deposits, including CDs, with all trading banks and savings banks.

60. This led the Treasurer at the beginning of 1985 to abandon monetary targets, at least temporarily.

61. M_1 is defined as currency in circulation plus current accounts with all trading banks.

2 The UK Financial System

1. Normally taken to subsume overseas banks, consortium banks and 'other British banks'.

2. This was replaced by the *'monetary sector'* (see *BEQB*, Mar 1983 for the list of institutions covered) in November 1981, which was defined to include all recognised banks and licensed deposit-taking institutions (as defined under the 1979 Banking Act), the National Girobank, the Trustee Savings Banks, the Banking Department of the Bank of England and certain banks in the Channel Islands and the Isle of Man.

    The final revision to official statistics (explained in *BEQB*, Dec 1983, pp. 562–3) occurred in September 1983 when 'British banks' were redefined to comprise a new 'retail banks' group, 'accepting houses', as now, and a residual 'other British' category–*see* Table 2.1.

3. The amount of notes that may be issued is affected by the Currency and Bank Notes Act 1954. According to this Act, the Issue Department can only issue notes to the value of gold held unless the Treasury authorises otherwise. In practice, however, because little gold is held by the Bank, authorisation is automatic, so that fluctuations in the public's demand for notes can always be met, notification being duly given to Parliament.

4. On the mortgage front, many building societies are still using gilt trading profits to cross-subsidise their traditional mortgage lending business, thereby holding down margins, and foreign banks and insurance companies have improved their competitiveness and innovativeness (e.g. the provision of loans at rates linked to movements in LIBOR and 'chain-breaking' mechanisms) as a precursor to raising their own market-share, particularly at the top end of the market. And, in respect of the provision of unsecured loans, the post-flotation TSB and building societies (Johnson, 1986) are likely to prove major competitors.

5. Likely to be carried a stage further in the near future with the offering of share discount broking facilities and the management of 'Personal Equity Plans' (an innovation of the 1986 Budget).

6. The day, 27 October 1986, when fixed commissions are abolished on

share trading in the UK – see Exhibit 2.1 (p. 142–3). Apart from Lloyds, each of the big four clearers have already bought into stockbrokers and stockjobbers in preparation for the event, and all are determined to become gilt and equity market makers.

7. A move induced by the supervisory authorities' actions to raise capital requirements which, unfortunately for the banks, are now spreading to embrace off-balance-sheet activities as well.

8. A phased reduction in first-year capital allowances was announced (they were cut from 100 per cent to 75 per cent in March 1984 and were then to fall to 50 per cent by end-March 1985 and to 25 per cent by end-March 1986) together with a gradual cut in the rate of corporation tax applied to the clearers (it was to fall from 52 per cent in 1984 to 35 per cent by end-March 1986).

9. This will also be the case for finance houses who will further suffer from a slowdown in the demand for consumer credit (due to the 'over-gearing' of borrowers and the diminishing effect of the abolition of hire-purchase terms control in 1982) and fiercer competition for the business from the building societies and the TSB in particular.

10. For example, two of the largest, Kleinwort Benson and Morgan Grenfell, announced increases in pre-tax profits for 1985 of 35 per cent and 40 per cent respectively.

11. Morgan Grenfell, following a merger in 1985 between its property services arm and Michael Laurie & Partners, chartered surveyors and estate agents, is another merchant bank intent on boosting its activities in the mortgage and allied retail financial services field.

12. Allen, Harvey & Ross merged with Cater Ryder to form Cater Allen in 1981; Jessel Toynbee merged with Gillett Brothers in 1982; Clive merged with Page & Gwyther, the discount broker, in 1983 to form Clive Discount.

13. For example, to allow the smaller houses to participate more fully in bill operations with the Bank, where the average size of deals had greatly expanded, to diversify into more capital intensive activities (e.g. acceptance credit business) and to enable them to secure economies of scale (e.g. in computing) and generally reduce overheads.

14. Smith St Aubyn, for example, lost £15 m., three-quarters of its net worth, in 1981 as a result.

15. Under Section 4 (b) a banker was defined as 'any such person carrying on a banking undertaking as may be declared by order of the Treasury to be a banker for the purposes of this section'.

16. The form of this schedule was revised in Schedule 2 of the 1967 Companies Act.

17. The London and Scottish clearing banks, among others, have relinquished exemption so that the status is now principally confined to accepting and discount houses.

18. Exemption prior to 1967 was confined to those banking and discount companies with Schedule 8 exemption under the 1948 Companies Act.

19. The list was effectively closed pending the repeal of the licensing provisions of the Moneylenders Acts and their replacement by provisions incorporated in the 1974 Consumer Credit Act.

20. For example, the criteria used in assessing applications for Section 123 certificates under the 1967 Companies Act were purely functional and did not involve assessment of the quality of business undertaken by the applicant company and so possession of a certificate represented only a very limited 'recognition'.
21. In effect, this meant those DTIs 'authorised' under the 1947 Exchange Control Act and 'recognised' as exempt from the provisions of the 1963 Protection of Depositors Act under Section 127 of the 1967 Companies Act.
22. The ratio of total deposits to capital (adjusted where necessary).
23. The ratio of total deposits to short-term assets.
24. For example, lending ceilings both restricted the growth of balance-sheets and improved the quality of loans by favouring the less-risky borrower, the clearing banks' interest-rate cartel effectively limited the erosion of profit margins, and hire-purchase terms control acted to maintain the cash flow of finance houses and to improve the quality of their loans.
25. The imposition of a minimum reserve-assets ratio on all banks and large finance houses, by ensuring a certain level of holdings of prime liquid assets (Hall, 1983, ch. 2), did, however, perform some prudential function, although one can question its usefulness as a device for ensuring liquidity adequacy because of the rigidity of the requirement, i.e. an average rather than a minimum holding is required for this purpose.
26. Those outside the network of monetary controls had grown in size relative to 'controlled' institutions (primarily the clearing banks) although, to be fair, many of the clearers had established subsidiaries to compete with these institutions in what were termed the 'parallel' money markets.
27. Lending to property companies by 'secondary' banks rose by a factor of six during the period November 1971 to November 1973.
28. Non-bank wholesale depositors channelled the withdrawn funds largely towards the clearers, thereby, on the one hand, limiting the latter's exposure to a liquidity crisis of their own (although, at one stage – December 1974 – the National Westminster Bank found it necessary to deny rumours that they were receiving Bank support under the 'lifeboat') and, on the other, making the clearer's contribution to the 'lifeboat' possible through the recycling of such funds.
29. In June 1984 the Bank announced that discussions, focusing on liquidity, foreign-exchange exposures, asset quality and management information and control systems, with the UK branches of overseas banks (initially the smaller ones) were to be held more frequently than annually and that the information required in their statistical returns was to be extended (e.g. to cover branch profitability, large deposits and exposures) to bring them more into line with the supervisory arrangements covering UK banks. The move was made in the light of the liquidity pressures that some banks of debtor countries were facing and amidst fears that some branches of foreign banks were lending money to their home country to effectively finance balance-of-payments deficits. Closer liaison with the parent bank and the 'parent' regulatory authority was also foreshadowed.

30. The only requirement (Section 40 of the Banking Act) made of overseas deposit-taking institutions establishing a *representative office* in the UK is that the Bank be notified within one month of its establishment. In practice the Bank expects to be consulted in advance of the establishment of a representative office and to be assured that this has been undertaken with the knowledge of the parent supervisory authority. Representative offices are not authorised to accept deposits and are expected to restrict their activities to promoting their banking activities only.
31. Special investigations can, however, be commissioned by the Bank if suspicions have been aroused.
32. In the case of applications from overseas institutions (i.e. branches of foreign banks) the Bank also seeks assurance from the relevant overseas supervisory authority that they are satisfied with the quality of its management and its financial soundness. Additionally, in the case of subsidiaries and consortium banks, letters of comfort, designed to extend shareholder responsibility beyond that arising from their limited-liability status, are sought from any institution (bank or non-bank) or person controlling at least 15 per cent of the voting power of a bank. Similar assurances may be sought from controlling third parties.
33. To qualify as a 'recognised bank' the applicant should have enjoyed a high reputation and standing in the financial community for a certain length of time.
34. Justification for most of the deductions is given in the *BEQB* Sep 1980, p. 327. The exclusion of premises, however, does appear unfairly to penalise those with large investments in premises given that ownership rather than, say, sale-and-lease-back arrangements is likely to strengthen the depositors' position.
35. Obligations in this area are imposed on the UK by the European Communities Consolidated Supervision Directive, adopted by EEC countries in 1983.
36. The capital base comprises: (1) amounts partly or fully-paid up on issued share (ordinary and non-redeemable preference) capital and share premium; (ii) loan capital (up to a third of the total capital base net of outstanding goodwill and subject to straight-line 'amortisation' in the last five years of life) which is fully subordinated to other creditors (including depositors) and which has an initial term to maturity of at least five years and involves no restrictive covenants; (iii) general bad debt provisions, less any associated deferred tax asset; (iv) general reserves (including 'inner' reserves) plus the balance on the profit and loss account; and (v) minority interests, when included in accounts as a result of the consolidation of subsidiary companies not wholly owned.
37. These are now deemed to be more appropriately considered within the risk-asset ratio.
38. To attempt to take account of additional forms of risk would only serve to complicate the calculation without necessarily enhancing the validity of the risk measure.
39. Credit risk is the risk that claims may not be redeemable at their due dates at book values; investment risk is the risk that the market values of marketable claims may fall below book values; and forced-sale risk is the

risk that additional losses will actually be incurred because of the forced sale of assets at prices below book values.

40. The Bank's first paper (March 1980) was widely criticised by the banking community for the rigidity of its proposals and for its failure to recognise the role to be played by liability management in the liquidity management process. The Bank's prime aim was to ensure the liquidity adequacy of the banking system as a whole and, to this end, it proposed an 'integrated test' for all recognised banks and LDTs. The measure was to consist of two parts, one satisfying the need for immediate liquidity (e.g. to meet withdrawals of sight deposits) and the other meeting the liquidity needs arising because of unforeseeable difficulties experienced in the financing of known future commitments. Accordingly, a tentative scale of liquid-asset cover was suggested for both 'gross *maturity-uncertain* liabilities' and the net liability position arising from *maturity-certain* liabilities and assets. For the latter requirement the suggested liquid-asset cover varied according to the maturity band (from 'one to eight days' up to 'over one year') into which the (net) liabilities fell: the nearer to maturity the greater the proportion (which ranged from 90 per cent down to 5 per cent). For maturity-uncertain liabilities a 25 per cent cover was suggested, and 100 per cent cover was demanded against both 'gross market deposits from banks up to one month' and 'irrevocable undrawn standbys given to banks' on the grounds that, in the hands of the counter-party bank, these are treated as ('secondary') liquid assets so that avoidance of 'illusory' growth in the system's liquidity becomes necessary. The coefficients tentatively suggested were based on the assumption of a point of indifference between bank holdings of maturity-uncertain liabilities and maturity-certain liabilities lying somewhere between three and six months. Finally, for the protection of the system as a whole, banks were further required to hold part (40 per cent on average) of their estimated need for liquidity in the form of 'primary' liquidity (mainly cash, bankers' balances at the Bank of England and paper eligible for rediscount at, or as collateral for loans from, the Bank) as distinct from other classes of asset representing 'secondary' liquidity (i.e. near-cash or other readily marketable assets).

Apart from the apparent willingness of the Bank to specify arbitrarily chosen detailed norms in its proposed liquidity measure, the criticisms were mainly concerned with the distortions that would have been created, especially in the interbank and Eurocurrency markets, and the inequities that would have resulted, notably between 'retail' and 'wholesale' (e.g. non-clearing) banks. Concern about the impact on the interbank market was voiced because of the implications of the proposed scale of liquidity cover for different types of activity. For the recommended 100 per cent liquidity cover against interbank deposits up to one month would have, *ceteris paribus*, retarded growth in the interbank market by raising the effective relative cost (e.g. *vis-à-vis* CD issues) of obtaining funds through this medium. Moreover, the differential ratios applied to 'wholesale' business, as between bank and non-bank wholesale, would have undoubtedly caused non-bank deposit business to trade at a premium. Inequities would also have resulted from the lower coverage sought against maturity-uncertain liabilities which would have favoured the 'retail' banks at the expense of the 'wholesale' ('non-deposit') banks. Debate about the likely outcome for the Eurocurrency markets centred on two fronts. First, it was argued that Eurocurrency business would, despite the Bank's efforts to prevent it, move to other, less-regulated, centres as a result of UK banks exploiting, through their overseas branches, any differences in the liquidity requirements levied at home and abroad, and as a result of UK branches of overseas banks losing the privileges (i.e. lax surveillance) previously enjoyed with respect to their sterling business. Second, on a point of equity, it was suggested, again despite reassurance from the Bank, that foreign bank branches in the UK would continue to enjoy a competitive advantage over locally incorporated banks due to the prospect of the Bank failing to ensure equitable treatment between the two groups.

Having digested the weight of criticism of its first proposals the Bank, in a major but unadmitted climbdown, subsequently dropped the suggested liquidity measure, based on the distinction between maturity-certain and maturity-uncertain liabilities, and both the 'primary' and 'secondary' liquidity requirements. The detailed system of liquid-asset cover was also dropped and, instead, the Bank preached the virtues of a case-by-case approach, but with the caveat that 'it believes it possible to achieve a common basis of measurement which may then be applied after due consideration to...' the particular circumstances of each bank (*BEQB*, Mar 1981, p. 41). This materialised in the 1982 paper discussed in the text as a measure incorporating 'a series of accumulating net mismatch positions in successive time bands'. Across-the-board norms were eschewed and the role of liability management in the liquidity management process was formally recognised.

41. Taken to subsume licensed DTIs throughout this section.
42. I.e. 'one which offers security of access to liquidity without undue exposure to suddenly rising costs from liquefying assets or bidding for deposits' (*BEQB*, Sep 1982, p. 399).
43. This, following a separate assessment of the *overall* level of maturity transformation undertaken, eventually leads to the establishment and subsequent monitoring of agreed guidelines.
44. This is superior to the previous system adopted of relating some measure of deposit liabilities to the available stock of a class of assets defined as 'liquid' because it obviates the need to arbitrarily distinguish 'liquid' from 'non-liquid' assets, takes account of modern asset and liability management techniques for controlling liquidity, and avoids the problem of rendering liquid holdings illiquid by requiring observance of a minimum ratio.
45. For commitments which are not due to be met on a particular date, an 'appropriate' proportion, paying due regard to the bank's historical drawn-down experience, of outstanding commitments will be included as a liability in the first maturity band.
46. I.e. the extent to which they can be sold for cash quickly (or used as security for borrowing) at little or no penalty cost.
47. The more marketable the asset the lower the discount.

48. Hitherto the Bank had attempted to ensure that these banks' head offices performed this function.
49. In the first three years of its existence eight cases arose requiring payments to be made by the Board. These concerned depositors with Merbo Finance, First Guarantee Trust Company, Trinity Trust and Savings, Goodwin Squires Securities, Chancellor Finance (UK), St Martin-le-Grand Securities, Castle Court Trust, and Bremar Holdings, Cross & Bevington's Finance and Eastcheap Investments.
50. The Review Committee, in June 1985, proposed that this Treasury power be removed.
51. Otherwise a 'moral hazard' would be created whereby investors had a financial incentive to deposit with the institution offering the highest prospective yield, irrespective of the level of risk incurred by the institution in its business operations.
52. A circular detailing the Bank's view on what constitutes 'adequate' was sent out by the Bank in December 1974 and an extract from this is reproduced in *BEQB*, June 1981, p. 237.
53. The Bank, nevertheless, includes both dealing and structural positions in the aggregate foreign-currency position included in the risk-assets ratio used by the Bank in the assessment of capital adequacy, and expects to be consulted on any part of a position that a bank wishes to be classified as structural.
54. i.e. the difference between assets and liabilities.
55. As defined for the purposes of computing a bank's risk-assets ratio (see p. 90).
56. I.e. the net foreign-currency *liability* position.
57. Measured as the sum of its net short open dealing positions, spot and forward taken together.
58. The limits applied before exchange controls were dismantled in October 1979 are set out in *BEQB*, Dec 1975, pp. 355–6.
59. As for other subject institutions, the returns must provide, in contracted currency amounts, the net spot long or short position and the net forward long or short position in each currency at the close of business on the reporting day. The return should also incorporate a report on each occasion during the reporting period that the agreed guidelines were exceeded.
60. The UK is one of only a few countries to apply specific supervisory requirements to *deposit* concentrations also. The requirement is that individual deposits accounting for 5 per cent or more of the deposit base must be reported, on a quarterly basis, to the Bank.
61. In June 1985 the Review Committee proposed a complementary 25 per cent of capital limit on all individual exposures to non-banks and on loans to groups of 'closely related' borrowers.
62. Country risk is monitored by the Bank on a consolidated, worldwide basis and the creditworthiness of individual debtor countries is also independently assessed. No standardised guidelines are specified, however, the Bank preferring to ensure that adequate internal assessment, control and monitoring systems exist, aiding this process through the dissemination of relevant information (Cooke, 1982, pp. 11–12).

63. In the case of loans to countries engaged in debt-rescheduling the Bank's response has been to engineer a rise in provisions through moral suasion.
64. Citicorp acquired Seccombe, Marshall & Campion.
65. For example, for prudential purposes, the houses were subject to guidelines limiting the size of their total books to thirty times their 'resources' (capital and resources) and the size of their bond books to eight times resources. Additionally, as a means of conserving their capacity to operate in the sterling market, their foreign-currency book was limited to three times resources. Finally, for monetary policy purposes, the houses were subjected to a public-sector debt ratio which later gave way to the 'undefined assets multiple' (Hall, 1983, ch. 2).
66. The only subsequent amendments occurred in November 1984 (see *BEQB*, Dec 1984, pp. 461–2) when the system was extended to cover positions in futures markets and other forms of forward commitment and more favourable treatment was given to certain very short-term and highly liquid assets with a month or less to run until maturity. The alteration in the gradation of risk attaching to short-term paper was consistent with the planned supervisory arrangements for the new gilt-edged market.
67. Comprising: ordinary paid-up share capital; non-redeemable, paid-up preference shares; share premium account; capital and general reserves; profit and loss account; contingency and other reserves; profit/loss in current year to date including unrealised appreciation/depreciation (net of tax payable) in respect of current year. The following items are then deducted: net book value of fixed assets; goodwill; book value of interest in subsidiaries and associated companies; unsecured loans to parent company or fellow subsidiaries.
68. The foreign-currency book multiplier no longer applies, but, because an open foreign-currency position exposes a house to exchange-rate risk, it is incorporated (subject to an added risk weight of 2) within the added risk-class framework.
69. The first $7\frac{1}{2}$ per cent of 'liquid assets' (i.e. any assets other than mortgages and fixed assets) must be held in short-term public-sector securities or on deposit with named banks; the next $7\frac{1}{2}$ per cent may be invested in medium-term public-sector securities; and anything above 15 per cent may be invested in long-term (i.e. up to twenty-five years to maturity) public-sector securities.
70. Societies are also obliged to maintain liquid funds equivalent to at least $7\frac{1}{2}$ per cent of total assets.
71. The functions/powers of the Registrar involve the following. First, although he has no discretion to refuse registration if the conditions specified in the 1962 Act are met (nor to require the winding up of societies, nor to enforce mergers) he does possess the power to stop a society advertising for or taking deposits if he is not satisfied that its business is being conducted along prudent and conventional lines. (The most recent example where this power has been exercised occurred in August 1983, when the Chief Registrar revoked the right of New Cross Building Society to accept public funds, allegedly for exceeding the 'special advances' limit and for 'financial mismanagement'. Second, he

monitors societies through their annual accounts and directors' reports, through a special annual return, through quarterly revenue returns and through monthly cash-flow statements and reports of liquidity positions. The return includes, among other things, details of organisation, rates of interest paid and charged and the type of mortgage business undertaken. The monthly cash-flow statements are not audited and have been submitted on a voluntary basis since 1973. Third, he is responsible for 'designating' societies as suitable for trustee investment, according to the appropriate legislative requirements.

72. This requires, among other things, that its founder members, numbering at least ten, subscribe for shares to the total value of at least £5000 which must be left in the business for at least five years. It also forbids advertising during the first financial year of operation and in the following year.

73. Although work on the present liquidity observation ratio has been suspended.

74. In December 1984 the European Commission submitted proposals for a directive on mortgage credit.

75. Since the 1985 Budget, when the £30 000 limit on individual shareholdings with any one society was removed, investor choice has been widened. However, since then the Chief Registrar has operated guidelines which limit, according to the size of its balance-sheet, the proportion of a society's total share investments that may be held in balances over £250 000.

76. The Spalding Report thought that societies, subject to satisfying certain reserve requirements, should have the right to seek 'recognised bank' or LDT status (as defined under the 1979 Banking Act) or, alternatively, to establish a company through which they can offer 'banking' services. The need for the assumption of 'wide' banking powers has thus been toned down in the BSA's submission, as has the demand for the right to establish a 'banking' subsidiary. (The provision of legal powers, as envisaged by the government, allowing societies to engage in unsecured lending, is now thought to satisfy the 'banking' aspirations of most and in a much more straightforward fashion.)

77. In April 1985 the 'composite tax rate' agreement (whereby 'depositors' are paid interest net of tax levied at a rate just sufficient to yield the same revenue to the Inland Revenue as if depositors had paid tax individually) was extended to banks; societies' profits from trading in gilts have been, since February 1984, treated as trading income (as is the case for the banks) rather than capital gains and thus are taxed at the full 40 per cent (38 per cent for smaller societies) corporation tax rate whereas before they were tax-free if the gilts were held for at least a year and a day; and the corporation tax rate paid by banks is to be progressively reduced to 35 per cent (although leasing privileges are to be phased out at the same time) by end-March 1986.

78. Building societies are classified as mutual bodies as ownership pertains to their customers, both 'depositors' and borrowers, rather than to equity shareholders, as is the case for bodies corporate. As a result of not having to make provision for distributions, however, this allows societies (*ceteris*

paribus) to operate on finer margins than other deposit-taking financial intermediaries.

79. In fact the Anglia Building Society, in conjunction with ICL, launched the first, large cashless shopping experiment in the UK in Northampton in October 1985.

80. A number of links have been established between banks and building societies in attempts to combine the convenience of banking facilities (cheque books, overdrafts, standing orders, direct debits, credit cards, etc.) with the high interest paid by societies for retail savings. The motivation of the bank is normally to extend its penetration of the retail savings market or to increase the usage made of its clearing facilities nationally, while the society is usually seeking to accommodate customer demands for the provision of an extensive range of payments services.

81. In constructing the new supervisory regime the government was keen to ensure that any new services permitted should not prejudice a society's main business and that too rapid a rate of diversification was not allowed to taint the movement's reputation (especially for financial soundness) in the eyes of the general public.

82. As administered under the 1979 Banking Act.

83. The reasons for the secular decline in capital ratios are given on p. 158.

84. *Capital allowances*. The first-year allowances on plant, machinery and assets were cut from 100 to 75 per cent on 14 March 1984, fell to 50 per cent on 31 March 1985 and will become zero on 31 March 1986. An annual allowance of 25 per cent will then apply.
    Corporation tax. The rate was cut from 52 to 50 per cent for 1983/4, to 45 per cent for 1984/5, to 40 per cent for 1985/6 and to 35 per cent for 1986/ 7.

85. Reserve transfers made by Barclays, Lloyds, Midland and National Westminster to cover the enlarged deferred-tax payments were £543 m., £465 m., £230 m. and £570 m. respectively. (The merits of this move, and the subsequent restoration of capital positions, are questioned in Barge, 1985.)

86. This is only to be expected given their exposure to many of the same basic pressures, but differences in profitability and strategy (e.g. in relation to possible expansion in securities business at home and abroad and to investment in new technology) can create disparities. A clear example of this was Midland Bank's reluctance to emulate Barclays's March 1985 rights issue as a means of improving its gearing ratio because of its weak share price (largely resulting from the losses experienced by its American subsidiary Crocker National Bank).

87. Discretion is, however, likely to be exercised for banks playing significant roles in the primary and secondary markets for such securities.

88. A further problem in 1984 was the strength of the US dollar which caused a significant deterioration in capital ratios for those banks with large dollar-denominated asset portfolios.

89. Asset disposal runs the risk of impairing the liquidity and quality of the portfolio.

90. Earlier perpetual FRNs issued in 1984 by National Westminster, Bar-

clays and Standard Chartered (they were termed *junior* subordinated floating-rate loan stocks because they ranked between subordinated debt and equity) were not accepted as primary capital because there were no provisions for treating the issues as equity in the event of the issuing bank experiencing financial difficulties. However, with the apparent softening in the Bank's approach to the classification of FRNs for the purposes of computing primary capital ratios – see the text – the issuing banks now hope to get their earlier issues accepted. (Standard Chartered, in fact, in August 1985 tried to boost its primary capital by offering inducements to investors to swap the existing notes for new ones which incorporate a provision requiring conversion into preference stock should the issuing bank get into financial difficulties.)

91. A definition of capital, comprising the highest quality components, favoured by banking supervisory authorities in the US and adopted by the Bank in 1984. In the UK context it appears to include (no precise definition has yet emerged from the Bank) shareholders' funds plus general reserves plus general provisions against loan losses plus minority interests plus (since May 1985) qualifying FRN issues.

92. The Lloyds issue was followed by similar issues from Midland ($750 m.), National Westminster ($1 b.) and Standard Chartered (£150 m. Euro-sterling bond issue). Midland made a further $500 m. issue in August 1985 on the same terms as its May issue.

93. A statement made by Peter Cooke, Chairman of the *Basle Committee of Supervisors*, in May 1985 (*BEQB*, June 1985, p. 221).

94. Interest payments are tax-deductible but dividend payments are not. Moreover, front-end fees in the bank FRN market have now come down to $\frac{1}{2}$ per cent or so.

95. Even Midland Bank made a dividend payment despite the 40 per cent fall in pre-tax profits (largely caused by Crocker) recorded in 1984. This was due to the adoption of what some regarded as 'creative accounting' (optimistic provisioning on the 'non-Crocker' portion of the balance-sheet and the use of the proceeds from the sale of Crocker's headquarters in San Francisco) to generate a nominal profit.

96. The review was completed in March 1986 ('Off-Balance-Sheet Business of Banks'), but detailed capital requirements for off-balance-sheet activities are not to be promulgated until nearer the end of the year. The review contents itself with identifying and qualifying the risks attaching to off-balance-sheet activities.

97. NIFs and RUFs were first developed in the Euromarkets as techniques for underwriting the short-term security issues of corporate bodies, thereby ensuring the continued availability of short-term money through the medium term (seven to ten years) for corporate borrowers. They represent an attempt to reconcile leaders' preferences for liquidity with borrowers' preferences for medium-term finance. Typically a group of underwriting banks will guarantee the availability of funds for the medium term by agreeing to either purchase any unsold short-term notes issued by the borrower at each roll-over date or to provide a stand-by credit. If the borrower is a bank the paper is normally in the form of a certificate of deposit and for non-bank borrowers, in the form of

promissory notes. A contingent liability is therefore incurred by the underwriting bank as the borrower might, at some stage during the term of the contract, run into financial difficulties and even default.

98. Often banks continue to manage the ceded asset package which may involve them, even if they are immune from direct exposure to future portfolio losses, in incurring continuing contingent exposures. Additionally, asset disposal may adversely affect the quality of the remaining balance-sheet portfolio.

99. The Bank also asks that these facilities be included in borrowers' existing credit limits.

100. The commitment fees are so low because of the intense competition in the market and the underwriting banks' confidence in the soundness of the borrowers. The great attraction of the business to the banks is due to their desire to hold assets in a more liquid form, to allow for increased flexibility in the management of their asset portfolios (as a result of their experience with the rescheduling of international loans) and to boost fee income as a means of improving the return on assets.

101. Since the Bank's warning in April 1985 about the low level of fees, they have been on an upward trend. Moreover, some facilities have since been agreed which contain clauses within the contract allowing the participant bank(s) recovery of any costs incurred as a result of any relevant regulatory changes.

102. In a dealing capacity the advantage of possessing marketable assets has to be offset against the volatility of security prices in reaching a decision, which might necessitate a higher or lower capital requirement than for more 'normal' banking operations.

103. This would require convergence on the definition of 'capital' and hence on the regulators' treatment of inner reserves, subordinated debt (including FRN issues), bad-debt provisions, deferred tax provisions, minority interests, etc. Harmonisation of accounting conventions and fiscal systems would thus be required.

104. Those subject to less-stringent capital controls are able to operate on lower interest margins and hence gain a competitive edge over other banks. This may then create pressures for a further decline in capital ratios as banks subject to stricter regulation press their supervisors to relax controls to allow them to compete more effectively with those subject to less-stringent regulation. This may be conceded in order to retain a healthy market-share at 'home'.

105. By, for example, ensuring that all supervisory authorities adopt the consolidation principle, and so remove the incentive for business to gravitate to areas of perceived supervisory 'laxity', and the (revised) guidelines of the Basle 'Concordat' governing the division of supervisory responsibilities between parent and host supervisor.

106. An inadequate supply of 'liquid' assets, even if unintended, will restrain balance-sheet growth as effectively as any monetary control device.

107. Costs arising from delays in restoring the liquidity of deposits in the event of a financial collapse or assisted merger can be substantial.

108. Which may tempt the authorities to extract some form of 'payment', additional to complying with any reporting or other supervisory re-

quirements, through moral suasion in order to restore competitive equity *vis-à-vis* non-bank deposit-taking intermediaries.

109. A further moral hazard is created if the premium payable by an institution is not related to the level of risk incurred through its business operations because, once again, certain institutions might be encouraged to take more risks in the knowledge that the consequences of a disastrous outcome will be shared by all. (To a degree, however, this is mitigated by management fears of the likelihood of adverse shareholder/supervisor reaction.)

110. As the success of the scheme depends on the strength of the contributing members (assuming the schemes are industry-run), deposit insurance cannot be used in isolation from other supervisory techniques to guarantee the nominal value of deposits. In this sense deposit insurance imposes an additional burden on subject institutions unless measures are taken to reduce the supervisory effort elsewhere. For example, the existence of deposit insurance may obviate, to a large degree, the need for official lifeboats.

111. This overlooks, of course, the externalities of Bank failure and the fact that (witness the problems experienced by National Westminster during the fringe banking crisis of 1974-5) *all* banks mutually depend upon confidence prevailing in the banking system. Moreover, to the extent that competition is affected, it can be argued that the result was merely to redress the previous balance which favoured the clearers, privileged by the market's perception of the existence of a stronger implicit government guarantee of their deposits than was the case for those of other banks.

112. On depositor protection grounds it is not clear why only sterling deposits were covered by the scheme.

113. The limits applied before the abolition of exchange controls in October 1979 were designed to protect UK reserves rather than the banks.

114. The Bank's approach to the international debt crisis has been to exhort (and coerce where necessary) banks to maintain, at least in the short run, their inter-bank lines to countries involved in rescheduling, so as not to risk precipitating the feared loan defaults or moratoriums, while, at the same time, encouraging them to boost bad-debt provisions (even at the expense of dividend distribution) and their capital bases more generally. Presumably, given the length of time it would take to completely 'write off' doubtful sovereign loans (for both Lloyds and Midland, for example, exposure to Latin America alone is considerably greater than their capital base), the authorities are looking to a non-inflationary upturn in the world economy (despite the apparent downturn in the US economy), a fall in the US dollar and a fall in interest rates to alleviate the debtors' problems. In the longer term some switch in the financing of deficits to official agencies (e.g. the IMF and the World Bank) is favoured. Others, however, are less sanguine about the success to be reaped from *ad hoc* rescheduling and IMF-imposed adjustment, and urge more radical solutions. Ideas on this front embrace increased co-financing between commercial banks and official agencies (Cook, 1983), the establishment of an international deposit insurance scheme, a supra-

national lender of last resort and a private safety-net (Dale, 1982), the provision of a facility for discounting problem loans and improved collection, analysis and dissemination of relevant information (e.g. through the Institute of International Finance and the Ditchley Institute).

115. In the event the Bank decided in May 1985 that provisions of £245 m. were necessary to cover the losses incurred. This resulted in the Bank and the other participants to the 'lifeboat' contributing half of the shortfall each. With the capital reserves and bad-debt provisions of JMB standing at £130 m. at end-September 1984, and taking into account the parent company's contribution of £50 m., this amounted to a sum of £32.5 m. each. Although the scale of the provisions is thought adequate, this will remain subject to review on a quarterly basis until March 1986 when the indemnity agreement signed by the banks in March 1985 is due to expire.

116. JMB is a member of a group of five big gold bullion dealers which jointly 'fix' the price of gold twice-daily in London.

117. The Bank's contribution, if called upon, will come from the Banking Department's reserve which led the government to claim that taxpayers' money was not involved (see also *BEQB*, Dec 1984, p. 473). However, a fall in reserves might necessitate an increase in the tax on banks (i.e. through an increase in the $\frac{1}{2}$ per cent of eligible liabilities, non-operational cash requirement), which is likely to be borne by shareholders and consumers of financial services alike, and lower banking profits by the Banking Department will result in a reduced contribution to the Exchequer, which may subsequently affect Budget planning.

118. In May 1985 this was converted into capital in the shape of £50 m. ordinary shares, £25 m. redeemable shares and £25 m. subordinated loan stock dated 1995. The capital is to be recovered if and when JMB is returned to the private sector, which is expected to be in 1986.

119. i.e. one for which the net present value of the discounted future cash flow proves negative.

120. It was rejected on the grounds that the Bank *might* not have been able to contain the likely ensuing confidence crisis and also because the provision of the necessary liquidity in the form of gold would have necessitated recourse by the Bank to the government-owned gold reserves held in the Exchange Equalisation Account or to government guarantees for the borrowing of gold from other sources. Although ruled out on the grounds of impracticability, given the short time available within which a decision had to be taken, it is not obvious why this type of liquidity provision should have posed such an insuperable problem.

121. Some evidence to support this view had apparently been gleaned on 1 October, even before JMB's problems had been announced, when banks in the Far East were said to be refusing to deal with first-class British banks, some of which did not operate in the bullion market.

122. A problem that would have been compounded by the loss of confidence felt by foreign governments and central banks responsible for large gold deposits in the London market. (Similar 'sensitive external ramifications' had weighed heavily in earlier decisions made by the Bank to

acquire Slater Walker Ltd and Edward Bates & Sons Ltd – *BEQB*, June 1978, pp. 235–8.)

123. An added attraction of Johnson Matthey Bankers to foreigners is its refining capacity and, of the 'Gold Ring' members, JMB is unique in operating such a process.

124. Although not specifically mentioned in the Bank's report on the JMB affair, it is conceivable that it was seriously concerned about the possible impact of JMB's collapse on Midland Bank, because of its equity links (then 60 per cent) with Samuel Montagu, another operator in the London bullion market. Problems on this score would have compounded Midland's difficulties in handling the losses incurred by its American subsidiary Crocker National Bank.

125. The approach adopted by the 'Control Committee' of the Bank of England and the English and Scottish clearing banks during the fringe banking crisis was set out in the *BEQB*, June 1978, pp. 233–9. Before agreeing to provide the support the Committee required to be satisfied that: (i) the company seeking support was currently trading solvently and, on the basis of best estimates possible at that time, was likely to remain solvent provided it received liquidity support; (ii) the company exhibited sufficient banking characteristics to justify support and had attracted a significant level of deposits from the public; (iii) the company did not possess any institutional shareholders whose interest in the company was such that they might properly be expected to provide the necessary support. Where other financial institutions were involved, either as significant shareholders or as large depositors, they would be pressed to contribute by increasing their lending or, at the very least, not withdrawing their deposits. A margin over LIBOR ($1\frac{1}{2}$ per cent–2 per cent) was generally charged, according to the perception of risk involved, although account was taken of the need not to prejudice the chance of the supported company severing its dependence on support funds and re-establishing its position in the market. Security, when available, was taken when deemed appropriate.

126. Although Johnson Matthey plc was capitalised at £126 m. at the close of business on 12 July 1985, following publication of pre-tax profits for the 1984/5 financial year of £20.1 m. (after allowing for extraordinary losses – the £50 m. once-and-for-all payment towards the rescue of JMB and £102 m. consolidated net assets of JMB written off in March 1985 – of £152 m.), this relatively healthy state of affairs does not indicate the pressures faced back in October 1984. For, at that time, given its exceedingly large level of market borrowings, Johnson Matthey was unable to raise even the £50 m. demanded by the Bank without the help of Charter Consolidated.

127. Although this is precisely why the fine detail relating to the nature of likely Bank support available to financial institutions experiencing financial difficulties is not publicly disclosed (Wallich, 1977, p. 95, and McMahon, 1977, p. 108), allowing market operators to form judgements on the basis of recent historical experience is unlikely to secure a more desirable outcome.

128. In seeking to reassure the market that the JMB rescue was exceptional,

the Chancellor proclaimed that 'If you are under any impression that any bank which gets into difficulties will automatically be rescued, this is certainly not the case. The banking community should be well aware of that.' (House of Commons, 20 June 1985.) In a similar vein the Bank asserted that 'there should be no presumption that the failure of any bank would be thought to carry such risk for the system that it would be rescued' (Bank of England, 1985, p. 38).

129. Judging by experience, the Bank is also most reticent about applying the *caveat emptor* principle to 'large' depositors, especially if they are foreign.

130. Subsidiary issues relate to the competence of senior Bank supervisory staff (JMB was allowed to produce its March 1984 quarterly return, due in April, in June 1984 and then to postpone a meeting between its directors and the Bank, planned for July, until August), the adequacy of existing supervisory staff numbers and their training (the Bank admitted that JMB's regular returns did contain some clues to the developing crisis which might have been picked up earlier, e.g. the rapid growth of the commercial loan book, the large and growing exposures to less than first-class names and a declining risk-assets ratio), and the adequacy of existing links (the chain of command runs from the Cabinet to the Treasury to the Bank, but the Bank retains a large measure of independence) between the Bank and the Treasury – clear demarcation of responsibilities in the JMB case would have been beneficial.

131. Although the finance houses, the major group of LDTs, have always insisted that they suffer from the public's perception, despite the Bank's repeated assertion that the distinction in status with a recognised bank need not imply a distinction in creditworthiness or financial standing, that recognised banks have a stronger implicit government guarantee of support than LDTs. This, they argue, requires payment of a premium for deposits of a given term.

132. '... the controls and systems were inadequate; ... the organisation and management of the commercial banking and credit monitoring activities had serious shortcomings; ... insufficient attention had been given to the concentration of risks involved. Security was not required from borrowers ... and even when security was required the steps necessary to give the bank title to the security were not always taken properly. The need for provisions against bad and doubtful debts was not assessed with the proper degree of caution and the judgement of management in approving so many loans which have required substantial provisions was clearly defective.' (Bank of England, 1985, pp. 34–5).

133. The Bank expects to be notified of any single non-bank exposure amounting to over 10 per cent of a bank's capital and, depending on factors such as the standing of the borrower, the nature of the bank's relationship with the borrower, the nature and extent of security taken and the bank's expertise in the area of lending undertaken, will specify an appropriate additional capital cover. Breaches of the guideline are, however, commonplace and the Bank condones this on the grounds that a 'rule' would be too constricting.

134. Complicating factors in JMB's case were the non-reporting of certain

large exposures and the persistent understatement of the size of the two largest exposures. In its 1985 Annual Report the Bank claims that the reported figures for these two exposures at end-June 1983 were 15 per cent and 12 per cent of capital compared to the 'true' figures of 26 per cent and 17 per cent respectively, and at end-June 1984 were 38 per cent and 34 per cent compared to the 'true' figures of 76 per cent and 39 per cent respectively.

135. Leaving aside the JMB case, Financial Intelligence and Research (1984) found that one in five LDTs had not filed accounts for more than two years despite the Companies Act requirement that reports be filed within seven to ten months (depending upon the kind of business undertaken) of the end of the financial year. This is even more disturbing in the light of the additional requirement to report to the Bank within six months of the end of the financial year.

136. Both the Bank and Johnson Matthey plc are suing JMB's auditors, Arthur Young, for substantial damages arising from their alleged negligence.

137. A move towards supervision *by function* rather than by type of institution faces the same difficulty.

138. This is to include measures to ensure that statistical returns are lodged with the Bank on the due dates. The Committee suggests that late submissions prompt immediate action from the Bank in the form of a visitation and, perhaps, an inspection of the books.

139. The Bank of England issued two consultative documents on proposals to reform banking supervision on 19 July 1985. The recommendations included: abolition of the two-tier authorisation system for deposit-takers, with the minimum net-asset requirement raised from £250 000 to £1 m.; limiting large exposures to single non-bank or 'closely related' groups of borrowers to 25 per cent of capital (in addition, all exposures to non-banks of over 10 per cent are to be reported); broadening the powers of the Bank to obtain and disseminate information; limited independent checking (e.g. by the banks' auditors) of prudential information; amendments to the Deposit Protection Scheme involving an increase in the level of protection offered, an increase in the minimum level of contribution, and removal of the Treasury's power to exempt overseas institutions under certain circumstances. A further consultative document, dealing with proposals to introduce a line of communication (seven types of 'dialogue' were distinguished) between the Bank and auditors, was published in August 1985. It considered various ways in which supervisors could obtain information directly from auditors without undermining the latter group's primary duty to their bank clients. To preserve this relationship the Bank suggests that a legal duty might be imposed on individual banks to require their auditors to exchange relevant information with the supervisors, but occasions might still demand an exchange of information over the heads of the banks. Auditors will likely be asked to submit, annually, a report (distinct from the management letter given their clients) and will also be required to audit the banks' quarterly returns made to the Bank at the latter's request. Finally, it was proposed that the UK branches of overseas

banks should employ a UK-based accountancy firm to audit their quarterly returns made to the Bank and to check the adequacy of their control systems. (Most of these proposals were confirmed with the publication of the 'Banking Supervision' White Paper in December 1985, the government making it clear that it would legislate if non-statutory guidelines on supervisor/auditor dialogue could not be made to work satisfactorily.)

140. One could do worse than adopt the Campbell Committee's (Campbell Report, Canberra, Australia, 1981) preferred functional approach to prudential supervision in Australia which embodies the following guiding principles: (i) financial institutions should be allowed to fail; (ii) a liquidity safety-valve should be available to financial intermediaries; (iii) investors should receive reasonable protection against fraud and mal-practice; (iv) there should be a 'fair' and well-informed market in securities, the government's role being to ensure disclosure of relevant information; (v) entry requirements should be concerned solely with the issue of depositor protection; (vi) requirements should be applied in a flexible manner, leaving intermediaries with maximum freedom to adjust to changing circumstances, and should aim at ensuring competi-tive neutrality among intermediaries; (vii) regulations should not impair the provision of a reasonably full spectrum of risk/return investment opportunities, including a 'safe haven' for the small, unsophisticated investor.

141. This is in spite of the large-scale equity withdrawal (*BEQB*, Sep 1982 (a)) that occurs, allowing for the diversion of housing loans to other areas of consumption.

142. I.e. a desire to ensure that fiscal provisions and regulations cause minimal disturbance to the competitive balance existing between groups of deposit-taking intermediaries. The restrictions to be imposed on asset portfolio composition and on access to the wholesale market (where funds can frequently be borrowed more cheaply) must lead to a questioning of the government's resolve on this issue.

143. Despite the Bank's desire to see some auditing of banks' prudential returns the Registry does not perceive this to be necessary for building societies. (In a consultative document issued on 20 August the Registry did propose, however, that auditors submit a confidential annual report covering compliance with the law in respect of the effectiveness of its controls over its staff, assets and liabilities, and in the quality and accuracy of information about its business. Additionally the auditors must disclose exclusively to the Registrar whether all the details of the annual accounts accord with the records and are to be empowered to converse with the Registrar without seeking the society's permission.)

144. Although the Registrar revoked New Cross's right to accept deposits from the public in August 1983, for alleged 'financial mismanagement' and breaches of the 'special advances' limit, an ensuing secret legal battle delayed its ultimate closure (its interests were eventually acquired by the Woolwich) until January 1984. The event illustrated the Regis-trar's inability to protect *existing* depositors (from illiquidity) as they had to wait until March 1984 before they could withdraw their funds.

145. Additional proposals concern the protection of newly formed companies from predators during the first five years of corporate life and limitation of abuse in the distribution of accumulated reserves (or, more precisely, the associated benefits).
146. In his report for 1983 and 1984 (published in October 1985) he criticised the fall in societies' additions to reserves from 0.88 to 0.66 per cent of average total assets in 1984 and maintained that their reserves, averaging 4 per cent of total assets, would not be sufficient to allow them to undertake the new activities to be sanctioned.
147. For example, in the handling of financial futures and risk more generally.
148. Currently (the largest) societies are able, subject to discussions with the Chief Registrar, to tap the wholesale market through issues of sterling CDs, Eurosterling floating-rate notes, yearling bonds and index-linked stock and through the taking of time deposits and syndicated loans. For both CDs and time deposits the maximum term to maturity allowed is one year. Interest-rate 'swaps' are also sanctioned. Under the new Act societies are to be allowed to raise up to 20 per cent of their funds from the wholesale markets, although the Commission has the discretion to vary this, subject to a ceiling of 40 per cent.

Appendix   The Prudential Regulation of Deposit-taking Financial Intermediaries: An Overview

1. I.e. the extent to which savings gravitate towards outlets offering the highest risk-adjusted rates of return.
2. E.g. with respect to official requests for statistical returns and the general provision of information and the 'costs' (which ultimately may be borne by borrower and/or lender) associated with compliance with prescribed balance-sheet ratios and authorised business behaviour.
3. The regulatory authorities are occasionally faced with the dilemma of whether or not to support 'non-viable' intermediaries in the interests of preserving the stability of the financial system as a whole. (This also gives rise to an issue of *moral hazard* – see pp. 162).
4. I.e. the extent to which costs are minimised for a given level of service provision.
5. For a discussion of the causes and possible solutions to the international debt 'crisis' see Black and Dorrance, 1984.
6. The issue normally narrows to one of weighing up the advantages, in terms of flexibility, low administration costs and minimal interference with standard business practice, of self-regulation against the doubts over effectiveness that non-statutory regulation undoubtedly encourages.
7. Discussions on this point usually focus on the need to preserve as far as possible *competitive neutrality* within the financial system, a requirement that sorely taxes regulatory authorities across the globe.
8. For further discussion of some of the issues involved see the Gower Report (*Review of Investor Protection*) (1984) and the Wilson Report (*Report of the Committee to Review the Functioning of Financial Institutions*, Cmnd 7937, HMSO, 1980) ch. 21.

9. Minimal requirements should perhaps cover capital adequacy and managerial competence, but the list often extends to embrace criteria of 'economic necessity', adequacy of existing service provision, etc. With respect to foreign bank entry the principle of reciprocity is also frequently applied.
10. Some host authorities demand 'letters of comfort' from parents even though the legal force they carry is often of minimal value.
11. Apart from depositor protection, capital is also concerned with the provision of the basic structural foundations of the enterprise and the maintenance of confidence in the soundness of the intermediary.
12. For a good non-mathematical discussion of risk analysis see Revell, 1975, chs 7 and 8.
13. The requirement of the authorities to specify what constitutes a 'disaster' situation also entails their deciding at what level of disaster they will intervene to support the system in order to preserve overall financial stability.
14. The Bank of England's line was modified as recently as May 1984 (as outlined in a letter sent to the British Bankers Association) when it was decided to exclude bank holdings of loan capital from the capital figures used for monitoring purposes by the Bank. The intention was to allay fears that bank purchases of each other's loan capital were masking the need for further improvements in capital ratios as contributions made by retained profits fell due to the erosion of profit margins on international lending and to heavy general provisions for bad and doubtful debts, especially with respect to foreign loans. The move reflects concern that subordinated debt is not permanently available to cushion losses, is subject to interest and redemption payments and can only be used to absorb banks' losses in the event of liquidation.
15. There are strong arguments for confining the list to only those acceptable as collateral for loans from or eligible for rediscount to the central bank in recognition of the fact that only these assets represent liquidity for the system as a whole under all prospective conditions.
16. Whereas specification in the form of a minimum is likely to facilitate the operation of the control system it fails (like all simple ratios) to take account of the maturity structure of balance-sheets or differences in asset marketability. Moreover, those assets held to meet the prescribed minimum can no longer perform a liquidity function by definition! A system employing averages would overcome the last problem, but at the cost of loss of predictability of liquid holdings.
17. Some supervisors insist on the provision of cash-flow forecasts to gain an insight into immediate future management plans.
18. This raises a further problem, however, as volatility in the flow of funds to the wholesale money markets (for example in the international interbank market during 1982/4, in the US wholesale market in May 1984 following the Continental Illinois scare and in the UK during the 1974/5 fringe banking crisis) can cause unexpected funding difficulties even for soundly managed enterprises. What then constitutes a 'prudent' level of liquidity in this form?
19. Although more common as a monetary control device, interest-rate

controls (normally ceilings) are sometimes justified on the grounds of consumer protection, in the spirit of anti-usury laws, or as a requirement for financial stability, as unfettered competition is assumed to manifest itself in volatile interest rates, more risk-taking and hence industry instability.

20. Disclosure requirements for deposit-taking financial intermediaries vary between countries and even within countries between types of institution (e.g. the UK). While full disclosure of 'true' profits, capital reserves and provisions might be welcomed by shareholders, present and prospective, institutions are sometimes excused in the belief that it might lead to unnecessary speculation and hence financial instability. Why this should not occur when information is deliberately withheld and investors have only rumour and guesswork to act on is not at all clear however.

21. For example, large loans, property investment or loans secured on property-related collateral, loans granted for the purpose of speculation, loans to (investments in) related companies, net foreign-exchange exposure and loans denominated by industry and country borrower.

22. Although the spirit of the controls can often be avoided when separate limits apply to foreign governments, their agencies and instrumentalities.

23. The application of the principle of *caveat emptor* to the more wealthy is usually endorsed on the grounds that relatively rich depositors are better placed to assess investment risks.

24. If complete protection is granted up to this ceiling a *moral hazard* issue arises in the shape of the encouragement given to (small) depositors to ignore risk assessment in the distribution of their wealth between deposit-takers.

25. Flat-rate contributions as a percentage of deposits are the norm, but, occasionally, positive discrimination in favour of the large banks occurs on the assumption that they are the least likely to become susceptible to loss of confidence (although the Continental Illinois scare in May 1984 would point to the fallacy of this argument).

26. Where no central bank exists (e.g. Hong Kong) support operations are normally mounted, with or without official encouragement, by the largest commercial banks.

27. Monetary policy objectives are likely to become subordinated to prudential concerns in such circumstances, e.g. target 'overshooting' in monetary growth may have to be tolerated, at least in the short run, though this need not herald the initiation of future inflationary pressures as it is mainly satisfying the public's increased desire for liquidity.

28. For this very reason fine detail about the nature of the likely (including assisted mergers and caretaker management) support facilities available is not disclosed (Wallich, 1977, p. 95; McMahon, 1977, p. 108).

29. This is because, rationally or otherwise, access to last-resort facilities will be seen by the public as conferring a higher degree of official protection on those lucky enough to come under the umbrella, thereby imposing a competitive disadvantage on those not so favourably treated.

30. In *Canada* concerns relating to loans to Dome Petroleum (an enterprise experiencing difficulty in the energy sector) forced the Bank of Scotia, the world's fiftieth-largest bank on some measures, to proclaim that 'any

concerns about the bank's stability and financial strength are unfounded'. Similar reassuring statements issued on behalf of the *US* bank (the eighth-largest), the Continental Illinois Bank of Chicago, proved to be more hollow, however. Difficulties at the Continental Illinois had first surfaced in July 1982 following the collapse of Penn Square Bank with whom it was heavily involved in syndicated oil and gas loans. After making provisions of $220 m. for doubtful loans acquired through Oklahoma City Bank a loss of $60.9 m. was reported for the second quarter of 1982, the biggest quarterly loss ever made by an American bank. Further losses incurred on energy and industrial loans, together with an inability to make adequate provision against foreign loans, culminated in the $7.2 b. 'lifeboat' operation launched in May 1984. The Continental Illinois was not the only US bank to be hit by domestic difficulties. Crocker National Bank (owned by Midland Bank, UK) reported substantial losses in 1983/4 (largely due to non-performing domestic property loans, but sufficient to cause the comptroller of the currency in March 1984 formally to seek details on how management planned to resolve the bank's problems), as did Chase Manhattan of New York in the second quarter of 1982 following the collapse of the securities dealer Drysdale Government Securities. Finally, in *West Germany*, problems were experienced by banks heavily involved in lending to the ailing electrical goods manufacturer AEG–Telefunken and other industrial giants. The most notable casualty was Schroeder Muenchmeyer Hengst, which was rescued by a group of banks having made, through various offshoots, loans totalling DM800 m. to the troubled IBH group. Each of these examples suggests that banks' internal control procedures were incapable of ensuring an adequate degree of diversification within domestic loan portfolios.

31. Bankhaus I. D. Herstatt closed its doors on 26 June 1974 following the incurring of large losses on foreign-exchange speculation (especially in the forward market). Its closure resulted in a virtual standstill in foreign-exchange trading in the preceding few days due to the uncertainty created by the Bundesbank's handling of the affair. At the centre of the controversy was the Bundesbank's decision to close Herstatt during banking hours yet allow inter-bank clearings on behalf of Herstatt to proceed at the Frankfurt clearing centre resulting, owing to time differentials between continents, in settlement being only half-completed. The losers were mainly US institutions, but the danger was there for all to see – time-zone differences threatened same-day settlement. The reaction of the New York banks involved was to invoke their rights to recall, within one day, payments made through the system (the facility was designed to cover banks against the risk of their customers failing to deliver covering funds for payments made on their behalf that day). This only served to heighten uncertainty as such 'recall' action was interpreted by European banks as reneging on contractual commitments.

    The immediate outcome of the affair was a dramatic decline in foreign exchange and Eurocurrency (the need for a formal lender of last resort was called into question) trading, inter-bank depositors becoming more selective creating interest-rate 'tiering' on the market, inter-bank rede-

positing was curtailed and authorities in several countries raised reporting requirements. For example, German banks were required to submit
monthly reports on forward-exchange positions and proposals were
made to limit net open spot and forward positions to 20 per cent of their
nominal capital plus visible reserves. Spain, Switzerland, and Canada
also intensified their monitoring of foreign-exchange positions (the USA
had done so in 1973) and the Bank of England announced its intention of
extending the information requirements made on all banks operating in
London.

32. The Luxembourg-based Banco Ambrosiano Holdings (BAH), 68 per cent
of which was owned by the Italian bank Banco Ambrosiano, was
declared in default in July 1982 following legal proceedings enacted by
foreign bank creditors. The background to the problem lay in the loans
(up to $400 m.) made in 1980 by Banco Ambrosiano's Latin-American
subsidiaries (financed by BAH and other Ambrosiano companies) to a
number of Panamanian companies said to be controlled by the Vatican's
bank, Instituto per le Opere di Religione (IOR). The last mentioned was
also said to have guaranteed the loans. What the Panamanian companies
did with the loans is unclear, but it is alleged that they were used to buy
shares in BAH.

Following the formal announcement of default the assets of BAH were
frozen by Luxembourg courts (until 30 September 1982). Creditor banks,
believing BAH to be under the control of its Milan parent, hoped for
restitution either directly from the parent or indirectly through the Bank
of Italy. They were to be disappointed, for despite organising a support
operation for the parent, to stop a run on its deposits, in violation of the
spirit of the central bankers' gentleman's agreement on supervisory co-
operation BAH was ignored and the IOR, having issued 'letters of
comfort', was held morally responsible. Likewise, the Banking Commissioner in Luxembourg disclaimed responsibility on the grounds that BAH
did not take deposits from the public and therefore was not a bank!
Inactivity on behalf of the Luxembourg and Italian authorities and
intransigence by the Vatican led to a liquidity crisis, as no authority was
willing to assume a 'lender-of-last-resort' role. (Architects of the 'Basle
Concordat' deflected criticism also by pointing out that last-resort
lending issues were explicitly excluded from consideration in the document.)

The affair was resolved in May 1984, when the IOR agreed to pay
creditors of BAH $244 m. (60 per cent of the overall settlement on a claim
of $600 m.) in recognition of moral involvement and in return for
indemnification from further claims. The Nuovo Banco Ambrosiano
succeeded the 'old' Banco Ambrosiano on the liquidation of the latter.

33. In a Group of Thirty publication (*How Bankers see the World Financial
Market*, New York, May 1982), North American banks in particular felt
they suffered a competitive disadvantage as a result of relatively onerous
domestic requirements on permissible business activities, lending limits
and capital adequacy. The majority of both North American and
European banks surveyed called for greater harmonisation of regulatory
requirements generally.

34. For an illuminating discussion of the nature of the crisis, its causes and resolution see *The Secondary Banking Crisis, 1973–5* by Margaret Reid (Macmillan, 1982).
35. West Germany, Italy and Spain have been the most remiss in this respect.
36. Dale (op. cit. Group of Thirty, 1982) is also critical of the lack of guidelines relating to the monitoring and regulation of liquidity in the Eurocurrency markets.
37. Although the legal distinction between a subsidiary and a branch is clear (the subsidiary alone is a separate legal entity) the demands of some national and state supervisors have confused the picture. For example, New York state insists that foreign *branches* operating there must act as separate entities from their parents and that, in the event of liquidation, New York creditors are paid before the parent bank.
38. For example, the Banco Ambrosiano affair is sometimes raised as evidence to support the contention that supervisory authorities (in this case in Luxembourg and Italy) will subordinate the spirit if not the letter of the *concordat* to the demands of political expediency, with little regard for the international ramifications.
39. The *Basle Committee* has endorsed the following general principles in relation to the supervisory constraints imposed by bank secrecy provisions:
    (i) it is desirable that parent banks be permitted to have access to all necessary information about the operations of their foreign branches and subsidiaries;
    (ii) the law in the parent country should fully protect the confidentiality of such information as is passed to the parent authority and should limit its use to supervisory purposes;
    (iii) host and parent authorities should ensure that, subject to reciprocity and appropriate confidentiality, exchanges of information should not be hampered by banking secrecy regulations;
    (iv) information which parent authorities receive about their banks' foreign establishments should be open to verification in some way (in February 1984 a statement was issued by the International Federation of Accountants, in the joint names of itself and the Basle Supervisors Committee, which outlined the procedures to be used by banks' internal and external auditors in obtaining independent confirmation of financial and business relationships with other banks).
40. This reflects the supervisors' desire to reverse the trend of banks gravitating to the areas of supervisory laxity, a result also achieved through the adoption of the principle of consolidated supervision.
41. As occurred in 1979 when the US Federal Reserve formulated (though never implemented) proposals for imposing extensive reporting requirements on the US offices of certain foreign banks.
42. Where a bank is the parent company of a group containing intermediate holding companies the parent authority should either ensure that such holding companies and their subsidiaries are adequately supervised or, alternatively, prohibit the formation of such intermediate holding companies.

43. Parental supervision on a consolidated basis is necessary because the operations of foreign establishments may directly affect the solvency of parent banks which in any case have a moral commitment to their subsidiaries.

44. The defect in the 1975 *concordat* became apparent once agreement had been reached between central bank governors in 1978 that parent authorities should supervise banks on a consolidated basis. The danger was that host authorities would rely too heavily on the consolidated supervision of the parent in their supervision of locally incorporated subsidiaries of foreign banks.

45. Legally independent institutions incorporated in the country where their principal operations are performed and controlled by two or more parent institutions which are usually foreign though not necessarily banks. Typically ownership is held by a group of minority shareholders, although *effective* control may be exercised by one parent.

46. With respect to branches, parent authorities have due cause for concern since the branch's liquidity is frequently controlled by the parent, while in the case of subsidiaries and joint ventures account needs to be taken of any standby or other facilities granted or commitments entered into, e.g. through the provision of 'letters of comfort'.

47. The Committee consists of not more than three representatives from each member state and from the Commission and usually meets twice a year in Brussels. It came into operation in 1979 and, with technical assistance from the *Contact Group* when necessary, determines, along with the Commission, general policy guidelines relating to supervisory co-ordination.

48. 'Authorisation procedures for a credit institution should allow banks access to the entire common market, necessitating either the harmonisation of licensing conditions throughout the community or mutual recognition of national authorisation procedures; secondly, if branches are to be exempted from local supervision rules such as solvency requirements through the principle of home country rule, control and supervision techniques must be coordinated so as to avoid distortions of competition.'

49. Controversial issues tackled were whether banks should be allowed to maintain 'hidden reserves' (a maximum of 5 per cent of loans and advances was suggested), the imposition of a requirement for the production of consolidated accounts by banking groups and abolition of the requirement to produce branch accounts for community banks.

50. The directive establishes the principle that the home country authorities of banking groups must receive relevant information on the activities of all affiliates with a view to consolidating and centralising supervision. This requirement is additional to the controls exercised by host country authorities over each local affiliate.

References

1 The Australian Financial System

AGPS, *Australian Financial System: Final Report of the Committee of Enquiry* (The Campbell Report) (Canberra, Australian Government Publishing Service, 1981).

—— *Australian Financial System: Report of the Review Group* (The Martin Report) (Canberra, Australian Government Publishing Service, 1984).

BEQB, *The Nature and Implications of Financial Innovation*, Sep 1983.

BILSON, J. F. O., 'Australian Financial Reform: Implications and Alternatives', ch. 3 in *A New Financial Revolution* (Centre for Independent Studies, 1982).

'Campbell Symposium', *The Australian Economic Review* (Institute of Applied Economics and Social Research, University of Melbourne, 1st Quarter, 1982).

'The Campbell Report', papers presented to a Conference on the Campbell Report, *Economic Papers* (special edition) (The Economic Society of Australia, Apr 1983).

COHEN, A. M., 'Exchange Control and the Campbell Report', *Economic Papers*, special edition on 'The Campbell Report', Apr 1983.

CORRIGAN, C. D., 'What Happens to Merchant Banks?', paper delivered at the *Rydges Conference* on 'The Implications of the Campbell Report', 1982.

DAVIS, K., 'Regulation, Retail Financing and Credit Unions', *Bulletin of Money, Banking and Finance*, 1984/5, No. 3, Macquarie University, 1985.

—— and LEWIS, M., 'Monetary Tactics and Monetary Targets: A Guide to Post-Campbell Monetary Policy', *Economic Papers* (The Campbell Report), Apr 1983.

DAVIS, K. T., 'Reserve Requirement Changes as a Monetary Instrument', *Economics Department Working Paper No. 81–10*, University of Adelaide, 1981.

——'Financial Regulation in Australia', paper presented to the *13th Conference of Economists*, Perth, Australia, Aug 1984.

DONNELLY, M., *Deregulation: What it Is – What it Means for Building Societies*, Permanent Building Societies Association (NSW) Ltd, Sep 1984.

FRENKEL, J. A., 'The Collapse of Purchasing Power Parities during the 1970s', *European Economic Review*, **16,** pp. 145–65, Feb 1981.

GLOVER, D. G., *The Entry to Banking from a Building Society Viewpoint*, Centre for Studies in Money, Banking and Finance, Macquarie University, Apr 1983.

HALL, M. J. B., *Monetary Policy Since 1971: Conduct and Performance* (London, Macmillan Press, 1983).

HARPER, I. R., 'Some Speculation on the Long-term Implications of Financial Deregulation and Innovation', paper presented to the *13th Conference of Economists* (Perth, Australia, Aug 1984).

HOGAN, W. P., and SHARPE, I. G., 'On Prudential Controls', *Economic Papers*, Apr 1983.

MACFARLANE, I. J., 'Methods of Monetary Control in Australia', paper presented to the New Zealand Association of Economists Annual Conference, Massey University, 22 Aug 1984.

'Macquarie Banking Centre', 'Papers on the Treasury Bond Tender', Centre for Studies in Money, Banking and Finance, Macquarie University, Mar 1983.

—— 'Seminar on Bank Entry Criteria', *Economic Society of Australia*, Centre for Studies in Money, Banking and Finance, Macquarie University, Sep 1984.

PERKINS, J. O. N., *The Australian Financial System after the Campbell Report* (Melbourne University Press, 1982).

Permanent Building Societies' Association (NSW) Ltd, *Policy on Legislative Reform/Amendments*, Aug 1984.

R.B.A., 'Submission to the Committee of Enquiry into the Australian Financial System', *Occasional Paper No. 7*, 1979.

—— *Reserve Bank of Australia: Functions and Operations* (4th ed.), 1983 (a).

—— *Overseas Operations of Australian Banks*, 1983 (b).

——'Financial Intermediation', *Bulletin*, Apr 1985.

STEARN, G., and TRESS, R., 'Australian Bank Mergers of 1981: Their Motivation and Effects', *Bulletin of Money, Banking and Finance*, 1983–4, No. 2, Centre for Studies in Money, Banking and Finance, Macquarie University, 1984.

THURLOE, J., and VALENTINE, T. J., 'Financial Innovations and the Demand for Money', paper presented to the *Financial Innovations Conference* (Melbourne, Australia, 1984).

TOBIN, J., 'On the Efficiency of the Financial System', *Lloyds Bank Review*, pp. 13–14, July 1984.

VALENTINE, T. J., 'Campbell and the Critics', *Economic Papers*, Apr 1983.

—— 'Recent Australian Monetary Policy', *Bulletin of Money, Banking and Finance*, 1983/4, No. 3, Centre for Studies in Money, Banking and Finance, Macquarie University, NSW, Australia, 1984.

WOOD, G. E., 'Competition, Innovation, Consumer Protection and the Role of the Market: The Philosophy of the Campbell Report', ch. 4, part II, in *A New Financial Revolution*, Centre for Independent Studies, 1982.

2 The UK Financial System

AGPS, *Australian Financial System: Final Report of the Committee of Enquiry* (The Campbell Report) (Canberra, Australian Government Publishing Service, 1981).

BAIN, A. D., *The Economics of the Financial System* (Oxford, Martin Robertson, 1981).

Bank of England, 'The Measurement of Liquidity', consultative paper issued by the Bank of England in March, 1980.

—— 'The Measurement of Liquidity', consultative paper issued by the Bank of England in the summer of 1981.

—— *Bank of England, Report and Accounts, 1984*, June 1984.
—— *Bank of England, Report and Accounts, 1985*, June 1985.
BARGE, J., 'Goodhart's Law Strikes Again', *The Banker*, July 1985.
BAUMOL, W. K., 'Contestable Markets: An Uprising in the Theory of Industry Structure', *American Economic Review*, Mar 1982.
BEQB, 'The Capital and Liquidity Adequacy of Banks', Sep 1975.
—— 'Limits on UK Banks' Foreign Exchange Positions', Dec 1975.
—— 'The Secondary Banking Crisis and the Bank of England's Support Operations', June 1978.
—— 'Papers Submitted to the Wilson Committee', Sep 1978.
—— 'The Measurement of Capital', Sep 1980.
—— 'The Liquidity of Banks', Mar 1981.
—— 'Foreign Currency Exposure', June 1981.
—— 'Prudential Arrangements for the Discount Market', June 1982.
—— 'The Measurement of Liquidity', Sep 1982.
—— 'Mortgage Lending and the Housing Market', Sep 1982 (a).
—— 'The Role of the Banking Supervisor', Dec 1982.
—— 'The Nature and Implications of Financial Innovation', Sep 1983.
—— 'Competition, Innovation and Regulation in British Banking', Sep 1983.
—— 'Revised Presentation of Banking Statistics', Dec 1983.
—— 'The International Market for Floating-rate Instruments', Sep 1984.
—— 'Some Current Concerns of a Banking Supervisor', June 1985.
—— 'Change and Development in International Financial Markets', Sep 1985.
—— 'Change in the Stock Exchange and Regulation of the City', Dec 1985.
BIS, 'The International Interbank Market', *BIS Economic Papers*, no. 8, July 1983.
BOLEAT, M., *The Building Society Industry* (London, Allen & Unwin, 1982).
BSA, 'New Legislation for Building Societies', *The Building Societies Association* (BSA), Feb 1984.
—— *The Future Constitution and Power of Building Societies* (Spalding Report), Jan 1983.
CARTER, H., and PARTINGTON, I., *Applied Economics in Banking and Finance*, 2nd ed. (London, Oxford University, 1981).
COOK, J., 'Maintaining the Flow of Loans: The Co-financing Alternative', *The Banker*, May 1983.
COOKE, W. P., 'International Lending in a Fragile World Economy', paper presented to the *SUERF Colloquium*, Vienna, Apr 1982.
DALE, R., 'Safeguarding the International Banking System: Present Arrangements and a Framework for Reform', paper presented at the *SUERF Colloquium*, Vienna, Apr 1982.
DRURY, A. C., *Finance Houses: Their Development and Role in the Modern Financial Sector* (London, Waterlow Publishers, 1982).
Financial Intelligence and Research, 'UK Licensed Deposit-takers: Financial Status and Performance' (London, Feb 1984).
FOWLE, M., 'Should Bank Auditors and Supervisors Talk to Each Other?', *The Banker*, Apr 1985.
Group of Thirty, *Risks in International Bank Lending* (New York, 1982 (a)).
—— *How Bankers See the World Financial Market* (New York, 1982 (b)).

HALL, M. J. B., *Monetary Policy since 1971: Conduct and Performance* (London, Macmillan Press, 1983).

—— 'Money Market Management in the UK', *SUERF*, 1986.

—— *The City Revolution: Causes and Consequences* (London, Macmillan Press, forthcoming, 1987).

HMSO, *Report of the Committee to Review the Functioning of Financial Institutions* (The Wilson Report), Cmnd 7937 (HMSO, June 1980).

—— *Building Societies: A New Framework*, Cmnd 9316 (HMSO, July 1984).

—— White Paper on *Banking Supervision*, Cmnd 9695 (HMSO, Dec 1985).

—— *Report of the Committee set up to consider the System of Banking Supervision*, Cmnd 9550 (HMSO, June 1985).

HOUSE OF COMMONS, *The Building Societies Bill*, HC, 5 Dec 1985.

JOHNSON, C., 'Competing for Consumer Loans', *Lloyds Bank Economic Bulletin*, Feb 1986.

McMAHON, C., 'Central Banks as Regulators and Lenders of Last Resort: A View from the United Kingdom', in *Key Issues in International Banking*, Federal Reserve Bank of Boston, Oct 1977.

OECD, *The Internationalisation of Banking: The Policy Issues* (Paris, 1983).

REID, M., *The Secondary Banking Crisis 1973–75* (London, Macmillan Press, 1982).

SANTOMERO, A. M., and WATSON, R. D., 'Determining an Optimal Capital Standard for the Banking Industry', *Journal of Finance*, vol. 32, Sep 1977.

WALLICH, H., 'Central Banks as Regulators and Lenders of Last Resort in an International Context: A View from the United States', in *Key Issues in International Banking* (Federal Reserve Bank of Boston, Oct 1977).

WILSON, K. W., '*British Financial Institutions: Savings and Monetary Policy*' (London, Pitmans, 1983).

3   Financial Deregulation in Australia and the UK Compared

HALL, M. J. B., *Profits: Future Prospects for UK Clearing Banks*, Paper presented to the 4th Garderen Conference organised by the Rotterdamse Monetaire Studies Group (Holland, Garderen, 4 Apr 1986 (a)).

—— *Reform of the London Stock Exchange: The Prudential Issues*, Loughborough University Banking Centre Research Paper No. 24, Mar 1986 (b).

Appendix

BLACK B., and Dorrance, G. (eds), *Problems of International Finance* (London, Macmillan, 1984).

COLJE, H., 'Bank Supervision on a Consolidated Basis', *The Banker*, June 1980.

—— 'How Much Capital is Adequate?', *The Banker*, June 1982.

COOKE, W., 'The Communities and the Banks in the 1980s: Supervisory

Aspects – A Central Banker's View', a speech given at a British Bankers Association Seminar, Jan 1982.

—— 'Developments in Co-operation among Banking Supervisory Authorities', a paper presented at the Conference on the Internationalisation of the Capital Markets in New York, Mar 1981 and published in the *BEQB*, June 1981.

—— 'The International Banking Scene in a Supervisory Perspective', a speech given at the Financial Times World Banking Conference in London on 9 December 1982 and published in the *BEQB*, Mar 1983.

DALE, R., 'Basle Concordat: Lessons from Ambrosiano', *The Banker*, Sep 1983.

GOWER, L., *Review of Investor Protection* (Department of Trade and Industry, Jan 1984).

GROUP OF THIRTY, *Bank Supervision Around the World*, R. Dale (New York, 1982).

—— *How Bankers See the World Financial Market* (New York, 1982).

—— *Insurance of Bank Lending to Developing Countries*, H. Wallich (New York, 1984).

HEGGESTAD, A., and KING, B., 'Regulation of Bank Capital: An Evaluation', *Federal Reserve Bank of Atlanta Economic Review*, Mar 1982.

HENRIKSEN, O., 'How the EEC Influences Banking in Europe', *The Banker*, Mar 1983.

ICBS, *Proceedings of the International Conference of Banking Supervisors* (Washington, Sep 1981).

McMAHON, C., 'Central Banks as Regulators and Lenders of Last Resort: A View from the United Kingdom', in *Key Issues in International Banking* (Federal Reserve Bank of Boston, Oct 1977).

MAISEL, S. J., *Risk and Capital Adequacy in Commercial Banks* (Chicago, University of Chicago Press for the National Bureau of Economic Research, 1981).

OECD, *Costs and Margins in Banking, An International Survey*, J. Revell (Paris, OECD, 1980).

—— *The Internationalisation of Banking: The Policy Issues*, 1983.

REID, M., *The Secondary Banking Crisis, 1973–5* (London, Macmillan, 1982).

Report of the Committee to Review the Functioning of Financial Institutions (the Wilson Report), Cmnd 7937 (London, HMSO, 1980).

REVELL, J., 'Solvency and Regulation of Banks', *Bangor Occasional Papers in Economics*, no. 5 (University of Wales Press, 1975).

—— 'Capital Adequacy, Hidden Reserves and Provisions', ch. 13 in *UK Banking Supervision: Evolution, Practice and Issues*, ed. E. Gardner (London, Allen & Unwin, 1986).

TUGENDHAT, C., 'Opening up Europe's Financial Sector to Intra-community Competition', *The Banker*, Jan 1985.

WALLICH, H., 'Central Banks as Regulators and Lenders of Last Resort in an International Context: A View from the United States', in *Key Issues in International Banking* (Federal Reserve Bank of Boston, Oct 1977).

Index